'The significance of *DC Confiden...* [...] daily interaction between the US a[...] that things did not have to turn [...] his unique vantage point on Massachusetts Avenue, the ambassador saw that although Britain's reputation in a traumatised US soared to "stratospheric new heights" after the 9/11 al-Qaida attacks, the prime minister was unable to translate it into real influence on the Bush administration ... This book is a useful reminder that the debate about Iraq is about the present as well as the past'   *Guardian*

'This is the most interesting, credible insider account of the run-up to Iraq so far published. It is being made much of by the antis as definitive proof of Blair's awfulness'

Andrew Marr, *Daily Telegraph*

'This high-level account of the run-up to the Iraq invasion is thorough, credible and deflates the notion that Bush and Blair decided early on to go to war, come hell or high water'

Jim Hoagland, *Washington Post*

'The importance of the Meyer book is very great'

Peter Oborne, *Spectator*

'Blair emerges from Meyer's unique perspective as shallow and vainglorious ... a tragic indictment of the dysfunction of 21st century British government'   Andrew Stephen, *Observer*

'His inside story of Tony Blair's relationship with George Bush in the run-up to the Iraq war is laden with delicious detail. Peaceniks may be disappointed by the narrative: the war was right; Mr Blair did not lie; there was no secret deal to "whack Iraq" – but only the earnest will care'   Francis Elliott, *Independent on Sunday*

'Meyer's Washington reminiscences are sensational. He portrays the prime minister as a star-struck wimp and his cabinet as "pygmies"'

Simon Jenkins, *Guardian*

'A marvellously entertaining and readable book that deserves to sell as many copies as any airport paperback saga. It is already famous as perhaps the rudest volume ever written by an insider about New Labour's top talent'   Andrew Gilligan, *Evening Standard*

'In his wry and literate way, Meyer fleshes out the bones of what's been a pretty familiar skeleton ... His talent for comic observation and understated wit is a great bonus'

Matthew Norman, *Independent*

'This book is a fabulous queenie gossip. It's like Lance Price, but the difference is that Price was a third-grade government press officer and Meyer was a number-one Washington official'

Roger Alton, *Press Gazette*

'The delicious portraiture, razor-sharp character assessments and the sharing of undiplomatic discretions, are all beautifully, and often comically presented'   James Cusick, *Sunday Herald*

'The book does provide some valuable insights into British-American relations. The chapters on 9/11 and on the Iraq War are totally absorbing and often quite moving. The account of Blair's bonding with Bush after 9/11 is wonderfully – if a trifle gushingly – laid out'   Cal McCrystal, *Independent on Sunday*

'The book is of great value to anyone interested in diplomacy and foreign policy'   Bruce Anderson, *Independent*

'His honesty, tittle-tattle and tales of PM's shirts are to be applauded, not lamented'   David Banks, *Press Gazette*

'It may not spill the official secrets but it does provide plenty of colour ... Historians will find this book a useful addition to the archive material'   Sean Donlon, *Irish Times*

'The value of the book is that it gives a feel for the nuts and bolts of diplomacy and foreign relations – the networking, the gathering of intelligence, the analysis, the reporting home and the endless protection of a variety of national interests from bendy bananas to nuclear power'   Maurice Hayes, *Irish Independent*

'A masterpiece of elegance which places the stiletto between New Labour's shoulder blades with panache'   Clive Aslet, *Country Life*

'This is an important book about what it was like to be Britain's most senior and lustrous ambassador at a time when the prime minister enjoyed a direct line to the White House for which there are few precedents'   Martin Kettle, *Guardian*

'Never before has there been such a riveting and candid memoir of life behind the diplomatic scenes'   *The Middle East*

Christopher Meyer served as Ambassador of the United Kingdom to the United States from 1997 to 2003. He was a vital link in the important relationship between America and Britain, one of the closest periods since the Second World War. He had previously been British Ambassador to Germany and chief spokesman and press secretary for former Prime Minister John Major, and for Geoffrey Howe when he was Foreign Secretary. In 2003 Meyer was appointed Chairman of the Press Complaints Commission. He was knighted in 2001.

DC
CONFIDENTIAL

The Controversial Memoirs of
Britain's Ambassador to the U.S.
at the Time of 9/11 and the
Run-up to the Iraq War

CHRISTOPHER
MEYER

PHOENIX

A PHOENIX PAPERBACK

First published in Great Britain in 2005
by Weidenfeld & Nicolson
This paperback edition published in 2006
by Phoenix,
an imprint of Orion Books Ltd,
Orion House, 5 Upper St Martin's Lane,
London WC2H 9EA

5 7 9 10 8 6

A CIP catalogue record for this book
is available from the British Library.

ISBN-13 978-0-7538-2091-9
ISBN-10 0-7538-2091-9

Printed and bound in Great Britain by
Mackays of Chatham plc, Chatham, Kent

The Orion Publishing Group's policy is to use papers that
are natural, renewable and recyclable products and
made from wood grown in sustainable forests. The logging
and manufacturing processes are expected to conform to
the environmental regulations of the country of origin.

www.orionbooks.co.uk

To Eve and Catherine

Contents

Acknowledgements

I never had a burning desire to write any kind of memoir. But, last summer, as I was regaling my wife and family with old war stories for the umpteenth time, they urged me to write them down before my memory faded. So, early one morning in August last year, I sat down on the balcony of our flat in Megève and looked to the French Alps for inspiration. I had before me a French exercise book and a pack of Bic ballpoints. I put pen to paper and became instantly addicted. The addiction was to hold me in its thrall for over a year.

This is a book which is based largely on memory. I never kept a diary. As ambassador in Washington, I occasionally made jottings of words and phrases which I had used and to which I had taken a fancy. Some of these re-emerged in speeches and interviews which I gave later. A few are to be found lurking in the books of other authors – sometimes attributed, sometimes not – with whom I have been happy to cooperate. I have not sought access to the archives of the Foreign and Commonwealth Office or any other government department. I have checked certain details with one or two friends and former colleagues.

As I started to write I had no clear structure to guide me. I decided only on a loose chronology, which would start in 1994 when I went to Downing Street to work as John Major's press secretary; and end in 2003, when I left Washington as ambassador and retired from the Diplomatic Service. I have broadly stuck to the chronology. But, along the way, I found myself constantly diverted by reminiscence and reflection. The doors of memory would suddenly fly open and out would pop something that I had not thought about for years.

Nor did I start with a wish to convey some great message. But, as I wrote, certain broad themes began to emerge, almost of their own accord. With hindsight, as I put down my pen in relief at finishing the book, I realized that these were the vertebrae of

DC Confidential: the imperative necessity of retaining a clear-eyed vision of the national interest; the enduring relevance of diplomacy and embassies, when ease and speed of communication between capitals, stripped of context, can lead to facile and misguided judgements; the importance of knowing how to negotiate with friend and foe alike – when to stand and when to bend.

Another theme is my huge affection and admiration for America and Americans. I hope that this book may in some modest way contribute to a better understanding of this great friend and ally. It is not to be blithely uncritical to say that the world is a far better place for the existence of the United States.

A few good men and women have helped me with this book. My agent, Jonathan Lloyd of Curtis Brown, who so wisely led a novice author by the hand; my editor, Alan Samson at Weidenfeld and Nicholson, who both improved the text and displayed saintly forbearance as I missed deadline after deadline; Alan's assistant, Lucinda McNeile, who, with gentle firmness, took me through the painstaking detail of editing; our neighbours, Sue Lawley and Hugh Williams, who thought up the title *DC Confidential*. I am especially grateful to our good friends Barbara Taylor Bradford and Bob Bradford who took such trouble to help me make the transition from the clipped prose of the Civil Service to something which is, I hope, more entertaining to the reader. I am also immensely grateful to our good friends Claudine and Dennis Ward who so generously provided a refuge in the south of France from which several chapters of the book emerged.

As with everything else, I could not have written the book without the support of my wife, Catherine. She enters the narrative early on. The book is as much about her as me. More important, so far as America is concerned, it is a story of what we, as a partnership, saw, heard, felt and did together. She brought her keen judgement to the text, kept me going when I wanted to abandon the project, and had to put up with my all too frequent bouts of surly grumpiness while I wrestled with the writing. I am eternally grateful to her.

London, September 2005

We have no eternal allies and we have no perpetual enemies. Our interests are eternal and perpetual, and those interests it is our duty to follow.

LORD PALMERSTON (1784–1865)

War is nothing but a continuation of politics with the admixture of other means.

KARL VON CLAUSEWITZ (1780–1831)

There is nothing more difficult to plan, more doubtful of success, nor more dangerous to manage than the creation of a new order of things ... Whenever his enemies have occasion to attack the innovator they do so with the passion of partisans, while the others defend him sluggishly so that the innovator and his party alike are vulnerable.

NICCOLÒ MACHIAVELLI (1469–1527)

List of Illustrations

Sir Sean Connery
John Cleese and his wife (Greg E. Mathieson/MAI Photo Agency)
Jack Straw and Plácido Domingo (Greg E. Mathieson/MAI Photo
  Agency)
Lady Thatcher, Senator Jesse Helms and his wife (Lynn Horner
  Keith)
Donald Rumsfeld and Ben Bradlee (Lynn Horner Keith)
Steven Spielberg (Lynn Horner Keith)
Colin Powell and Rich Armitage (Rex Features)
Karl Rove (Rex Features)
Paul Wolfowitz
Farewell call on Dick Cheney (White House)
Farewell call on Colin Powell
Laura Bush's farewell lunch (White House)
The Bushes' farewell dinner (White House)

Foreword to the Paperback Edition

The controversy which attended the publication last year of the hardback edition of *DC Confidential* had many piquant ingredients. Together they created a succulent stew of exploding minister, harrumphing mandarin, provocative newspaper headline, and, most tasty of all – the garlic of political *affaires* – disinformation and smear from unnamed sources. Sprinkled on top were two Early Day Motions put down in the House of Commons, one of which urged me to publish and be damned, while the other called for my head as Chairman of the Press Complaints Commission for doing just that. One MP supported both Motions.

This was all a little unexpected for a book which had had some difficulty finding a publisher. It was the more surprising for my having followed the rules for the publication of books by retired diplomats. With the written consent of the Foreign Office, I submitted my manuscript to the Cabinet Office for clearance before publication. Official sources subsequently offered several explanations, on and off the record, for the bewildering contradiction between raising no objection to publication and the fuss made later. The explanations appeared to vary from week to week: the book had been read only by a junior member of the Cabinet Office; the Foreign Office had never seen the manuscript; I had delayed submitting the manuscript for clearance until just before publication, so facing the government with a *fait accompli*; I had threatened the government with lawyers. It was also alleged that I had ignored a personal appeal from No. 10 not to publish. All of this was untrue.

Officialdom went on to compound its confused handling both of my book and that of Sir Jeremy Greenstock (former British Ambassador to the United Nations and Tony Blair's representative in Iraq in 2003) by tightening the rules for civil servants and diplomats on publishing books, when all it needed to do was to apply the existing rules clearly and consistently, with equal treatment for politicans, political advisers and civil servants. Getting the balance right between what should remain undisclosed and the public's right to know is, of course, not an easy thing. But it is no answer to impose draconian restrictions on civil servants and diplomats, so that the only version of history to be written will be by politicians and their political advisers.

One of these days I may write an account of this bizarre episode, titled, perhaps, *Westminster Confidential*. Who knows, it could be of more than passing interest to a university politics class.

This paperback edition corrects a number of errors and repetitions spotted by eagle-eyed readers, several of them in America. I am extremely grateful to them. I am also grateful to the scores of people who wrote to me about the book. Their comments were overwhelmingly supportive. Most asked what the fuss was all about. I have tried to reply to all of them. I take this opportunity to apologise to those who may have slipped through my net and have had no acknowledgement.

April 2005

1

Vanity and Ambition

'We want you to get up the arse of the White House and stay there.'
So spoke the Prime Minister's chief of staff, Jonathan Powell, in the
splendour of one of Downing Street's reception rooms.

I was, as the Americans would say, a thirty-year veteran of the
British Diplomatic Service. Now, after all that slog, I was about to
reach the pinnacle of a diplomat's career and become Britain's
ambassador to the United States. Trust the blokeishness of New
Labour to reduce it to an anal metaphor (mind you, on entering the
Diplomatic Service, I had been enjoined by a military-looking type
of the old school to be 'as crisp as a fart').

It was all quite hard to believe. As I sat opposite this young,
tousle-headed chief of staff, who had once been my subordinate, I
had one of those can-it-really-be-me? moments. I had a modest
middle-class background. No member of my family had ever been
a diplomat; I had never had a burning desire to become one. My
uncle had made a lot of money as a quantity surveyor. For years it
had been assumed that I would follow him into the business. But
my uselessness with figures – I had scraped an O level in Maths –
and my total lack of interest in quantity surveying had ruled that
out.

When I was about seven, I found in my grandmother's attic one
of those illustrated, leather-bound histories of the kings and queens
of England, of which the Victorians were fond. My imagination
was immediately fired. History became my passion. When I was
twelve or thirteen, it took me to second place in a national competition for schools called the Townsend Warner History Prize. It
then carried me a decade later to a scholarship at Peterhouse,
the oldest Cambridge college, distinguished in equal measure for
eminent historians and scientists. I disappointed my professors
by not getting a first-class degree. I got instead what was called a

two-one. I always rationalized this by saying that the best diplomats are those with good second-class minds. Too much intellectual firepower can damage your common sense.

I had not a clue what I would do with my degree. The university careers advisory service suggested that I put my expensive education in the service of the fruit-and-vegetable business. They commended a company based in London and Sicily. This was on the strength of my telling them that I liked travel and had hitchhiked in Italy. I dismissed the idea with the arrogance of youth. I considered myself destined for higher things. I made also an irrational connection between fruit and veg and the chicken factory near Bath, where I had once worked as a student 'hole-cutter'. This task – three chickens a minute, seven hours a day – is too disgusting to describe. I was an interloper in a close-knit rural community, where archaic forms of English were still in use – 'thy' and 'bain't' – even among the German and Italian ex-prisoners of war, who preferred the chicken factory to returning to their homelands. They accepted me with a friendly curiosity. In due course I was to choose a career where success depended on the ability to be welcomed by alien communities.

I sometimes wonder what would have happened if I had gone into fruit and vegetables. I might now be sunning myself on the balcony of a fine Sicilian country house, surveying my empire of lemon groves and olive trees. Who is to say that this would not have been a better choice?

The careers advisory service also sent me to BP for an unpleasant and unsuccessful interview, where I was criticized for wearing a sports jacket and brown shoes. 'No gentleman wears brown shoes in London,' I was told. This remark was uttered just as the Beatles, Carnaby Street, and the Swinging Sixties were tolling the knell of the traditional English gentleman, so beloved by Hungarian *immigrés* and the French.

It was my Peterhouse supervisor, Maurice Cowling, who suggested the Diplomatic Service. I had my doubts. My mother and stepfather, an officer in the RAF, had led a peripatetic life. We had lived in Aden and Turkey, where our landlord had been hanged after the military *coup d'état* of 1960. That is one way of avoiding the rent. As a teenager, I had met Foreign Office people in these places, including one who hated the career. But Cowling convinced me. 'Take the exams,' he said. 'If you pass, you have a career, if you want to be a diplomat. If you pass, but decide to do something else, you will have a qualification of interest to any employer.'

I took the exams and tests in the spring of 1965. To my astonishment I came top. This more than compensated for having failed to get a first in my final university exams; and for the ignominy of having organized a May Ball that lost a large amount of money and led to the bacchanalian destruction of the Fellows' Garden. The experience had almost tempted me to get into the pop-music business. I discovered that I had a nose for talent and an ear for hits. I hired three bands, who at the time were either unknown or at the outer fringes of commercial success. One was called the Jokers Wild, a local Cambridge band that played every week at the Victoria Ballroom above the cinema in the market place. Their leader was David Gilmour, who went on to create Pink Floyd. Then there were the Paramounts, who later morphed into Procol Harum. Their 'Whiter Shade of Pale' was a global hit, which is still widely played today. I also hired Zoot Money's Big Roll Band. National fame largely eluded them, but Zoot was huge on the south coast for years.

As I basked in the success of getting into the Foreign Office, a letter suddenly arrived, inviting me to report for duty in early September. Real life loomed and I took fright. I was still not sure that the Foreign Office was for me. More to the point, I was reluctant to abandon the student's life. The college notice board carried a seductive advertisement for a one-year diploma in international relations from the School of Advanced International Studies in Bologna, Italy (subsequently renamed the Paul Nitze School, after one of its most illustrious benefactors). This was an American establishment run by the Johns Hopkins University in Baltimore. Because Bologna had a communist city government and was in Italy's so-called Red Belt, the rumour was, as I later discovered, that the school was funded by the CIA. The deputy director of the school was certainly a mysterious fellow with a crew cut who had no obvious academic or administrative functions. Much later, when I told a Soviet diplomat who had KGB written all over him that I had studied in Bologna, he replied, 'Ah! The spy school.'

I had little difficulty in persuading the Foreign Office to give me a year's deferment to go to Bologna. It liked the glossy brochure and the impressive set of courses. It also hoped I would learn Italian, which I did. Typically, it never took advantage of this to send me to our embassy in Rome. The best it could do was, later, to send me to Madrid on the grounds that the Spaniards, like the Italians, spoke a Latin-based language. In the end Spain, with the United States, proved the most enjoyable and fulfilling of my postings abroad. But that is another story.

Bologna was an idyllic interlude, in which my attention to advanced international studies was cursory at best. A year passed in travel around Italy and dancing with Italian girls in the little bars that dotted the hills around Bologna. I returned to London in the autumn of 1966. My year away had given me no fresh ideas about a career. Without further ado, I entered Her Majesty's Diplomatic Service and was posted to the West and Central African Department of the Foreign Office. I was made responsible for French-speaking African states. The prospect terrified me. There were so many of them. My head of department brushed my worries aside. 'No need to worry, old boy. We have damn-all interests in these places. The French have them sewn up.'

If Bologna did little to fire enthusiasm for the Foreign Office, it marked the start of my fascination for America. Most of the students and faculty were American. They were pulsing with debate over the war in Vietnam. I took a course in American history, did my first multiple-choice tests, ate my first Thanksgiving dinner and duly emerged with a diploma. I went on to spend the summer working for the American School in Switzerland. This was an American high school based in Lugano, which used to recruit its 'senior counselors' from the students in Bologna. It ran a two-month summer programme for American teenagers, overwhelmingly girls, which provided a distilled course in European culture. The job of a senior counselor was to drive a minibus, with eight girls aboard, on week-long excursions around Europe, returning to Lugano for much-needed rest between sorties. Hotels were forbidden. Camping sites were obligatory. The senior counselors were supposed also to be chaperones. It was a struggle to protect the American girls from the attentions of Italian and Spanish men. I was offered money for access to them in Rome and Barcelona. Our minibus was pursued all the way from Milan to Chiasso on the Italian–Swiss frontier by a car-load of Italian boys. The girls were torn between fear and longing. I still have ringing in my ears the Mickey Mouse song, rendered horribly by eight tuneless voices in the claustrophobic confines of a Volkswagen minibus. I learnt to purchase Tampax in French, Swiss, Spanish, Italian, German and Austrian pharmacies without batting an eyelid.

Almost twenty years were to pass after these adventures before I set foot on American soil. It used to be said that the most common dream experienced by the British people was to have tea with the Queen. Mine was always to go to America. I finally did it in 1985, when, as his press secretary, I accompanied Sir Geoffrey (now Lord) Howe, the then Foreign Secretary, to a UN meeting in New York. We stayed at the posh UN Plaza hotel on East 42nd Street. My first night I was so excited that I got up and went for a walk around the East Side. It taught me something about America that has remained with me ever since. So much was intensely familiar from movies and television; but so much was alien. This was a foreign country, not Britain writ large. It was a huge mystery, to be explored and explained. That first morning I had breakfast in John's restaurant, a diner on the corner of 42nd and 2nd Avenue: two eggs over easy, Canadian bacon, hash browns, toast, jelly, orange juice, coffee. I listened to the raucous conversation of office workers, policemen, waiters, postmen. I had finally arrived.

After that I travelled frequently to the US with Geoffrey Howe, usually to Washington and New York. Geoffrey had struck up a good relationship with George Shultz, the American Secretary of State. They both spoke in a low rumble, barely audible to their staff and sometimes to each other. On one occasion Howe tried to persuade Shultz to get the American military to buy a battlefield communications system called Ptarmigan. After Howe had made his pitch, Shultz replied bafflingly that the US would always support democracy in the 'Southern Cone'. What had he meant, we asked Shultz's staff after the meeting. 'The Secretary,' they said, 'thought that Sir Geoffrey was talking about Argentina.'

Geoffrey got it into his head that he could extract more value from his lightning trips to Washington if we took Concorde. It would add an entire afternoon to the time available for talks with the Americans. That was fine as far as the afternoons were concerned. But with a five-hour time difference working against us, by the time the working dinner arrived, we were all dead from jet lag. Shultz once had the idea that it would be nice to have the dinner on the old presidential yacht *Sequoia* and sail down the Potomac River.

Shultz and Howe decided to get away from matters of the moment and discuss long-term trends in world affairs. It was a balmy spring evening, with the sun setting over the Virginia shore. To the gentle throb of engines and the sound of swishing water was added the soporific rumble of the two Great Men, as they grappled with subjects like population control. The entire British team was soon asleep at the dinner table. Shultz and Howe would sometimes doze as the other spoke. I opened an eye to see that jet lag was contagious. American heads were drooping.

As my time with Sir Geoffrey drew to a close in 1988, he asked me what I wanted to do next. I said that I wanted to get to know America better. Our thirty-six-hour visits to the US had been tantalizing. I was more and more aware of the vast country that lay behind the east coast. I was also exhausted after spending four years dealing with the press. There was a programme at Harvard University which every year brought together from all over the world twenty or so foreign policy 'practitioners' – diplomats, businessmen, politicians and so on. The idea was to bring academics and practitioners together in a creative synergy. In reality, as I was to find out, most of the academics did not want to touch the practitioners with a bargepole, in case the real world were to burst in on the musings of the ivory tower. Each year, the Foreign Office sent someone on the course. I asked to go in the academic year 1988–9. Howe granted my wish. In due course I set off for Cambridge, Massachusetts, where Harvard is located, with my first wife and family.

Our arrival in August coincided with the final stage of the 1988 presidential election campaign between George Bush the father and Michael Dukakis, the Governor of Massachusetts. Dukakis was leading Bush by around fifteen points in the polls. In the end he was to be beaten heavily by Bush; but as we arrived, a number of Democrat-supporting Harvard academics were expecting to be called to Washington to serve in a Dukakis administration. Harvard proved to be a superb observation point as the campaign moved to its climax. I found myself living a political melodrama as the Dukakis campaign went down the drain, taking with it the hopes and ambitions of most of Harvard's academic community. I learnt lessons about presidential campaigns, which were to stand me in good stead when I was ambassador twelve years later. One of them was to pay little attention to the predictive power of the polls before the beginning of September. I became hooked on American politics and have remained so ever since.

When, after a few weeks at Harvard, I took a call from the Foreign Office asking me if I would like to stay on that side of the Atlantic and take up a posting at our embassy in Washington at the end of the academic year, I jumped at the chance. My family were delighted too. The alternative option of Eastern Europe, even as ambassador, was not so appealing.

We moved to the nation's capital in May of 1989. I was to stay for five and a half years until the end of 1993 in this, my first, Washington incarnation. It converted me in the eyes of the Foreign Office from a Russian to an American specialist, so paving the way for my appointment four years later as ambassador to the United States.

Which explains why, just before leaving for Washington in this second and more elevated incarnation as ambassador, I had gone to see Jonathan Powell, the Prime Minister's chief of staff. It was normal for senior ambassadors to get their marching orders from Downing Street. His crisp instruction was the most important briefing I received. Six months after New Labour's crushing election victory in May 1997, it was clear already that the Prime Minister's office would control relations with Washington. As in the days of another dominant Prime Minister, Margaret Thatcher, the Foreign Office was about to be relegated to second fiddle.

My thoughts went back to those years when the relationship between Powell and me had been reversed. He too had been in the Washington embassy in the early nineties. I was the ambassador's deputy, he a middle-ranking member of the staff, who reported to me. He was good: quick off the mark, with an astute understanding of American politics. His job in the embassy was to follow closely the presidential election campaign of 1992 between Bill Clinton and George Bush senior. He travelled around the US with both campaigns. This enabled him to get up the arse, as it were, of key figures in the future Clinton administration. This was to be of inestimable value to the Blair government.

At about the same time Tony Blair, sometimes with Gordon Brown, started visiting Washington. They were members of the Labour Party's Shadow Cabinet. They set out to forge close links with the New Democrats, the political and intellectual force behind Clinton. Blair and Brown were energized by Clinton's election victory in 1992. After long years in opposition they wanted to learn how to win too. The New Democrats warmly welcomed them. In the 1997 election much of New Labour's political strategy was borrowed from the Clinton campaign book.

Embassies are required to give all assistance to 'Her Majesty's Loyal Opposition'. So, Powell and I used to help Blair and Brown set up these visits. They were an odd couple: Blair effervescent and talkative, with a flashing smile and almost unnaturally youthful; Brown taciturn and brooding, with nails bitten to the quick. This gave the impression that Blair was the senior partner. But after a while, as you observed them, you began to ask the question that has bedevilled British politics for almost ten years: who is the organ-grinder and who the monkey?

Their visits were useful because they introduced me to the stokers in the New Democrat engine room: Al Frum, Sid Blumenthal, George Stephanopoulos, James 'the ragin' Cajun' Carville and others. Among those around Blair, I thought only Peter Mandelson, Alastair Campbell and, later, Jonathan Powell himself, matched these thirty-somethings for intellectual firepower and political imagination.

Gordon Brown was hard to read because he said so little. So was Tony Blair, perhaps because he talked so much. Eric Anderson, Blair's housemaster at his public school, Fettes, once said to me that all I had to know about Tony Blair was that he was a great actor.

After I became ambassador in Washington, I saw another side to Brown. Unlike other cabinet ministers, he never stayed at our embassy, nor any other, apparently. He would plant himself in a downtown hotel, frequently the Watergate, surrounded by a small band of advisers. I think he regarded ambassadors as the eyes and ears of Tony Blair. I can understand why this bothered him. Brown did not confine his American contacts to his economic opposite numbers, like the Treasury Secretary or the Chairman of the Federal Reserve. He built his own political network with the Democratic Party. He is, for example, a close friend of Bob Shrum, who was a senior adviser to both Al Gore and John Kerry in their presidential campaigns. Shrum was hired as an adviser to New Labour in the 2001 general election in Britain. His greatest claim to fame is his skill as a speech-writer and communicator. I may have detected his hand in some of Brown's speeches.

From time to time I was admitted to the Brown magic circle. I once went with Brown to New York, where he was to make a speech. He was terrific company. I was surprised at his voluble interest in American politics, on which he was a fair expert. He was friendliness and charm personified. Brown drafted and redrafted his text until the last moment.

I got another surprise on a later visit. I went with Brown to see Bob Zoellick, US Trade Representative in George W. Bush's first administration. Bob was an old acquaintance of mine: brilliant, tough-minded and acerbic. When deputy White House chief of staff, he was reputed to have fallen out with George W. over his father's doomed campaign against Bill Clinton in 1992. I heard George W. once say that Bob's bedside manner left something to be desired. He was the best National Security Adviser the US never had. He had a passionate interest in foreign policy and, though he brought his usual laser focus to the business of trade, he felt a little shunted out of the mainstream of things. Bob had a surprising knowledge of British nineteenth-century history, especially military. He immediately spotted that the abysmal 2002 remake of the movie *The Four Feathers* had the late Victorian British army incorrectly fighting in red, instead of khaki. I sent him a copy of the more accurate and far superior 1939 Korda version of the film.

Brown wanted to sell Zoellick on the notion of a European–American economic cooperation agreement. As far as I could tell, this sprang from his own political imagination, with minimal, if any, concertation with No. 10, the Foreign Office or anyone else in Whitehall. Zoellick was not buying. 'Gordon, come back when you have sold the idea to your European friends.' But the meeting was a great success. The two of them settled down to a knowledgeable and animated discussion of British prime ministers in the nineteenth century.

My final encounter with Tony Blair in this first incarnation in the Washington embassy was towards the end of 1993. Clinton was in his first year as President, and Blair had come to Washington to talk politics with the victorious Democrats. It had just been announced that I was to become Press Secretary to the British Prime Minister, John Major. I fixed a lunch for Blair with a bunch of high-powered

Democrat consultants and advisers in a private room at the Four Seasons Hotel in Georgetown. They had played big roles in Clinton's victory. They were cock-a-hoop. They hoped to get insights from Tony Blair into how the Labour Party intended to plot a similar course to election victory.

Blair was hesitant and banal. At the time he was Opposition spokesman on home affairs. This was the first occasion that I heard the slogan – the quintessence of New Labour – 'tough on crime, tough on the causes of crime'. Slogans were about as far as Blair got that day. He kept eyeing me nervously. I have always wondered if his reticence was just unformed thinking, or reflected concern that I would spill his beans to John Major and the Tories. If the latter, he had not yet grasped that civil servants like me had to be politically neutral, even in the job of Prime Minister's press secretary.

Jonathan Powell himself left the Diplomatic Service a year later to work full-time for Blair. And lo! here we were in Downing Street in the autumn of 1997, with him giving me instructions and not the other way round. Like most of my friends, Jonathan had thought me daft to go to work for John Major at the beginning of 1994, as the wheels started to come off his government. Not for the first time, I allowed vanity and ambition to get the better of me. But it all led indirectly to my becoming ambassador in Washington.

Geoffrey Howe had hired me in 1984 as his press secretary when I was working in our embassy in Moscow. He used to say that I was the only British diplomat in the Soviet Union who had been recruited by someone other than the KGB. My four years with Geoffrey were among the happiest in the Diplomatic Service. He was a fine Foreign Secretary, thoughtful, astute and meticulous. I knew little about the press at the time; but I grew to love newspapers in all their grubbiness and glory, where all human life met and the sublime and ridiculous were impossible to disentangle. I liked the company of journalists and came to count several as friends. I also learnt that if the choice lay between the story and friendship, the story would usually come out on top. In most cases this was not betrayal, but simple professionalism. It is striking how few politicians understand this. Journalists are held in low public esteem. More than a few deserve to be. But on the whole their profession is marked by an impressive ability to encapsulate accurately the essence of the story, often against a tight deadline.

It was on the strength of these four years lashed to Sir Geoffrey's mast that I was asked in late 1993 if I wanted to be John Major's press secretary. The call came from Sarah Hogg, who ran Major's Policy Unit in No. 10. She painted a glowing picture of life with the Prime Minister, deploying those descriptive arts which come so easily to estate agents. I was receptive. I was just finishing my first stint in Washington. I expected, with no great enthusiasm, to become chairman of the now notorious Joint Intelligence Committee. I agreed to come to London to be interviewed by John Major himself.

This was a bizarre event. I was ushered into the Cabinet Room. Major liked to work there, at the middle of the long table, under the portrait of Sir Robert Walpole, the first British Prime Minister. I had met Major once before, when he had come to Washington in 1989 as Margaret Thatcher's brand-new Foreign Secretary. There was an obscure row going on with the Americans about a hideous thing called chewing tobacco. This intensely carcinogenic substance is what you see American baseball players and good ol' boys in the southern US spitting out in long, brown streams. For some reason an American company produced it in the UK for export to Scandinavia, where this repellent habit had taken root. The British wanted to close the factory for health reasons. The Americans were resisting. I was impressed at how Major had got on top of this obscure brief in his very short tenure as Foreign Secretary. He obliged me to produce samples of the stuff. He interrogated me in depth on how to settle the dispute. Then, in a rapid change of gear, he gave, across the lunch table, a rather brilliant assessment of the situations in Russia and South Africa.

It was a different kind of Major who interviewed me four years later in 1993. He was tense, irritable and tired.

'Why do you want the job?' he asked. This was couched in tones suggesting that I had taken leave of my senses. I burbled pompously about how the Lobby – the collective name for the journalists who covered Westminster and Whitehall – conveyed a more pungent sense of journalism.

Major gave me a sharp stare. 'Pungent, pungent? Putrid, you mean?' On that felicitous note I was hired.

The calm and ever affable Gus O'Donnell, whom I was to replace (he is now Cabinet Secretary), ushered me rapidly from the Cabinet Room.

'We need to make an announcement today.'

'What?' I quavered. 'Surely we don't have to rush things.'

'Oh yes, we do,' said Gus firmly. 'It will leak. This place is like a sieve. We will do it at the four o'clock Lobby briefing.'

I realized later that Gus, who could not get out from under fast enough, was petrified that I would change my mind. I had discovered, to my alarm, that I was the sole candidate for the poisoned chalice. I was crowded with second thoughts. Too late. The deed was done that afternoon. In a moment of pure surrealism I awoke next morning to the gruff tones of Sir Bernard Ingham, Margaret Thatcher's long-serving press secretary and an old friend and mentor, talking about me on the BBC's *Today* programme.

A good friend, who remains prominent in public life, consoled me by saying that John Major's political fortunes could not sink lower, that I was joining his team at just the right time, that as things got better for him, I would rise with his tide and be able to share in the credit. Never has a prediction been more wrong.

2

The View from the Bunker

Nothing, but nothing, prepares you for working in Downing Street in intimate relationship with the Prime Minister.

Several things happen to you with shocking velocity. The pressure of events almost suffocates in its intensity. There is little time for reflection. Reflex replaces reasoned thought. You are cut off from the outside world. You function inside a combination of hothouse and bunker: a cramped eighteenth-century building, which housed what must have been the smallest permanent staff serving the leader of any major power.

You see more of the Prime Minister and your colleagues than you do of your family. Only the strongest marriages survive. My average day – by no means the longest in No. 10 – began at 5.45 a.m. and ended about 9.30 p.m. There were Saturdays and Sundays when I never got out of my pyjamas – awoken by some emergency and then having to handle it all day until it was time to go to bed. Exhaustion starts to distort judgement. You keep going on adrenalin and the thrill of being at the summit of things. In the end the attrition gets you. It is a far cry from the days of Sir Jock Colville, Winston Churchill's wartime private secretary, who noted in his diary that you knew there was a war on because everyone was working till 6 p.m.

Every morning I would report to John Major between 7.30 and 8 a.m. We would discuss the morning's press and how I was going to handle things for the rest of the day. This meant that I had to have read the morning's papers before meeting Major. When I arrived at No. 10, I assumed that there was a well-oiled machine that would deliver newspapers to my doorstep. No such machine existed. When I asked about arrangements for getting the papers to me before I left for work, the reaction was: 'You must be joking – make your own arrangements like everyone else.' As for getting the first editions the night before, it was as if I was asking for caviar and lobster in a fish-and-chip shop. It was suggested none too tactfully that I might like to pop down to Charing Cross or Victoria Station and pick them up myself.

Gus O'Donnell had been forced to make an arrangement with a newspaper shop near his home. I tried the same. I scoured Putney for a willing newsagent. I eventually found him on a council estate next to Putney Heath. As soon as the wholesalers had delivered the papers at the crack of dawn, Mr Patel, or one of his family, would descend Putney Hill and drop them on my doorstep. He never let me down. But the wholesalers were themselves often late. When that happened, I would have to finish reading the press in the back of the government car that fetched me every morning. It was horrible. Half my brain would be tuned to the BBC *Today* programme on the car radio, while by the time we got to Downing Street I was ready to throw up from car sickness.

It was typical of Downing Street. Tradition is one thing, amateurish improvisation another. It was very hard to shift the this-is-the-way-it-has-always-been-done attitude. It took an election victory like Blair's and a force of nature like Alastair Campbell's to sweep away the barnacles and cobwebs from the No. 10 press operation. How the gleaming new Campbell machine was used is, of course, quite another matter.

Even worse was the No. 10 coffee, a vile, feeble brew, which appeared to have been mixed with Bovril. I imagined vast stocks of wartime ersatz coffee, which, in the interest of public economy, were still being used by the managers of Downing Street. To the nation's shame this noxious fluid was offered by the Prime Minister to foreign dignitaries. I could read on the faces of a visiting French delegation the struggle between disgust and bewilderment, as the tepid liquid did dreadful violence to their palates.

My early-morning meetings took place in the Majors' bedroom. The prime ministerial quarters were then on the top floor of No. 10. 'Modest' did not do justice to this cramped, rather pokey accommodation, with its bland decoration. The dead hand of Civil Service furnishing ran throughout. The White House private quarters, which are not particularly grand, are palatial by comparison. The bedroom itself was comfortable enough, with a double bed, en suite bathroom, and enough room for three or four people to be seated, including on a bench at the foot of the bed, where I usually installed myself. I invariably arrived as the Prime Minister was getting dressed, but was always admitted no matter what stage this process had reached. It was some way removed from the levée of Louis XIV. Occasionally I was summoned into the prime ministerial bathroom, where, as I spoke, he would discharge some ablution. While all this was going on – and we were often joined by other No. 10 advisers, such as Alex Allan, his principal private secretary, or Howell James, his political secretary – Norma Major sat serenely in bed, in a nightgown, reading the papers and drinking a cup of tea. Norma, who was universally liked in No. 10, was a monument of good sense and calmness in a world that was permanently fraught.

It made me think of my great-aunt Sheila Minto. She had been one of Churchill's secretaries during the Second World War – what was known as a 'garden room girl', from the secretaries' room at the back of No. 10 giving on to the garden. She worked for every prime minister from Baldwin to Wilson. She was the one Churchill summoned to take dictation in the middle of the night. He used to say, apparently, that she did not mind his bad language. Sheila told me that he was usually in bed, sometimes in his bath, often with a brandy balloon and cigar. It was all totally decorous. My memory may be playing me false, but I think I recall her saying that once, in a moment of high inspiration, while dictating a speech, the great man stood up in his bath. True or false, Sheila was a no-nonsense Scottish woman who took things in her stride. Her shade hovered over me, as John Major prowled the bedroom in his shirt-tails, fulminating about something in the *Daily Mail* or *Sun*.

A couple of false dawns apart, John Major never got off the back foot in the two years I worked for him. I often felt overwhelmed by events. I had done well as the Foreign Office spokesman. But like a striker from the lower divisions who is bought by a Premier League club, I found scoring goals at the higher level a much tougher proposition.

It was Britain's humiliating ejection from the European Exchange Rate Mechanism in autumn 1992 that had done for Major's authority. At the time, I was in my first incarnation at the British Embassy in Washington. A few days after what became known as 'Black Wednesday', my first wife and I were invited by the ambassador, Sir Robin Renwick, to a small dinner at the embassy in honour of the

Chancellor of the Exchequer, Norman Lamont, and the Governor of the Bank of England, Robin Leigh-Pemberton, both of whom were subsequently sent to the House of Lords. After the Prime Minister himself, they were the two officials most involved in the debacle. It was a beautiful autumn evening. The table was set on the embassy terrace beneath the neo-classical portico with its great pillars. Candles were lit. Fireflies danced at the bottom of the garden, the size of a small park. Conversation was jovial. Maybe it was the magic of the dusk. Maybe it was the release of tension. But I could never understand how, after one of the worst days in post-war British history, Lamont and Leigh-Pemberton could be as light-hearted as they were that evening.

John Major was on the rack most of the time. He had launched, at the 1993 Conservative Party conference, a campaign with the slogan 'Back to Basics'. It was intended to denote a return to traditional standards in areas like crime and education. But there were those in the Party who wanted it to cover personal behaviour. I was told that, at a press conference shortly before I joined the No. 10 staff, Major confirmed, almost by accident, that he considered personal behaviour to be covered by 'Back to Basics'. The fat was in the fire. This was an invitation to the press to go after any Tory politician who had a peccadillo in his pocket. 'Sleaze' was born. Labour licked its lips.

I joined Major on the rack. Throughout 1994 there were repeated sleaze eruptions. A routine was established. On a Saturday afternoon, between 4 and 4.30, I would take a call from a reporter on one of the Sunday papers. Some poor, bloody Tory politician was going to be exposed *in flagrante* the next day. What did I have to say about it? I would call the Chief Whip, the Party Chairman, and the Prime Minister himself. They would establish whether the allegations were true. If they were, the sinner was expected to fall on his sword – and fast. My advice to Major was always to cut his losses as rapidly as possible. I was criticized for increasing the appetite of the press for more sacrificial lambs. But I thought any-thing was better than a long-drawn-out defence of a hopeless cause. By Monday morning the waters would have closed over the affair. It nearly always involved a political figure of only minor significance. Yet the Opposition had another shot in its locker for Prime Minister's Question Time; and the notion of a corrupt government, assiduously encouraged by the Labour Opposition, began to spread like poison through the country.

All the time John Major's small majority in the House of Commons was getting smaller, through death or desertion. The Tory Party was still in full nervous breakdown after the defenestration of Margaret Thatcher four years earlier. One symptom was the demonic self-destructiveness of the Eurosceptic rebels, who wanted Major to take a much harder line against Britain's further integration into the European Union. Their ferocious polemic and guerrilla warfare carried into the Cabinet itself, where discipline was lamentable. I preferred the dentist to briefing the Lobby on a Monday morning. It would be a bloodbath after a weekend of speeches and pronouncements by senior cabinet ministers like Ken Clarke, Michael Portillo and John Redwood. Together they managed to contradict each other as well as official government policy on Europe.

There was only one way to deal with this at the Lobby briefing: tell the hacks with an absolutely straight face that there was no inconsistency whatsoever between these various statements; that those who detected any were worse than angels on a pinhead; and go on repeating this bald economy with the truth until, as President Nixon used to say about the necessary repetitiveness of political campaigning, you wanted to throw up.

The Lobby briefings became a battle of wits between the journalists and me. Most of the time I thoroughly enjoyed these jousts. Nowadays it is all much more antiseptic and formal. No. 10 has its own briefing room and many briefings take place in the grand surroundings of the Foreign Press Association in Carlton Terrace. But in my day it was close-up and personal, hand-to-hand combat with the hacks. My office was the ground-floor, bow-fronted room looking on to Downing Street. In accordance with long-established tradition I would brief the Lobby in my office at 11 a.m., Monday through Thursday, when Parliament was in session (there was also a return match at 4 p.m. in a strange Victorian attic in the House of Commons where you expected to meet Anthony Perkins in his *Psycho* role). As many as twenty-five journalists could be crammed into my modest office. There were small chairs only for about half a dozen. The rest stood or sat on the floor. If it had been raining, there was an odour redolent of wet dog mixed with wet sock. I faced them, seated in a grand chair. An image of reading bedtime stories to my children would flash through the mind. I then briefed, seeking to explain and justify the policies of the day. This was invariably, and quite often justifiably, greeted with intense scepticism, as I sought to demonstrate the government's far-sighted wisdom and they smelled another cock-up.

After some ghastly political mishap had befallen the Government, the hacks would enquire with sadistic relish about the Prime Minister's mood. They hoped that through some remark, some sigh, some facial twitch, I would reveal a dramatic decline in prime ministerial morale. Whatever the true state of affairs, I would invariably reply in the same way: 'The Prime Minister is in robust/vibrant/sparkling good form' (the Blair equivalent is 'firing on all cylinders' or 'up for it'). I would deliver this with all the fervour at my command. That was not always easy. It often followed my ritual execution earlier in the morning at the hands of a Prime Minister in robust/vibrant/sparkling shoot-the-messenger form.

As if John Major did not have enough problems with his own side – Government, Party, back-benchers, and Margaret Thatcher, to name but four – from the spring of 1994 he faced a resurgent Labour Party under its new leader, Tony Blair. This mortal combination of forces was just too much. Repeated reshuffles, denying the Whip to recalcitrant back-benchers, the extreme step in 1995 of resigning the Party leadership and standing for re-election – all these stratagems provided only the most insubstantial toe-holds in an inexorable slide down the political glacier.

In a last-ditch attempt to get a grip, John Major made Michael 'Tarzan' Heseltine Deputy Prime Minister in 1995. Heseltine was a heavyweight who, in normal circumstances, would have been a serious contender for Major's job. But his pro-European credentials, combined with the role he had played in bringing down Margaret Thatcher, made him anathema to many in the Tory Party. He was no natural ally of Major's. His appointment was some kind of Faustian bargain, but I could never work out who was Faust and who the Devil.

Heseltine was given the task of bringing strategic coherence and discipline to government and party. To accomplish this, he took for himself in Whitehall an office of immense proportions, in which five-a-side football would have been possible. The room was furnished with plump sofas and a single high-backed chair in the middle. At the morning strategy meetings Heseltine sat on the chair as if on a throne. The rest of us, politicos and civil servants, sank almost horizontally into the sofas. Though unmatched in their comfort, they only emphasized our submission to the Sun God, with his golden mane of hair.

These were strange meetings. Heseltine would summon other cabinet ministers to account for the presentation of their policies. Brian Mawhinney, the Party Chairman, would flash his shark's teeth and pour withering scorn on the civil servants. Tony Newton, Lord President of the Council, would bring us simple truths, harvested from other commuters on the train from Essex. Mighty grids and plans were commissioned so that the government could seize back the agenda from New Labour. All of this activity withered in the harsh light of political reality.

It was a measure of the pressures on Major that he found respite in the intractable problems of Northern Ireland. The cares of the world would fall from his shoulders on our many visits to Ulster. He immersed himself in the history of the province. To the consternation of police and security men, he plunged into crowds, Catholic and Protestant, and was greeted warmly by almost all. Here he was the bold statesman and natural-born politician who, if he had been able to duplicate this form on the mainland (as I never ceased to point out to him), would have swept all before him. Major did not mind tough negotiation, at which he excelled, and appeared impervious to physical danger. But what crippled him, and diminished him in Westminster and the country at large, was the spite and personal nature of the attacks that he had to endure.

His resilience under fire was nonetheless remarkable. He was never the boring, grey man of caricature. He was temperamental, passionate and thin-skinned. He concealed this in public with an iron self-discipline. He was the devil to work for. But you had to like and admire him.

Nowadays, I choke on my toast when I hear politicians and others complaining about the 'breakdown in trust' between government and media, for which, so they tell me, journalists are largely responsible. Of course, a lot of the criticism in the press is partisan. It is meant to be. Sometimes it is terribly unfair. But this is a free press operating in a democracy. As the government's spokesman, I came to realize that the power of government to control and shape the flow of information is overwhelming and potentially dangerous. 'Spinning' – briefing the press to put the government in the best possible light – is the second oldest profession. The notion that objectivity and accuracy would be better served if government were able to transmit its policies directly to the voters, unmediated by journalism, is specious and self-serving. There is no policy without politics; and no politics without bias and distortion.

Nor is there a Westminster without politicians and journalists cohabiting in an incestuous relationship of lunches, dinners and off-the-record briefings. Politicians are the first to come running when journalists snap their fingers. It was ever thus. In reality, as an editor of the *Sun* once admitted to me, newspapers have little effect on how people vote. Politicians would do themselves a favour if they were less sensitive to what is written about them and less eager to ingratiate themselves with editors and proprietors.

And pigs might fly.

3

Nothing Personal, Jean-Luc

John Major suffered two ghastly torments in particular. One was Europe, the other the press. Often the two were in tandem. The Conservatives tore themselves to pieces over Europe, egged on by some of the newspapers. The Eurosceptics claimed to be defending the legacy of Margaret Thatcher, with whom Major was compared unfavourably. Lady Thatcher was widely believed to be encouraging them. Nostalgia for the Thatcher era, and bad conscience at having got rid of her, ran like poison through Conservative veins. The Tories rapidly forgot that the very quality of strong leadership, impervious to criticism, which they professed to admire in Thatcher and find wanting in Major, had been seen only a few years previously as purblind obstinacy, leading to her downfall.

The bitter enmity inside the Conservative Party between pro- and anti-Europeans underwrote Major's longevity as Prime Minister and Party leader. In the spring of 1994 there was a smell of conspiracy in the air. I wondered whether he would last the summer. But the Party was simply unable to coalesce around a figure to replace Major. The two most heavyweight candidates were Michael Heseltine and Kenneth Clarke. Both were ardent pro-Europeans and so anathema to a large number of Conservative MPs. The less heavyweight figures of Michael Portillo and John Redwood, the leading Eurosceptics, aroused an equal and opposite resistance among the pro-Europeans in the party. The only credible compromise candidate was John Major himself.

Major exhausted himself in the futile effort to find a middle way between the pro- and anti-European factions. In 1994, in, of all places, the sun-kissed island of Corfu, as my hotel brochure described it, I assumed involuntarily a leading role in this Manichean melodrama. It was all the fault of Jacques Delors.

Delors was to retire as President of the European Commission at the end of 1994. The Commission is the executive body which runs the European Union on a day-to-day basis, proposing and implementing the rules and regulations that govern the Union. Delors was a hate-figure for the Eurosceptics. The *Sun*, the top-selling daily British tabloid, once ran the front-page headline: 'Up Yours, Delors'. He was seen as the arch-apostle of European integration and enemy of Britain's national identity. He had clashed often with Margaret Thatcher. For the British, he had also committed the unpardonable sin of being French. Finding a successor to him was therefore a hot political potato of the first order.

As usual, France and Germany tried to stitch things up in advance. They decided that the Belgian Prime Minister, the rotund Jean-Luc Dehaene, should be the new Commission President. He was considered by the French and Germans to be eminently amenable to their interests. They expected the rest of the EU to fall in behind without too much argument. But the British Eurosceptics, once they had answered the question 'Jean-Luc who?', went for him with a vengeance. The tabloids mocked him. Dehaene was a Delors clone, they screamed. He committed the even more unpardonable sin of being Belgian: Prime Minister of a joke country, which had refused to sell Britain ammunition during the Falklands War and in whose capital, Brussels, the monstrous regiment of Eurocrats marched to the beat of the French and German drum.

The decision on Delors's successor was to be taken at a summit meeting of European leaders in Corfu in June 1994. The vote had to be unanimous. There were other candidates in the field, but Dehaene was the favourite. Britain would have preferred the Dutch Prime Minister, Ruud Lubbers, but somewhere along the line he had ruined his chances by getting on the wrong side of Chancellor Kohl of Germany. We would also have backed Leon Brittan, one of the British Commissioners; but he was an outside candidate.

Major set off for Corfu to a loud chorus of demands that he should veto Dehaene. The whips were telling Major this would do wonders for party morale. I could see that it would throw a juicy bone to the press, especially to Major's tormentors in the Murdoch and Rothermere empires. The problem was that, Lubbers and Brittan aside, the possible successors to the Great Delors were for the most part a bunch of political pygmies. Dehaene was in truth no better or worse than the alternatives.

I did not know which way Major would jump. He had already made it known to other governments that to foist Dehaene on the EU in this way was unacceptable. But would he veto on the night? I kept the Lobby at bay by nodding and winking that we were being canny by keeping our cards close to our chest. This was the flimsiest of material. I needed urgently to be able to give clear guidance to the press. Otherwise they would write their stories on the basis of, heaven forfend, French or German sources. European summits were furnaces of competitive briefing by the national spokesmen.

It was all to be decided at a dinner in a hotel in the hills behind Corfu town. The issue was considered so sensitive that only presidents and prime ministers, and their closest advisers, were invited by our Greek hosts. I meantime dined in a pretty harbour-side restaurant with the Sunday Lobby, the political journalists who wrote for the Sunday papers. I was fairly confident that before coffee either Major would come back or word would descend from the hills of what had been decided. A very long and well-lubricated meal came to an end with no news. The Sunday hacks were restless. I was worried. It was getting late and this was the big story of the summit.

Major finally returned at around 2 a.m. We gathered in his hotel suite. There was Douglas Hurd, the Foreign Secretary, who had challenged Major for the Thatcher succession: urbane, a little aloof, a former career diplomat and the occasional writer of thrillers; John Kerr, my old friend and our ambassador to the EU, who was a master of its Byzantine politics; Sarah Hogg, the head of the No. 10 Policy Unit, who had been with Major a long time and had helped him beat Neil Kinnock in the 1992 election; and me. Ken Clarke, the Chancellor of the Exchequer, was also part of the British delegation, but I have no recollection of seeing him in Corfu.

I was agitated. What had happened? Major told a long, bizarre story of a dinner and discussion, chaired so ineptly by the ailing Greek President Papandreou that several prime ministers had thought the meeting over when it was not and had had to be recalled when their cavalcades were already driving home. 'Get to the point, get to the point,' I muttered to myself. I was boiling with impatience. It was already at least 3 a.m. A crowd of journalists was waiting for me in the press centre in Corfu town.

Then we got to the climax. The meeting had finally broken up without a final decision. Discussion would resume the following morning. But, in his flat and undramatic way, Major recounted a conversation with Kohl.

'Is Dehaene acceptable to you?' asked Kohl.

'No,' said Major.

Kohl asked again and Major gave the same answer.

'Right,' I thought, 'it has to be a veto. I must get to the hacks before the Germans do.' It was vital to get our take, or 'spin', into the reporters' notebooks first. I said so to Major.

'No. I don't want you to do that,' Major said.

'But,' I protested, 'you know Kohl's people. They will brief immediately. We cannot leave the press with a German account of a British veto.'

Major would not budge. There followed an inconclusive discussion. Major repeated that he had made clear to Kohl that he could not support Dehaene. But he did not want me to tell the press that it was a veto. I was baffled at first. But then I saw that it was the purest metaphor for his European predicament: a European Morton's Fork, with Major trying to find a middle way between the prongs.

After a while Major said in exasperation to no one in particular, 'You decide.' With magisterial ambivalence, Hurd interjected: 'The Prime Minister is tired, he needs to go to bed, and that's where I'm going.'

'Thank you very much for that useful guidance,' I thought sourly. I had just got another message from the press centre, imploring me to hurry up. Rumours of a British veto of Dehaene were beginning to circulate. The German briefers were reported to be advancing in force. The British hacks were getting mutinous. I huddled with Sarah Hogg and John Kerr outside the Prime Minister's suite.

'I have to speak to the press within the next hour. I cannot duck the veto question. I have to say, because that is what the Boss said he said to Kohl, that we will block Dehaene. I may have no cover from Major or Hurd, but I think we have no choice in the matter.' Sarah and John did not disagree.

I was less than happy as I drove into Corfu town; it must have been somewhere between 3 and 4 in the morning. I was on my own. I had visions of being disowned the next day if I said that Britain would veto Dehaene.

I entered the British briefing room at the press centre. It looked like the fag end of a binge drinking session. The place was packed. Some journalists were asleep. Some looked tired and emotional. Some were playing cards. There were beer cans on the floor. The air was thick with cigarette smoke. As I walked in, people rushed to their desks, fumbling for pens and paper. It was like a rowdy classroom when the headmaster walks in. I made them sweat a bit, offering a lengthy reportage on the dinner until I got to the nub: we would veto Dehaene. The hacks rushed from the room to file their reports. I was left alone with a microphone, my assistant, a snoring journalist, and scattered chairs.

A few hours later I emerged from my hotel room after a sleep as brief as it was disturbed. I immediately ran into a smiling Douglas Hurd. 'Jolly good briefing you gave last night to the press,' he said without batting an eyelid; 'I used the transcript for my *Today* interview a few minutes ago.' Douglas had confirmed the veto! I was swept with relief. Nonetheless, I arrived at John Major's suite with dark foreboding. I entered to find a chirpy Prime Minister, wreathed in smiles.

'I knew I had taken the right decision to veto Dehaene,' said John Major; 'the whips have just rung to congratulate me, the Party is delighted, and we have got exceedingly good headlines.'

'I'll be buggered,' I thought to myself. 'Politicians!'

John Major enjoyed it while it lasted. It did not last long. Once the veto 'triumph' had been gulped down and digested, the question 'If not Dehaene, who?' had to be answered. And the uninspiring answer was, *faute de mieux*, the Prime Minister of Luxembourg, Jacques Santer. It was impossible to demonstrate that Santer would be any better for Britain than Dehaene. But the British press, having gorged on 'Jean-Luc who?', had no appetite for 'Jacques who?' Santer's presidency was to end ignominiously amid allegations of corruption.

No hard feelings, I hope, Jean-Luc.

4

A Small Town in Germany

To become ambassador in Washington I had first to pass through Bonn in 1997. My qualification for becoming Britain's ambassador to Germany was as follows: a German O level acquired at the age of fifteen. I had never served in Germany. I had visited it rarely. I once had a girl friend from Hamburg. This triumph of Foreign Office career planning, to which I raised no objection, was pure expedience. I had been trained in the sixties as a Russian specialist. I expected to end my diplomatic days as ambassador to Moscow, where I had already spent two postings. But the Foreign Office found itself in a jam: its most senior German expert – Pauline Neville-Jones, now Dame, chairman of Qinetic and a former BBC governor – refused to go to Bonn. I was just about the only senior diplomat available to take her place.

I took my leave from No. 10 at the beginning of 1996 after exactly two years in the job. John Major did not want the idea to gain currency that I was fed up and jumping ship. The reason given for my departure, therefore, was the appointment to Bonn and the need to prepare for it. This did not wash, because I was not due to arrive in Germany until over a year later. So the assumption was exactly what Major wanted to avoid: that I had got out to avoid going down with a sinking ship. I was not too pleased with this interpretation either. In fact my understanding with Major had always been to stay with him for two years. More to the point, my marriage had collapsed, making concentration on the job impossible. But that was not something I wished to disclose publicly.

I had months of intensive German-language training in London. To my dismay I discovered that my ear for languages had deteriorated with the passage of the years. Languages that I knew already, especially Russian, kept forcing themselves into my attempts to speak German. My teacher asked me how come I spoke German with a Russian accent.

In the autumn I went to live incognito in Germany, firstly in Hamburg, where I lodged for a month on the banks of the Elbe with a charming divorcee and her daughter. My clapped-out Mini was, in Hamburg, something of a status symbol. I went to a couple of football matches, but the Hamburg team had slipped badly from its glory days with Kevin Keegan, known locally as 'Mighty Mouse'. Hamburg is reputed to be the most anglophile of German cities, despite the RAF's flattening it during the Second World War. It was certainly the case that tweed jackets and Church's shoes were ubiquitous. Everyone seemed to speak good English, including the large community of Turkish immigrants. At the football games the fans chanted in English. They even sang 'You'll Never Walk Alone', Gerry Marsden-style. Hell will freeze over before the Liverpool Kop sing in German.

I then went south to Ebenhausen, a Bavarian village just outside Munich. This was home to a think tank called the Stiftung Wissenschaft und Politik, which focused heavily on foreign policy. Its then director, the glamorous and high-profile Michael Stürmer, had invited me to do some research and learn some German along the way. This was bracing, both intellectually and linguistically. The Bavarian dialect is so distinct that it might have been a different language from the German that I had been speaking in Hamburg. This led to endless confusion. I lost half my underwear and shirts to the leisurely village laundry, when I failed to comprehend that it would take *eine gute Woche* ('a good week') to have them washed and ironed. The week was so good that it was actually two weeks before I saw my linen again. For some incomprehensible reason my shirts and boxer shorts had to be sent to Munich for laundering. Perhaps it was because they were foreign and needed, in Bavarian eyes, the most meticulous cleansing, of which only a big city was capable.

But there were compensations. I developed a taste for blood sausage, aka black pudding, and wheat beer. I read a paper to the think tank in which I argued, in German, that the twin processes of widening and deepening in the European Union – that is, enlarging membership and centralizing decision-taking – were ultimately irreconcilable and would end in tears. My shocked German audience dismissed this as the typically eccentric vapourings of an unreconstructed English Eurosceptic. Then there was the strange case of the Ukrainian army delegation who took part in a conference on military matters at the institute. I was intrigued that none of the delegation had a Ukrainian accent and very few a Ukrainian surname. They sounded like typical Soviet Russians. Later, after a few drinks, we discovered that the Ukrainians had all been officers in the Soviet Army in Germany. I wondered where their loyalties really lay.

Finally, in March 1997, I arrived in Bonn, a single man, to take up my appointment. I expected a full four years. I was looking forward to moving the embassy from Bonn to Berlin, where the German parliament had voted by a narrow majority to reinstate the capital. I would have been the first British ambassador in Berlin since 1939.

My brief, seven-month sojourn in Germany was an intense experience, professionally and emotionally. I threw myself into getting to know the country. I travelled to almost all the *Länder*, or regions. In speeches and interviews I took my chances with my brand-new German. This led to numerous embarrassments, the most common being that when I finally got to the verb at the end of the sentence – which is where the Germans usually put it – I could not remember how I had begun. But this, and going out with German women, were the fastest way of getting to grips with the language.

The Germany that revealed itself to me was a mass of contradictions. Actually, most countries are. The trick is to find out what they are, and why. Having fought two world wars against the Germans in the twentieth century, it was easy to forget that they had been a unified nation for little over a century. Regional diversity was deeply ingrained. So was the line between the northern Protestant and southern Catholic traditions. Edmund Stoiber, the Prime Minister of Bavaria, once told me that politically he felt he had more in common with London than with Bonn. There is a war memorial in Munich to the Bavarians who fought alongside the French against the Prussians in the Napoleonic Wars.

There was a marked division, which no German liked to talk about, between those who had lived in the old communist East Germany – the 'Ossis' – and those who lived in the rest of the country – the 'Wessis'. Following Germany's reunification in 1989, the Wessis resented the tax they had to pay to help subsidize the East. I was told that a trillion Deutschmarks had been transferred to the East, of which around two-thirds was being spent on welfare payments. The Ossis resented the higher standard of living in the West and the fact that they had to live on handouts from Bonn. Some nurtured an ill-concealed nostalgia for their communist past, in which consumerism had played little role. I found myself in many a strained conversation between Wessis and Ossis.

Germany's conservatism was suffocating. So its equal and opposite indulgence in anarchy and the wilder side of life came as a shock. In 1997 there was endless debate about whether to allow shops to open for a couple of hours on Saturday afternoons. Sunday opening was beyond the pale. By Saturday mid-afternoon the only action to be found in German towns was in the cafés. Here the middle class flocked for their traditional tea and cream cakes. I dreaded a wet Sunday afternoon in Bonn.

Yet some weekends a rather vibrant German anarchist movement would loot a supermarket or two in Berlin. In the early evening German television gave you oompah bands in leather shorts; in the later hours an obsession with specialized forms of sex, in which leather again played a leading role. The gardener in the ambassador's house in Berlin, now the official residence, used to parade before me, pushing his lawnmower in tight leather shorts, oiled legs and what looked like a codpiece.

If you wanted rock'n'roll, it would probably be provided by an ancient British heavy metal band or David Hasselhof from *Baywatch*, God forbid. I once saw a Japanese ballet in Hamburg, which comprised three nude males standing motionless, while a fourth male, dressed in a woman's nightie, crawled back and forth across the stage. The performance was received with thunderous applause from a large audience, who, to all outward appearances, were paid-up members of the tea-and-cream-cakes brigade.

My assignment in Bonn began inauspiciously. The German government under Chancellor Helmut Kohl had given up on John Major's administration. It was not just British Euroscepticism, but the well-founded belief that the Tories were poor, limping creatures who would soon be put out of their misery by the electorate. The Germans also assumed that, with the demise of Major, I would be sacked by his successor. That would have been the German way. I was quite worried. No one knew how a Labour government would behave after eighteen years in opposition. There was a fear among Britain's senior ambassadors that those most closely associated with the outgoing Conservatives – like me – would be for the chop.

In the event, nothing of the kind happened. Labour's crushing victory in May 1997 enormously enhanced my position and possibilities in Germany. Blair's triumph was almost as dramatic for the Germans as it was for the British. Suddenly the UK was on the map again. This coincided with a moment of doubt in the German government about the wisdom of launching the euro on its due date of January 1999.

Helmut Kohl, the Jabba the Hutt of German politics, had devoted his career to two projects: the reunification of Germany and the unification of Europe inside the European Union. It was always interesting to hear Kohl talk about this to a German audience. The rationale for reunifying Germany needed little explanation; that for a united Europe needed more. Kohl belonged to the last generation of politicians who had a personal memory of the Second World War. Much of what he had to say was couched within the framework of an historic reconciliation between Germany and France and the elimination of war from the continent of Europe. In a meeting with Kohl I told him that my father, an RAF pilot, had been killed in the war. He had been posted missing in action a week or so before I was born. Tears filled his eyes and, having asked whether my mother was still alive, he handed me a small gift for her.

Sewn into Kohl's public rhetoric was the idea that Germany's destiny was to lead Europe; but that, against the background of Nazism, this could be accomplished only within the constraints on national sovereignty provided by the European Union. This alone would inoculate against the fear elsewhere in Europe of what the Soviet propagandists used to call 'German revanchism'.

I doubted that for some in France any amount of inoculation would suffice after four major wars against the Germans in one hundred and fifty years, in two of which they had been crushed and in another almost bled to death. More than once senior French officials emphasized to me how important it was for Britain to play a full role in Europe to counterbalance the Germans. I used to hear exactly the same argument in reverse from the Germans.

When I arrived in Germany in March 1997, the next step in the

European project was the introduction of the euro. Strict rules had been drawn up to establish eligibility for membership. This had been largely driven by the Bonn government. It needed to be able to reassure German voters that it was safe to abandon their beloved Deutschmark and that their savings would not be debauched by the new currency. In early 1997 the Germans went wobbly. It looked as if their level of government debt would breach one of the key rules. The Italians were in even worse shape. Perhaps the whole thing should be put off a year, muttered the political class.

The Italian question – real enough – was useful camouflage for German worries about their own economy. A rigid labour market and huge welfare costs were knocking the shine off the German economic miracle, driving down productivity and driving up unemployment. A debate raged – it still does – about the relative merits of the German economic model and that of the 'Anglo-Saxons', the US and UK. Jürgen Stark, at the time the deputy German Finance Minister, was blunt with me in a private conversation. He said that the Italian economy, at least in the north, was actually performing better than the German. It was a huge gamble for Germany to adopt the euro before liberalizing and reforming its economy. Yet, he continued, the euro was essential as an alibi for pushing through painful reforms that would otherwise be politically unacceptable.

This was a failed prediction. The Germans, French and others have preferred to weaken the eurozone's disciplines rather than make the necessary reforms. I was frequently asked in interviews why Britain had been able to liberalize its economy and Germany not. I used to say that Britain had reformed a failed economy. The Germans had the much tougher political task of reforming an economy which had delivered post-war recovery, stability and prosperity. Nothing concentrated the mind more than looking into the abyss. In Britain we had done that in the 1970s. Germany had yet to look into the abyss. It still hasn't.

As this debate ebbed and flowed, enter a new British government, brandishing gleaming European pretensions.

5

New Labour Has Landed

'Is this for real?' my German friends asked about Tony Blair's strongly pro-European rhetoric following his election victory in May 1997. 'Or is this a rerun of John Major's failed ambition to be at the heart of Europe?'

There was a profound wish across the German establishment that it should be for real. The litmus test would be the new government's intentions towards the euro. Would it honour its commitment to hold a referendum on giving up the pound and, if so, when?

In my brief seven months as ambassador successive visits by Robin Cook, the new Foreign Secretary, Peter Mandelson, an ardent pro-European who had become Minister without Portfolio (i.e. odd-job man for the government), and Tony Blair himself, encouraged the Germans to think that this time it really would be different.

It was not, of course, though at the time that was not obvious. Sitting in Bonn, I even detected a vibration from London that Blair might be considering a quick euro-referendum in the autumn of 1997, to cash in on the new government's soaring popularity. But it was not to be. Instead, the government constructed an elaborate argument around the need for the British and eurozone economies to converge more closely before our membership could be contemplated. There was much talk about the economic cycles being out of sync. It was quite convincing for a while. In reality it masked a failure of political will.

A week or so after the general election, the late Robin Cook paid a lightning visit to Bonn, after a similar stop in Paris on the same day. This encouraged him to hint in public at a three-nation directory of the European Union, comprising Britain, France and Germany. To the French and German political elites this was heresy. Their commitment was to an EU driven by the Franco-German motor. They did not want the awkward Brits trying to elbow their way in. I heard much German tut-tutting afterwards.

Cook, a man more to be admired than liked, put in a bravura performance. His German opposite number, Klaus Kinkel, took Cook to a little restaurant called Kinkel's (no relation) in Kinkel-strasse. There we had a traditional German lunch for that time of the year of white asparagus and white wine. Kinkel, who sported a nifty Tony Curtis hairstyle, had been in office for years. He was surrounded by advisers and a mountain of briefs. Cook had with him no briefs that I could detect, just a notepad with a few jottings. If you had not known, you would have thought Kinkel the novice and Cook the man with years of experience. It was admirable. People in the Foreign Office told me later that Cook was idle about reading his briefs. If that was so, he managed to conceal it through a natural intelligence and a lucid, forensic style of exposition.

A month later Tony Blair himself came to Bonn for an afternoon's talks with Chancellor Kohl. Of all the Blair visits I hosted in Bonn and Washington, this was the most light-hearted. Blair was accompanied by his closest advisers: Jonathan Powell, chief of staff; Alastair Campbell, spokesman; Anji Hunter, special assistant to the Prime Minister; and John Holmes, the career diplomat who served as his Foreign Policy Adviser. They were still in the first flush of electoral victory. There was something almost touching about the excitement that ran through all of them. It was still an age of innocence, which would, of course, quickly pass. We had a sandwich lunch in my office, sprawling around, shooting the breeze, discussing how to handle Kohl.

As we drove in my armoured Rolls-Royce to the Chancellor's office, Blair asked me, 'How are you getting on?'

'Well, really well,' I replied. 'But when I am in the Rolls, I have to pinch myself that this really is me.'

'Tell me about it,' said Blair with his boyish smile. 'How do you think I feel?'

I can remember almost nothing concrete emerging from Blair's meeting with Kohl. But that was not the point. Each was feeling his way with the other, Blair the *ingénu*, Kohl the Grand Old Man of European politics. Kohl was obviously fascinated by this young whippersnapper. He showed to Blair, as he always did to me, a genial, rumbling condescension, in which anecdote and reminiscence played a large part.

I never had a meeting with Kohl which did not involve his telling me some story about Margaret Thatcher. I got the impression that he had been seared by his encounters with her. He once told me at enormous length his version of the notorious Austrian tea-shop story (there is another version told by Charles – now Lord – Powell, who was then Thatcher's foreign policy adviser). He and his late wife Hannelore had gone to have tea with Lady Thatcher at her summer holiday home in Austria. What had been intended by Kohl as a purely social event turned into a harangue by her about something political – or at least, so he claimed. Kohl decided that he had had enough, made an excuse about another engagement, and he and his wife took their leave. They went straight to a café to have tea and cakes. Meanwhile, Lady Thatcher and Sir Denis had decided to take a walk in the town. As they passed the tea-shop, they saw through the window the Kohls tucking in. Kohl laughed volcanically when he got to the pay-off line.

On another occasion Kohl told me how disconcerting it was to have tea at No. 10. Margaret Thatcher would bustle around with teapot and cakes. Then, just as Kohl was beginning to relax, like Jekyll and Hyde she would switch from *hausfrau* to Prime Minister and try to skewer him on something like European agricultural subsidies. In these stories I always detected a sense of hurt on Kohl's part, like a suitor rebuffed.

There is a book to be written about Margaret Thatcher's relations with male foreign leaders: Gorbachev, who always blushed when he saw her; Reagan, who, to the irritation of his staff, rarely resisted her advocacy (this in part explains Thatcher's less-than-happy relationship with Reagan's successor, George Bush the elder, whose advisers were determined to cut the British Prime Minister down to size); President Samora Machel of Mozambique, whose infatuation with her was such that he once entrusted Geoffrey Howe, on a visit to Maputo, with an enormous box of frozen prawns to give her; Mitterrand, who said of her that she had the lips of Marilyn Monroe and the eyes of Caligula.

After Blair's meeting with Kohl, I flew back to London on the No. 10 aircraft. The weekend was coming up and I was in hot pursuit of the woman who is now my wife. Alastair Campbell and

I talked about handling the press. It was all very easy-going. 'These are people I can do business with,' I thought to myself. I think that this was the view throughout the Civil Service. People had got fed up with the exhausted Conservative government and prayed for a change. New Labour looked so fresh, promised so much and fired the enthusiasm of most civil servants. Soon after the election, Blair played a masterstroke in sending the Civil Service a message of thanks for helping New Labour ease its way into government. It does not take much to win over civil servants. They like to be thanked – it does not happen very often – just as they prefer a strong minister to a weak one (ministers who complain that they cannot control their civil servants are simply not up to the job). This was a good start; but it proved just another New Labour honeymoon that would end in tears.

New Labour's sister party in Germany was the SPD, the Social Democratic Party. It was powerfully impressed by Blair's victory and the rhetoric of the Third Way. To a degree it was destabilized also. Years previously the SPD had 'reformed' itself and discarded a load of Marxist baggage. But New Labour and Tony Blair were very different animals from the SPD and its leftish leader Oskar Lafontaine. All eyes were on the forthcoming German general election in 1998. Lafontaine's chances were not highly rated. The SPD looked enviously westward: Blair in power in London and the socialist Lionel Jospin in Paris. There was much talk about the need for a new leader. Who was the SPD's Tony Blair or Lionel Jospin?

I went to see the jovial, sharp-tongued Lafontaine. I noticed that his outer office was replete with good-looking women. 'I am fed up,' he complained to me, 'I am fed up with being compared to the British and French prime ministers. Do they want me to change my name to Tony Jospin?' 'Better than Lionel Blair,' I thought to myself.

In the end, it was Gerhard Schröder, Prime Minister of Lower Saxony, who took control of the SPD and went on to become German Chancellor. He did so on the back of a political campaign that preached the virtues of the New Centre, a German variant of the Third Way, but even more vacuous. I first met Schröder at Hanover airport in early 1997. We were both waiting to greet the Duke of Edinburgh, who was to open the British pavilion at the trade fair. This was the occasion when the Duke, instead of referring in his speech to Kohl as *Bundeskanzler*, called him *Reichskanzler*, a title last used by Hitler. In the audience a pulse of predatory delight passed through the British press, one of horror through the German dignitaries.

Schröder asked me to sit with him in his car, as we waited on the tarmac. 'How friendly,' I thought. Then, for fifteen minutes, Schröder proceeded to pump me relentlessly on how New Labour had taken power: strategy, tactics, slogans. You could not help liking this cigar-smoking, backslapping opportunist. Years later Blair and President George W. Bush found to their discomfort that Schröder was not a man to bet your mortgage on.

It was a pity that Schröder was unable to meet Peter Mandelson, who visited Bonn very soon after Blair. He was much better placed, as an architect of Labour's victory, to explain to Schröder how it had been done. I organized a dinner for Mandelson. I invited a wide range of members of the German parliament. He gave a fine exposition of New Labour's genesis, principles and ambitions. No one did the Third Way/New Labour riff better. An SPD parliamentarian asked Mandelson what was the single most important step taken to make Labour electable. 'You have to break the organic link with the trade unions,' replied Mandelson. There was a sharp intake of breath around the table. 'We could never do that here,' said the SPD man.

Later Mandelson and I travelled to the airport to catch a flight to Munich. We were going to one of the Club of Three meetings organized by Lord Weidenfeld. These brought together the great and the good from Britain, France and Germany. Mandelson ruminated on the lack of discipline in the old Major government: so many leaks, so much backstabbing; how could I have stood it, when I worked in Downing Streeet? New Labour would never be like that. 'Wait for the stormy weather,' I said. 'That's the test.'

I was having a good time in Bonn. Britain and Germany had become important to each other once again. The flow of politicians and businessmen in each direction sent a shot of adrenalin through the embassy. Most people assume that when I got the call to transfer to Washington, I could not leave Germany fast enough. It was not like that. Of course, I wanted to go to Washington, the pinnacle of a diplomatic career. But I had invested so much effort in getting to grips with Germany. I regretted that much of this would go to waste.

Today, for example, my German language is sadly decayed. I was just beginning to get beneath the surface of German life. It was fascinating. For the most part I liked and was stimulated by the Germans. I left Germany with regrets and considerable affection. These sentiments were not wholly unconnected with meeting and wooing my wife-to-be on the banks of the Rhine. But it was precisely her experience that was to turn my warm feelings about Germany into disenchantment.

6

Catherine's Story

Germany was where I met my wife, Catherine. I first encountered her in April 1997 when she called on me in Bonn in my official capacity. She wanted my help.

Before arriving in Bonn I had been warned by the Foreign Office about the case of Catherine Laylle (her maiden name). It was pointed out to me that the issue was a private dispute between estranged spouses. Any assistance to be given her either by the embassy or the consulate in Hamburg was to be strictly limited.

Soon after arriving in Bonn, I received a letter from Catherine, asking if she could come to see me. Accompanying the letter was a copy of her book *Two Children Behind a Wall*.* I asked my staff to get instructions from London on how they wanted me to handle Ms Laylle. I put her book aside without opening it.

Typically, weeks passed without a reply from the Foreign Office. To my embarrassment, before I had had the chance to answer her letter, Catherine telephoned me. I was put on the defensive. I knew that she was media-savvy and that she had the support of MPs in London. I agreed on the spot to a meeting at the embassy. Catherine was coming to Bonn anyway, to see if she could persuade any German MPs to help her. (She failed.)

Shortly before the meeting I finally opened her book. There were the usual photos in the middle. These revealed a very attractive woman. I was instantly enthused at the prospect of meeting her. As is normal in the Diplomatic Service, my staff proposed that one of them should accompany me at the meeting – to take a record, answer technical questions on family law and so on. 'No, I will see her alone. It's always for the best in cases like this,' I said. Then I added shamelessly, 'You need the personal touch when you can't

* Later substantially revised and published in America as *They Are My Children, Too.*

offer much in the way of practical help.' I blush to think of it. For all the wrong motives I did the right thing by meeting Catherine Laylle.

In case things got difficult, I told my private secretary John Krauss (Meyer and Krauss: it sounded like a firm of German lawyers) to interrupt the meeting after about thirty minutes.

'She's here,' said John.

'Show her up,' I replied.

The door opened and in came this very pretty, fragile-looking woman.

'Good afternoon, Miss Laylle,' I said, grinning fatuously (thinks: 'Much better-looking than her photos'). 'Have a cup of tea.'

Catherine was as businesslike and determined as she was good-looking. I rapidly realized that she was well versed in the evasions and half-truths of bureaucrats, lawyers and politicians. This was not a woman to be trifled with.

She told a shocking story, the details of which I was later able independently to corroborate. Her estranged German husband had, in contravention of a custody agreement and an English court order, kept their two sons, aged nine and seven, in Germany, when they had visited him in the summer holidays of 1994. He would neither return the children to London nor let Catherine have access to them, save under the most closely supervised conditions in his home town in Lower Saxony. The rare visits she was able to make, during which a third party – usually a German bureaucrat – was invariably present, had become an intolerable ordeal for both mother and children, as, no doubt, they were intended to be. The spurious justification for these inhuman conditions was that Catherine herself might kidnap the children.

The German courts behaved with systematic bias against someone who was not German. In Britain things were little better. The Lord Chancellor's Department, responsible for judicial matters, including the enforcement of the Hague Convention, had been in turn unsympathetic, misleading and obstructive. This later prompted Catherine to make a formal complaint of maladministration to the Parliamentary Ombudsman against the Lord Chancellor's Department.* She won her case in 2005 and the Department was forced to

---

* Now the Department for Constitutional Affairs.

apologize. I myself raised Catherine's case with the then Lord Chancellor, Lord Mackay, only to have it dismissively brushed aside. His successor, Lord Irvine, was no improvement. It seemed to Catherine and me that it was more important to the Lord Chancellor's Department to maintain solidarity between judiciaries than to uphold the rights of a British subject.

The likeable Geoff Hoon, then a junior minister in the Lord Chancellor's Department and later Blair's Defence Secretary, sent an unhelpful letter to Catherine, for which he had the good grace later to apologize to her privately. The Foreign Office eventually tried to help, thanks in particular to a few gallant individuals, but found its hands tied by the Lord Chancellor's Department. It talked about not interfering in the administration of justice in another country.

Because Catherine carried both a French and a British passport, she had sought help in Paris as well. In contrast to the British government, the French had been active on her behalf, though so far to no avail. Catherine's problem was very familiar to the French authorities. Many mixed French–German marriages had ended with the German spouse taking the children to Germany, with the French spouse unable to locate, still less to have access to, the children.

'I have lived in Britain for over thirty years, I am a British citizen, and I have been paying British taxes for most of my adult life,' Catherine said with fierce indignation and determination. 'Both my children are British subjects. Surely I can expect at least as much help from my own government as from the French.' I did not know how to reply. My instructions from London, such as they were, gave me little latitude. I had tea and I had sympathy, but that was about it.

'Miss Laylle,' I said (I begin to blush again at the memory), 'the only practical way forward is for you to reach an understanding with your husband. But I very much comprehend how you feel. I am legally separated from my wife, I have two sons as well, and it would be beyond bearing not to be able to see them.' I was, of course, sending a double message: 'I feel your pain – and by the way, I am available.' That was certainly how Catherine heard it.

We had a long meeting. We had much in common. We discussed things other than her tragic case. She is half-Russian and I had begun life in the Foreign Office as a Russian specialist. We discovered that, twice in our lives, as in a Pasternak novel, our paths had almost crossed in Moscow: once in 1968, when she had been visiting her aunt, a notable dissident writer; and again in 1984, when, on the day of Yuri Andropov's death, she had been in the Russian Writers' Club, and I had been laid up with flu in my flat a quarter of a mile away. After about half an hour John Krauss, as instructed, knocked on the door and came in to tell me that I had another appointment. I told him to bugger off.

With the greatest difficulty I stopped myself from looking at Catherine's legs. I succumbed to the temptation only as she was leaving my office. She told me later that she was instantly aware of this. She sensed my eyes boring into her calves like red-hot pokers. I was very gratified by what I saw. The plain truth was that I was enormously attracted to Catherine. I later discovered that the feeling was mutual. How was I to follow up without abusing my position? I assumed that Catherine would send me some letter of thanks for seeing her and this would give me an opening. She did and it did.

We started talking regularly on the phone. In one of these conversations I asked her when she would return to Bonn.

'But I have no reason to come,' she said.

'Oh yes, you do,' I replied. 'You have an invitation from Her Britannic Majesty's Ambassador to the Federal Republic of Germany.'

From then on Catherine's visits to Bonn became increasingly long and frequent. We got to know each other on the banks of the Rhine and the Moselle and over weekends in Berlin. I had never liked Berlin before, which I found drab and too communist in style. But Catherine introduced me to a world of small cafés and restaurants. We took long walks in the country around Potsdam and along the banks of the Wannsee. We bought Soviet memorabilia and Palekh boxes from the Russian street market by the Brandenburg Gate. We saw a superb production of *Mother Courage* by the Théâtre de la Complicité in a former bus garage in the old communist sector. Berlin went from drab to romantic in the twinkling of a Mills and Boon eye.

For a while the course of true love ran pretty smoothly. I do recall an evening of panic spent in the presence of the late, great violinist Yehudi Menuhin. My relationship with Catherine was at an early stage. I was a tad insecure. She was in London. We had a telephone date that evening at ten o'clock. Catherine demanded punctuality. Yehudi Menuhin was staying the night and he and I were to dine alone at my residence. Just as I thought dinner was about to end in good time for me to call Catherine, Yehudi drew from an inner pocket a plan for global peace, which he wished to send to the leaders of the world. He insisted on reading it out.

'What do you think?' he asked, as he finished reading.

'Terrific. Eloquent. Just the ticket,' I replied.

'It's not quite right,' said Yehudi. 'It needs some improvement. If you don't mind, let's go through it together line by line. It will benefit from your expertise.' The ingratiating smile on my face hardened into a frozen rictus.

We worked on the text at Yehudi's deliberate pace. I, blazing with the ardour of a new love, was in a fever of impatience and frustration. At last we finished the text. Yehudi Menuhin and I bade each other good night. I raced to the phone. Too late. No reply. Despair. Where was she? I did not sleep a wink. I called the following morning as early as decency allowed. A genial Catherine answered, curious to know how I had got on with Menuhin. She had assumed that I had been unable to get to the phone because of my guest. I exhaled a sigh of relief. As my grandmother used to say: there is no fool like an old fool.

It had been a long, long time since I had experienced the daft emotional roller-coaster of courtship. It was exhilarating for both of us. But our ever-present companion was the dark shadow of Catherine's case and the loss of her children.

In the beginning I could not completely believe Catherine's account of how she had been treated by the German courts and the British bureaucracy. Surely this was the overwrought reaction of a distraught woman? Surely reason could be made to prevail? Things could not be that bad, that inhuman, could they? Surely not. Later on, when I was more familiar with her case, I came to realize that it was far worse than even she had described.

At the outset I saw myself as the calm and rational force who would dissipate the bitterness between the estranged spouses and so resolve the matter. It just needed a little common sense. What vanity! In fact, things were only to get worse. At first I thought my approach was working. Catherine and her husband divorced in

September 1997. I attended the hearing; exchanged a few gruff, manly, but not unfriendly, words with her ex-husband; and saw to my satisfaction that, as part of the divorce settlement, a programme of increasingly liberal contacts between Catherine and her children had been finally agreed before the judge.

That was the start of a chapter which was to last almost a decade and include our time in Washington. It merited in full the overworked term 'Kafka-esque'. In the process it destroyed most of my feelings of sympathy and friendship for Germany.

The German courts and the Youth Authority set a pattern. Having been advised by her German lawyers to surrender her custody rights in return for access to her sons, Catherine would apply to the courts for a programme of contacts with her children, with the ultimate aim that the boys should spend time with us in Washington. A programme would be agreed in court, with an elaborate schedule of times, dates and places. On one pretext or another none of these programmes was ever implemented as agreed, or even at all. Catherine would appeal to the court. The judge would refuse to enforce the agreement on the grounds that, though drawn up in court, it was not legally enforceable, unlike custody arrangements. Despite this, the judge would then tell Catherine that she had no choice but to reapply to the court for a new programme of visits! Catherine and I went round this course several times, but were never able to break out of the judicial catch-22. Each application to the court required our physical presence in Verden, transatlantic air fares, and, of course, legal fees.

To add to the emotional and financial stress, agreeing dates for a hearing was made as difficult as possible. Little regard was paid to our ability to get away from Washington. We were summoned under pain of being fined if we did not appear. Delay was built into the system. Once we were told that the judge had left on maternity leave. No hearing could be held until she had been replaced. Months passed before this happened. We were then told that the replacement needed time to familiarize himself with Catherine's case. In the end it took eight months to secure a date for a hearing. We flew to Germany. No sooner had we arrived at our Hamburg hotel than we were told that the hearing had been cancelled. This was to happen again.

In court there appeared to be no official taking the record. We sometimes found it impossible to reconcile the oral summing up with the later, definitive written judgement. Though both of us spoke German, we asked for, and were provided with, court interpreters. They were useless. I recall a Ghanaian and a Kurd, each of whose German was worse than mine. The Kurd arrived late and unbriefed. 'What's this case about?' he asked me. I told him. 'What's the German for custody?' he asked again.

So Catherine and I found ourselves like hamsters endlessly pedalling the wheel of German 'justice'. This served a German argument which was used time and time again to trump Catherine's rights as a mother. We were repeatedly told that it was the children's wish not to see her. Yet even the psychological tests ordered by the courts showed that it was the months, if not years, of enforced separation from their mother, under influences ill-disposed towards her, that had made the children increasingly alienated from Catherine. They were told, among other things, that Catherine had abandoned them. As time passed their alienation deepened still further. Thus the German argument strengthened that it would be all too much for them even to go on holiday with Catherine. It was the strategy of the self-fulfilling prophecy, and it was successful. Catherine was later to discover, when she met other parents in the same plight, that her experience was part of a familiar pattern followed by the German authorities in cases of this kind.

Catherine has now resumed contact with her sons, but no thanks to the German authorities or any British government intervention.

This was the dark side to our five and a half years in Washington. Alongside the excitement and sheer hard slog of representing Britain in the United States was Catherine's permanent worry about her sons' well-being. I will never forget our first Christmas together in 1997. With my sons James and William, we went to the Caribbean island of Antigua. I was keenly aware of the cruel contrast between Catherine's harrowing solitude as a mother and my happiness in the company of my sons. She was never able to relax or to enjoy the sun and the sea. Her attempts over Christmas to speak to Alexander and Constantin were repeatedly rebuffed by those who answered the phone. The consolation was that, in sharp contrast to the ineffectiveness of the British bureaucracy, the first thing that Americans asked, when they heard Catherine's story, was how they could help. In due course, the Americans, from Presidents Clinton and Bush downwards, were to give Catherine enormous moral and practical help. If only for this reason, we have the deepest affection for America and the quite astonishing generosity of spirit of its people.

We did not start out in Washington with the intention of publicizing what had happened to Catherine, though we knew that sooner or later it would follow us across the Atlantic; the priority was to settle in and get a grip on the job. But within three months the story was out. My mother-in-law inadvertently spilled the beans to Bob Kaiser of the *Washington Post* at an embassy dinner. A week or so later, as Catherine and I were driving to Andrews Air Force Base to meet Tony Blair on his first official visit to the US, we heard that the *Post* planned to run a big story on Catherine and her children the next day. We were aghast. This would look as if we had deliberately contrived the publicity on the back of the Blairs' visit.

I called the late Kay Graham, the owner of the *Washington Post*, from the car. By all means run the story, but not tomorrow, I implored. Kay said, as she always did, that she no longer had influence over the paper's editorial policy, but she would put in a call. As a result, it was agreed to pull the story in return for Catherine's giving the *Post* an exclusive interview on a later date. The deal was struck just as we arrived at Andrews.

Our nerves had been stretched to breaking point. But it was the start of a new phase, in which the battle to raise awareness of parental child abduction across frontiers became an integral part of Catherine's mission in Washington.

7

The Hand of God

It was either late 1996 or early 1997 when I ran into Sir John – now Lord – 'Machiavelli' Kerr in the corridors of the Foreign Office. He was then ambassador in Washington. I was in my final preparations for going to Bonn.

As usual Kerr was thinking several steps further ahead than anyone else.

'How do you fancy succeeding me in Washington?' he asked. 'There's going to be an election soon, Labour will win, and in the summer John Coles will retire as (Foreign Office) Permanent Under-Secretary. I want to replace Coles and put myself in the running to become Cabinet Secretary to the new Labour government.'

'What on earth are you talking about?' I replied. 'I have just flogged my guts out learning German and am about to leave for Bonn.'

'Are you telling me that you'd prefer Bonn to Washington?' asked Kerr pointedly.

'Er, no. But this is sheer fantasy.'

'Well, we'll see. But you are by far the best candidate.'

John Kerr and I went back a long way – to Moscow in 1968. This was when I had succeeded him as the ambassador's private secretary on my first posting abroad. His ambassador had been Sir Geoffrey Harrison. He had been caught in bed with a Russian maid, trained and targeted, of course, by the KGB, the Soviet Union's redoubtable espionage service, where Vladimir Putin had cut his teeth. This penetration, as it were, of the embassy's defences had made those concerned with these things very jumpy.

Almost as soon as I arrived, I was taken to the embassy's secure speech room – where it was impossible (so it was said) for the KGB eavesdroppers to hear our conversation – to be given a stern briefing on sexual liaisons. This was delivered by the embassy's security man,

'Beetle' Williams, a character straight from the pages of Lawrence Durrell or John Le Carré.

'You're a young chappie and you're bound to have your flings, what? But remember one thing: Russia gels are absolutely taboo. The golden rules are: keep it female, keep it white, keep it single, and keep it in NATO. Any questions?' asked Beetle.

I had none. During my two years in Moscow I had cause to ask myself where girls from Scandinavia (the non-NATO bits), Yugoslavia (sort of communist, but non-aligned) and South America (white by Beetle's standards?) fitted into his formula. I did not seek his advice.

The KGB made a few unsuccessful attempts to suborn me. As the ambassador's private secretary, I arrived in Moscow rather full of myself. A mere twenty-four years old, I expected nonetheless to be entrusted immediately with important foreign policy tasks. So I was immensely deflated when, soon after my arrival, I was instructed to get the ambassador's dog vaccinated, to draw up a new system of paying the Russian kitchen maids (who immediately mocked my snooty St Petersburg accent), and, most important of all, to organize the embassy's Christmas cabaret.

This last task gave the KGB what it thought was its first opening. One Sunday afternoon I rehearsed in my flat a sketch based on the *Nutcracker Suite*. This required some of the largest and ugliest men on the embassy staff to be dressed in tutus and tights and to do a routine based on the 'Dance of the Sugar Plum Fairy'. There was much camping around. The following day I had the usual Russian lesson with my young, blonde lady teacher. She was provided by a Soviet organization, known by its Russian acronym UPDK, whose job was to service and report on foreign diplomats. It also provided maids, procured theatre tickets and made travel arrangements to those parts of the Soviet Union that were not closed to foreigners.

UPDK was regarded, rightly, as a front for the KGB. My maid, who never bothered to conceal what she was doing, would leave work early on a Wednesday to report on me to the *vlasti* – the authorities. She and I would joke about it. On the staircase of the block of flats where I lived it was a regular occurrence to run into the fellow whose job it was to change the tapes in all the eavesdropping machines lodged in the roof. As to my Russian teacher, she produced a large illustrated book of male Russian ballet dancers. She leafed through the book, asking me whom I preferred and if I would like to meet any of them. I must have looked genuinely bewildered. Suddenly, my teacher blushed scarlet and said in Russian, 'They have misled me!' The KGB had obviously been eavesdropping on my rehearsal and drawn quite the wrong conclusion about my sexual preferences. A number of microphones were dug out of the walls when my flat later came to be redecorated.

With the ambassador's wife Betty Wilson I used to give advanced English lessons once a week to members of the English faculty of Moscow State University. The faculty was run by a tough old communist called Olga Sergeyevna Akhmanova, a peroxide blonde of the kind only to be found in the Soviet Union, where hair dyes were probably the by-product of toxic waste from aluminium smelting or tyre production. Olga Sergeyevna was among that elite of Muscovites who were 'licensed' by the authorities to mix with foreigners. They included Communist Party members, government officials, KGB intelligence officers and a *demi-monde* of artists, journalists and intellectuals, some of whom were genuine and some informers or *agents provocateurs* for the KGB.

Olga Sergeyevna had a talented group of teachers and lecturers beneath her. They were sad people. They spoke superb English but, under the repressive Soviet regime, had never been allowed to visit Britain. One day they suggested that some of their students should attend one of the classes. In the group was a blonde girl of stunning beauty. I became instantly besotted. All thoughts of Beetle Williams vanished. I had a way of getting to this girl. At the university were some British students on a programme under the auspices of the British Council. They used to mix with the Russian students from the English faculty. 'The blonde stunner? That's Svetlana,' they said in answer to my question.

We hatched a plot. I would get tickets for the Bolshoi Ballet and we would go in a group of six, including Svet (as she was called). We had a sublime, but totally innocent, evening at the ballet – don't ask me the performance – and took our leave on the steps of the theatre. The next morning, I was awoken before dawn by an agitated phone call from our cultural attaché, James Bennett. He in turn had been called by an even more agitated member of the university's English faculty. I had been seen in the company of Svetlana. She was the daughter of a high official. It was dangerous for him and his family if his daughter went around with a British diplomat. For her sake would I, please, desist?

I got a severe reprimand from Beetle. It almost brought me to my senses, but not quite. I sneaked one more tryst with Svetlana, when I gave her a lift to the Metro from the Taganka Theatre. Big deal, you will say – but in Moscow in the depths of the Cold War, it was.

That was 1969. There was an epilogue. Fifteen years later, on a second posting to the Soviet Union, I found myself in Baku, the capital of Azerbaijan, at that time part of the Soviet Empire. I was married, my wife was in Britain having our second son, and Svetlana was long since forgotten. I was attending a trade fair, at which there was a heavy British presence. At the Russian banquet to celebrate the occasion I was placed next to a female Russian interpreter.

'I know you,' she said. 'I studied English at Moscow University and came to your class once.'

'Really,' I replied, my early-warning radar switching to full alert.

'Yes, and do you know, I am still close friends with Svetlana. She has always remembered you. She is divorced and living in Moscow. You could go and see her. She is still very beautiful.'

'Look,' I said, in response to this deeply subtle approach, 'you know and I know that this cannot be. The KGB would be on to me in a flash (why beat around the bush?) and anyway I'm happily married.'

'But Svet is lovely. She wants to see you. And if you take the Metro, no one will spot you.' The girl obviously knew the ploy had failed and she said this with a cynical, amused twinkle in the eye. Soviet interpreters, like Intourist guides and UPDK, were notorious for working closely with the KGB. Here, I thought to myself, was the organization's famous long memory.

Whenever I see John and Elizabeth Kerr it brings all this back with a large dose of nostalgia for those early adventurous days as a diplomat. I had succeeded him in Moscow. I was now dismissive of John's plans for me to succeed him for a second time, on this occasion in the US. It was all too implausible. But when, in early 1997, I visited Washington to brief myself on US foreign policy just before leaving for Bonn, John and Elizabeth were once again insistent that I should aim to replace him if he returned to London.

I became deeply absorbed in my job in Germany. My love life had taken off at supersonic speed after meeting my wife-to-be

Catherine. Washington seemed as remote as the moon. Furthermore, when Tony Blair visited Bonn in June 1997, I had what seemed a definitive conversation with his chief of staff, Jonathan Powell. We were standing in line watching Blair and Kohl inspect a guard of honour. A posse of teenaged German girls were screaming frantically. Blair used to have this effect. I saw him do it to a group of Japanese girls in New York.

Jonathan Powell muttered to me, 'Who shall we send to Washington to replace Kerr?'

'I dunno,' I said.

'We would have sent you, if you hadn't just arrived here,' said Powell.

'Right,' I replied. My concentration was already wandering as the vast bulk of the Federal German Chancellor turned towards us.

By this time, in early June, pressure on my private life was beginning to grow. Catherine and I were creeping incognito around the Rhine and Berlin on her weekend visits. We did not want our relationship to become public for obvious reasons. We were very reliant on the discretion of the staff in my residence in Bad Godesberg, Bonn's sleepy little suburb. This was a large, tranquil villa on the banks of the Rhine, where you fell asleep at night to the muffled thump of passing barges. It was not a grand residence, but it was comfortable and welcoming and, unlike the ambassador's magnificent house in Washington, you could turn it into a real home. The staff were superb. The major-domo, Harry Jostes, had served a generation of ambassadors with firmness, tact and the highest standards. He had taken a dim view – revealed in the subtlest of ways – of a couple of earlier girlfriends before Catherine. When Catherine herself first arrived, he instinctively and immediately knew that she was the right one for me. He looked after her attentively and discreetly. In his own way Harry encouraged our relationship. During Catherine's first visit, he and the chef, Herr Schlacht, organized off their own bat a delicious and irresistibly romantic dinner by candlelight.

After her experiences in Lower Saxony, recounted in her book, Catherine was quite naturally reluctant to return to Germany. But the Bad Godesberg house afforded a secure, calming refuge; and when she did venture out alone, the burly Herr Hartman acted not only as chauffeur but as a reassuring, protective presence. For the first time since she had lost her children, Catherine felt safe and able to relax.

I knew that this period of tranquil courtship could not last. When we first met, anxiety and stress had reduced Catherine to a thin, exhausted woman. Now that her energy and strength were returning, she would soon want to go back into battle to secure access to her children. Divorces were looming on both our sides. I wanted to give her every support in her dealings with the German courts and in her public campaign to raise awareness of parental child abduction across frontiers. Yet how was I to reconcile this with my official position as ambassador to Germany? One of Catherine's friends told her that I must be mad to have chosen a penniless woman with so much baggage in the very country in which I was Her Majesty's representative.

I was soon going to have to share this problem with the Foreign Office. I could not see a way through. It kept us both awake at night. But, miracle of miracles, just as matters seemed to be coming to a head, I received a phone call from my boss at the Foreign Office, Sir John Coles. 'Hold on to your chair. It is not official yet, but we are going to transfer you to Washington to replace John Kerr,' announced Coles; 'any objections?'

'Any objections? Jesus Christ!' I thought to myself, 'there is a God in heaven.'

'No, John, no objections,' I said trying to stay calm. 'But please let me know when this is official. The Germans won't like it and they will need careful handling.'

'I agree,' said Coles, 'so meanwhile, keep this under your hat.'

Catherine and I have sometimes asked ourselves whether, despite the apparent difficulties, she would have had more success in the German courts if she had appeared before them as wife of the British ambassador in Germany. Maybe. But, at the time, the knowledge that we would be going to the United States was an answer to our prayers.

To this day, I am not at all clear how it was that the powers that be decided to send me to Washington. John Kerr always maintained that it was a cunningly laid plot by him and Robin Cook to keep the job in the Foreign Office. There were all kinds of rumours about outsiders being politically appointed. Another version is that it was all the work of Jonathan Powell and Alastair Campbell. Probably both accounts are correct.

My appointment to the United States did not stay confidential for long. Catherine and I were taking a Sunday walk along the Rhine when Alastair called me on my mobile. There had already been speculation in the press as to who would be appointed. My name had so far not featured in any of the reports.

'There has been a leak. Phil Webster will run the story of your appointment in tomorrow's *Times*. We need to agree how to respond,' said Alastair.

'A leak my foot,' I thought. Alastair must have given the story to Phil. This would irritate the Germans royally and there would be nothing I could tell them officially until the Americans gave formal agreement to my appointment. The Germans would be annoyed, not only that I was leaving early, but that they had to find out about it in the press.

Kerr called me. He was going to leave Washington at the end of September. He did not think our top bilateral embassy should be in the hands of a deputy for more than a month. I agreed to arrive in Washington at the end of October. Then I found out I could not extricate myself from Germany before the middle of October. So I had only two weeks between leaving Bonn and arriving in Washington. This was barking mad. Usually, newly appointed ambassadors will have an elaborate programme of appointments with all the relevant government departments and big companies. All this went by the board for America. Thank God, I knew the country well already. Another triumph for career planning.

There was another problem. Catherine got her divorce at the end of September. My own was still in train in a ghastly tussle over money. It was not clear to me that I would be free before leaving for the US. I did not want to start in Washington without Catherine at my side. I consulted John Kerr while he was still in America: 'Could we arrive in Washington, live in sin and still function as an ambassadorial couple, pending my divorce?' John thought hard, consulted his wife and daughters, and concluded that I could not – or if I did, I would be functioning under a serious handicap. This was wise advice. Washington is a deeply conservative place. Two European ambassadors who arrived after us with partners and not wives found themselves in difficulty until they were able to marry.

So I decided it would have to be marriage or bust. It was a close-run thing. I was divorced on Monday, a free man on Tuesday and Wednesday, got married at Chelsea registry office on Thursday with a job lot of guests, and left for the US with Catherine, now my wife, on Friday, 31 October 1997. Halloween. Most appropriate.

8

Lying Abroad

As you enter the grand office of the Permanent Under-Secretary at the Foreign and Commonwealth Office, at the north-west corner of the ground floor, you see to your left a small, dark seventeenth-century painting. It is a portrait of one of the founders of modern British diplomacy, Sir Henry Wotton. He was active in the service of his country in the late sixteenth and early seventeenth centuries. He was typical of his age and class: writer, politician, scientist, intelligence agent, poet and what the Victorians used to call 'diplomatist'.

Wotton was present in 1613 when the Globe Theatre in London was destroyed by fire during a performance of Shakespeare's *Henry VIII*. In a vivid letter to a friend he describes the dramatic event. A theatrical cannon had set fire to the thatched roof. Members of the audience rushed forward to put out the flames. This involved throwing beer over an actor whose breeches had caught fire.

A few years earlier, in 1604, Wotton had been appointed ambassador to the Doge in Venice by King James I. The King had ascended the throne in the previous year, having descended from Scotland, where he was already King James VI. Fate had dealt him this fortunate hand because his predecessor on the English throne, the glorious Elizabeth I, had died without children. James was next in line to the throne by virtue of his descent from the Tudor King Henry VII. As George W. Bush was reputed to have said in another context, James belonged to the lucky-sperm club.

James was intelligent, witty, bisexual, and obsessively interested in matters of Church and State, like most of the political class in those days. He lacked what we would call today common sense. He was known to his contemporaries as 'the wisest fool in Christendom'. He once told the Bishop of London: 'I care not a turd for thy preaching.' James fathered the unfortunate Charles I, beheaded in 1649 after his defeat by Oliver Cromwell in the English Civil War.

As Wotton made his way to Venice through Germany, he stayed the night in Nuremberg with an English friend, Christopher Fleckmore. Wotton, wit that he was, wrote in Fleckmore's guest book, in Latin, his famously ambiguous dictum which, for diplomats, continues to echo down the centuries: 'An ambassador is an honest man sent to lie abroad for the good of his country.'

When King James got to hear of this a few years later, he did not see the joke and fired Wotton. In due course Wotton was able to worm his way back into James's good books. The result was a mission to Bohemia to keep an eye on James's daughter, the Princess Elizabeth. Wotton dedicated to her one of his few surviving poems, 'You meaner beauties of the night'. This small gem of early seventeenth-century literature suggests a greater intimacy between Wotton and the Princess than James might have wished.

As Wotton looks down from his cloud on today's ambassadors, he sees that, behind all the changes in technology and communication, the essentials remain the same. An ambassador and an embassy exist to advance the national interest. There is no other justification for their existence. Stripped to its core, this means safeguarding British security and British prosperity. In the USA it is not a simple task.

The first thing that British diplomats must do is to take an unsentimental look at the 'special relationship'. It is a phrase sustained by a curious conspiracy. American presidents are briefed to use it in the presence of British guests because, they are told, the British are profoundly attached to it. The British press, where Pavlov's dogs rule, stoke the conspiracy. A quick and easy way into a story about Britain and the US is to take the temperature, yet again, of the 'special relationship' and usually to declare it dead or dying. The number of press stories over the years pronouncing the demise of the relationship has been rivalled only by those asserting Britain's isolation in Europe.

The relationship has had a more chequered history than the mythology allows. The term 'special relationship' was unknown before the Second World War. It grew out of the wartime collaboration between Churchill and Roosevelt. Thereafter, it has had its ups and downs. Even during the Second World War there was much hard pounding between Washington and London. The wartime diaries of Field Marshal Lord Alanbrooke, the Chief of the Imperial General Staff and Churchill's main military adviser, vividly describe the tensions and arguments in the alliance with the United States. There was then a style of tough-minded, hard-hitting negotiation between the British and Americans. From this a common strategy against the Nazis was forged. It did not in the least damage the warm spirit of the Atlantic Charter. It is light years distant from the way the British government negotiated with the US administration before the war in Iraq.

The temperature of the post-war British–American relationship has had very little to do with whichever party has been in power in London or Washington. After all, Churchill was a Conservative, Roosevelt a Democrat. Personality and policies have been what has mattered. Macmillan (Conservative) got on well with Kennedy (Democrat). Wilson (Labour) got on badly with Johnson (Democrat), and refused to send British troops to Vietnam. Thatcher (Conservative) was very close to Reagan (Republican). She got on much less well with another Republican, George Bush the elder, with whom she disagreed on German unification. Major (Conservative) got on very well with Bush the elder (Republican), much less well with Clinton (Democrat), with whom he had differences over Bosnia. Blair (Labour) has got on famously with both Clinton and Bush the younger (Republican), and no doubt would have done the same with a President Kerry (Democrat).

When ambassador in Washington, I would not allow the phrase 'special relationship' inside the embassy. I was worried that my staff would approach their work with a set of delusions: that Britain's relations with the US were different in kind from those with any other country; that the Americans would therefore grant us special benefits, unavailable to other nations; and that, as a result, developing a relationship with the US of advantage to Britain would require less effort than with other governments. I wanted our diplomats to take nothing for granted.

A phrase like this must be deployed with great caution. It merits use only to describe those very few relationships where a foreign government has the ability significantly to influence US politics and, through this, the direction of US foreign policy. Only Israel, Taiwan, Saudi Arabia and the Irish Republic have shown this quality consistently over the years. It is measured as much by influence in the US Congress as with the US administration itself. America's rock-solid support for Israel over the years is founded on vast, instinctive pro-Israel majorities in both Senate and House. The hostility of the US administration to the EU's decision to sell arms to China reflects the implacable opposition of pro-Taiwan congressional majorities. The grip of Irish nationalism on domestic politics in America is the stuff of a later chapter.

British influence has rarely been in this category. It came close when Margaret Thatcher was Prime Minister, because of her warm personal and working relationships with both President Reagan and Senator Jesse Helms, the all-powerful Chairman of the Senate Foreign Relations Committee. It has come near under New Labour, thanks to Tony Blair's close ties with two American presidents. But the British Government has lacked the will fully to exploit the leverage.

None of this is to deny an instinctive warmth and affinity of outlook between many in America and in Britain. The US is a country in which Catherine and I have always felt comfortable.

There are certainly areas where the British–American relationship may be uniquely close. Forty-eight hours after 9/11 all three British intelligence chiefs – those of the Secret Intelligence Service, the Security Service and the Government Communications Head-quarters – were sitting on my terrace in Washington, having just flown the Atlantic to see their opposite numbers. The controversy over Saddam Hussein's weapons of mass destruction notwith-standing, the quality of British intelligence is such that it balances to a degree the enormous superiority in resources available to American intelligence agencies.

As the senior non-American partner, we have invested billions in an American military aircraft, the Joint Strike Fighter, which ten years or so hence will be the backbone of our Air Force and Navy. In my time, Britain and the US had been for years each other's largest foreign investor. Almost half of all American investment in the EU was to be found in Britain. British investment in the US – more than Germany's or Japan's – generated around a million American jobs. One of the things that allowed the British gov-ernment to take its time to decide whether to adopt the euro had been the absence of pressure from the American investor to enter the eurozone. Had it been otherwise, the euro would have replaced the pound sterling before you could say Gordon Brown.

Then there are the intangibles. They are important, but harder to measure. The instinctive reaction of British people to support America in its hour of need after 9/11 gave a huge boost to the notion of two countries bound by common values. Tony Blair's willingness to take a lead on terrorism and Iraq has aroused enormous admiration in the US. But how far can we take this idea that ties of history, language, intellectual tradition, family, have given Britain and America a reservoir of common interests and reflexes greater than that of other countries with the United States?

The answer is: some way, but less than a generation ago, and even less than a generation before that. I was struck forcefully by something I observed in my last twelve months in the US, following 9/11. Older Americans – those with some kind of memory of the Second World War – saw the British–American alliance against terrorism as a reaffirmation of the natural order of things. How many times did I hear, especially in the great American heartland away from the coasts, that when the going gets tough, America and Britain have only each other to rely on?

The reaction of younger people was usually different. There was gratitude and emotion for our support. But I had the impression that Britain as closest ally had come as a revelation. I found this especially in American universities, where I spoke to student audiences regularly: the mythology of the 'special relationship' and its history were *terra incognita*. I had the feeling that with these millions of younger Americans Britain was opening its account. They included the tides of new immigrants, largely Asian and Spanish-speaking, remote from the traditions and history of the Anglo-Saxon world. The 2000 census is compulsory reading for any student of American affairs.

Every year, in September, I used to address new arrivals at the embassy, with their families. The core of my message was always the same: think of the US as a foreign country; then you will be pleasantly surprised by the many things you find in common with this most generous and hospitable of peoples. Think of America as Britain writ large and you risk coming to grief; American attitudes to patriotism, religion, crime and punishment, schooling, sex, the outside world, can be very different from those of Europeans, including the British. For the novice British diplomat it comes as a shock to discover that most Americans, whether Republican or Democrat, sophisticate or redneck, believe that their country's actions in the world are intrinsically virtuous; and more fool those countries that do not recognize this. The attitude of Britain's Victorians was very similar.

I sought regularly and in vain to get the Foreign Office to grasp this message and to draw the conclusion that if it was right to train cadres of specialists in the EU, the Middle East, Russia and China, as we do, then it was also right to create an American cadre, which we do not do. The US is too complex, too diverse, too dynamic, too foreign, too vital to almost every British interest you can think of, to be left to *laissez-faire*, to the attitude that the British–American relationship will take care of itself.

Catherine and I benefited from the stock of goodwill in the relationship. We sensed it whenever Margaret Thatcher was in the presence of Americans; or when the memory of Winston Churchill was invoked, which was often, including in the White House; or, after 9/11, when, from one side of America to another, the mere fact of my being announced as Britain's ambassador brought audiences to their feet, stomping and cheering. What more surprising accolade for an Englishman than to be greeted, as I was, on the electronic scoreboard at the Yankee Stadium, during the fourth game of the 2001 World Series between the New York Yankees and the Arizona Diamondbacks?

We sensed the goodwill when, each year in late October, over one hundred US admirals and senior naval and marine officers, often accompanied by the US Secretary of the Navy, would come to the embassy for an elaborate and formal dinner to celebrate the life and death of Admiral Lord Nelson. We would hold the dinner as near as we could make it to 21 October, the anniversary of the battle of Trafalgar in 1805, in which Nelson defeated the combined French and Spanish navies, only to lose his life to a French sniper. The evening began with a band of the Royal Marines beating retreat in the embassy gardens, against a background of floodlit trees and bushes and Washington's pitch-black semi-tropical night. Serried ranks of American naval guests, resplendent in dress uniform, watched the ancient ceremony on the terrace beside the massive portico columns. During dinner, a gargantuan affair of many courses, after toasts had been drunk to the Queen, the President and Nelson himself, chocolate replicas of Nelson's ships of the line would be piped in, each borne aloft by a youngster from the Royal Navy catering school. The evening ended with the singing of shanties and the playing of the 'Posthorn Gallop'. The admirals and I would then repair to the drawing room, where the evening wound down in the gentle imbibing of malt whisky.

The origins of this Anglo-American celebration are lost in the mists of time. Different sailors give you different explanations. When I first came to Washington in the 1990s, the Americans had taken over Trafalgar Night. The first dinners that I attended were held at the US Navy Yard museum or at the US Marine barracks. As ambassador, I was determined to repatriate the ceremony to the British embassy. The two navies were very happy for me to do so and I presided over five in a row. The curious thing about this evening of warm Anglo-American fellowship and goodwill was that Nelson's Royal Navy regularly pressed American seamen into the involuntary service of His Majesty King George III; and that the US Navy played no part in the battle of Trafalgar, an engagement which took place not long after the War of Independence and not long before the War of 1812, when Britain and America fought each other bitterly.

The goodwill was an important factor in the British embassy's having a range of influential contacts across the US administration and Congress. They were the envy of other embassies and sometimes of American officials themselves. But it takes you only so far. There is no substitute for expertise which matches that of the formidably well-prepared American official; or for the ability to 'speak' American: to know how to connect with Americans in a way that invites their trust and cooperation. At the right moment there is no substitute for being as tough and direct in negotiation as the Americans are invariably with us.

Americans have a striking ability to compartmentalize their sincere affection for Britain from their single-minded pursuit of national interest. Even at the height of the *bonhomie* of a Trafalgar Night dinner, the top American admiral warned me of the negative repercussions for Britain if our defence arrangements in Europe led to the leakage to the French and others of American military and intelligence secrets shared only with us. British diplomacy was once very good at this compartmentalization. This was why the French called us, with sneaking admiration, '*perfide Albion*'. Today Britain needs to reacquire some of these old arts.

It sticks in the craw to say it, but we could learn a thing or two about negotiating from Sinn Fein: past masters at taking an implacable opening stand; at making it appear always for the other side to move first; and, when concession becomes unavoidable, at selling it for the highest price, preferably twice or more.

Britain's inability in 2001–2 to block tariffs on imports of British steel into the US, to secure a UK/US transatlantic air services agreement with fully reciprocal benefits, and to bring to a conclusion prolonged negotiations to liberalize the export to the UK of US defence equipment – all this was at least in part the result of a failure in London at the highest level to have a clear vision of the national interest and to negotiate accordingly.

The vision has been blurred by the excessive attachment of the British foreign policy establishment to fashionable notions of the post-modern state, international community and multilateralism. These are not without merit, interest or use. But for the cold-eyed realists of Washington, Moscow, Beijing and New Delhi they are second-order concerns. These four capitals, perhaps with Tokyo, will decide the fate of the world in the twenty-first century. It is precisely with them that we have to win the argument, if we are to achieve our great multilateral ambitions for the environment, nuclear non-proliferation and the curtailing of weapons of mass destruction. That argument will not be won, unless the cost–benefit analysis for the Americans, Russians, Chinese and Indians unambiguously satisfies their unsentimental vision of the national interest.

Lord Palmerston told the House of Commons in 1848, in a much misquoted phrase: 'We have no eternal allies and we have no perpetual enemies. Our interests are eternal and perpetual, and those interests it is our duty to follow.' Applied to the United States, this eternally wise observation leads to clear conclusions.

Whether you like it or not, there is almost nothing that the United States, as the sole superpower, does that will not affect Britain for better or worse. It is not just the Federal government in Washington. It is also the US Congress, whose independence as the legislative branch is enshrined in the American Constitution. This makes it an actor in its own right across the full spectrum of public policy, including foreign affairs.

It does not end there. So vast is the US, so huge its economy, that decisions taken in many of the fifty states of the Union by the Governor or his legislature can touch British interests. That is why, under the authority of the ambassador, we have consuls-general and consuls in many of the major cities, looking out for British interests. Each consul-general – in New York, Chicago, Los Angeles, San Francisco, Houston, Atlanta, Boston – is responsible for a group of states, whose gross domestic product and concentration of British economic interests are larger than most sovereign states with full-blown ambassadors. California, the last time I looked, was the world's fifth-largest economy, broadly the same as the UK. Our consul-general in Chicago covers an area which is larger economically than Britain itself.

To safeguard British interests in this massive country calls for eternal vigilance, expert and energetic staff, and the creation of networks of influence among the political, business and media elites. In my time as ambassador much energy was wasted in London in debate about the areas on which Britain's representatives in the US should concentrate: notably, should it be the business sector or should it be the politicians? Dumb question. As with the ambassador in Washington, so with the consuls-general in the great American cities: you had to do everything, to cover all the bases. It was all a single piece of elaborate machinery and you had to be familiar with each of its moving parts. If you knew the top politicians, it helped get in with the business leaders; and vice versa. If you knew the editors and leading journalists in the broadcast and print media, not only was this a source of indispensable information, it gave you a platform from which to influence opinion – and to get in with the politicians and business leaders. It was all mutually reinforcing.

Peter Bacon in Houston, Robert Culshaw in Chicago, George Ferguson in Boston, and Paul Dimond and Peter Hunt in Los Angeles performed these roles brilliantly in my time, understanding instinctively and as well as any ambassador what needed to be done. Unfortunately, today's Foreign Office sees these jobs as low-hanging fruit in the perpetual search for spending cuts, resulting more often than not from the mismanagement of the department's budget at the centre.

Sir Henry Wotton would have understood instantly the importance of this activity. We were engaged in upholding Britain's security and prosperity in multiple ways on a daily basis: persuading Americans that it was a better path to peace in Northern Ireland to rally behind Tony Blair's efforts than to give money to the IRA; helping a British company clinch a deal or overcome regulatory and political hurdles, designed to favour the American competition; pressing the Defense Department to buy British military equipment; persuading Congress to postpone the requirement to carry biometric passports until Britain was ready to issue them; and so on.

None of this activity is very glamorous. But today it is the meat and drink of everyday relations between states; and it cannot be carried out at several thousand miles' range. It needs people on the spot: feet on the ground, faces across a table, a tennis court, on a golf course, eyeball to eyeball. This is how Americans do business. It is the normal practice of great multinational corporations.

There is an argument that speed of communication and the ability of ministers and civil servants to talk direct or video-conference with their counterparts across the Atlantic remove the need for expensive diplomatic establishments. Speed and technology are certainly powerful weapons in the diplomat's armoury; but without quality and context, information delivered fast is without merit. Ambassadors can exploit instantaneous communication to make their contribution to policy debate in London in real time. They can help shape policy rather than being its mere recipients and mouthpieces. It may not be quite as heady as in the days of Sir Henry Bartle Frere, the British High Commissioner in South Africa, who, in 1879, was able to start the Zulu War almost on his own initiative, thanks to the slowness of communication with London; but the replacement of the sailing ship by digital, encrypted, electronic communication gives an ambassador an instrument of enormous influence, if he or she knows how to use it.

Direct diplomatic contact between London and foreign capitals has increased enormously in the last twenty-five years. It is indispensable to modern diplomatic relations. But it needs to be used with care and can be more trouble than it is worth. British officials in London are attracted to dealing directly with their counterparts in Washington like moths to a flame. This has its dangers. It can lead to tunnel vision. Policy formulation in Washington involves so many actors that the views of one individual or one department can be just that. American officials are not slow to try to inveigle their British counterparts into a supporting role in the interdepartmental battles which are a permanent feature of Washington's bureaucratic life.

Jack Straw used to pride himself on the intimacy and frequency of his contacts on the phone with Colin Powell. They were a very valuable line of communication. But Tony Blair was right to be irritated from time to time by what he saw as Powell's attempts through Straw to pray the British government in aid in his battles with Cheney and Rumsfeld for the President's ear.

At their best, direct contacts, particularly at the level of Prime Minister and President, are like a flash of lightning across the landscape. That is important; but it is not enough without the constant illumination that a good embassy should provide.

I used to be asked, usually by MPs, why Britain needed a staff of around four hundred souls in Washington, in addition to the two hundred and fifty-odd to be found in our consulates. My reply went something like this: 'Government, parliament and business require us to be expert in almost every area of public policy. We are expected to report on, and to influence, American policy on: trade, aid, agriculture, the economy, defence, the environment, energy, science, education, law and order, welfare, health, narcotics, and transport. We also have staff who promote US investment into the UK and help UK investors in the US; look after distressed British subjects; issue passports and visas; analyse, and report on, US politics; represent Scotland and Northern Ireland; maintain close relations with the US armed forces; and liaise equally closely with all branches of US intelligence and the FBI. All of this is in addition to staff who pursue the traditional Foreign Office agenda: relations with the US and third countries; the UN; weapons of mass destruction; Iraq and the Middle East; international crises of one kind or another; terrorism; war and peace, and so on. I have under my wing people from almost every Whitehall department. Those from the Foreign Office comprise less than 15 per cent of the total.'

That usually shut them up. I could hear Sir Henry cheering.

9

The Great House

Massachusetts Avenue starts in a rather sordid area near Washington's Union Station and then heads north-west towards the posh white suburbs. Along the way, in a matter of a few miles, you pass maybe twenty churches of every conceivable denomination. Each of these is packed to the rafters on Sunday, in stark contrast to Britain's churches. Massachusetts Avenue also takes you through an area called Embassy Row. As it emerges from central Washington, acquiring trees and elegance, the Avenue is flanked by clusters of embassies. The Row is famous enough to be a tourist attraction in its own right.

Just before you reach the Naval Observatory on your left, where the Vice-President has his official residence, you come across the buildings of the British Embassy. You cannot miss them, because they are big and fly the Union flag. More to the point, lying back from the pavement there is a full-size statue of Sir Winston Churchill, with one foot on British soil – the grounds of the Embassy – and one on American.

There are advantages and disadvantages in having the Vice-President as neighbour. On the one hand the embassy benefits from the very tight security around his residence. On the other you can be disturbed by the helicopter, which he frequently uses to fly in and out of the Observatory. Dick Cheney was more considerate than Al Gore. When Gore was Vice-President, the helicopter engines would idle interminably, because he appeared to have caught President Clinton's habit of always being late. Apart from the noise, the embassy grounds would fill with rich, carcinogenic wafts of kerosene.

There are two British embassy buildings: the ambassador's residence and the embassy offices. They offer a sharp contrast in styles. The offices are a dreary monstrosity from the late fifties, the exhausted creation of post-war brutalism that makes them a cousin to the Arndale Centre in Wandsworth.

The residence is another matter altogether. It is the work of the early twentieth-century architect Sir Edwin Lutyens. He is renowned for his country houses in Britain and his public buildings in New Delhi, built for the British Raj. In one of those rare moments of cooperation between Foreign Office and Treasury, Lutyens was commissioned in the twenties to design and build a new embassy in Washington. The intention was to combine residence and offices in a single building; but the embassy staff increased so enormously during the Second World War that it was decided to build a separate set of offices.

The residence is a magnificent structure, which, unlike its miserable companion, has seen its reputation grow with the passing of the years. Lutyens, in his mischievous, original way, gave the building different architectural styles for its three main aspects. Viewed from the gardens its columns and terrace recall an *ante-bellum* mansion from the Deep South. From another aspect it resembles a Queen Anne country house. When you arrive at the covered entrance – the *porte cochère* – and see the sweeping double staircase, flanked by life-size portraits of English kings and queens, there is an allusion to a medieval castle.

Inside there are several splendid public rooms: a ballroom which we used for very large dinners, lunches, concerts, seminars and receptions – but never for a ball; a drawing room, used again for receptions as well as for house guests, which, because of its east- and south-facing aspects, was bathed in sunlight most of the day; a dining room which could seat thirty-five; and my favourite, the library, where I would work and read when not in the office. In all of these rooms there were working fireplaces, where throughout the winter we had log fires, filling the house with that slightly scented perfume of burning bark and pine needles. Upstairs there were bedrooms that could accommodate a dozen house guests.

The challenge for Catherine and me in all this splendour was to create a home. We had an apartment upstairs which was located on the same corridor as the guest bedrooms. There was not much privacy. On arriving, as newly-weds, we found to our embarrassment that our apartment had three doors opening on to the corridor and that none of them could be locked. Some of the domestic staff had got into the habit of walking in without knocking. In fact, a few of the veterans among them had come to consider themselves as the permanent occupants of the Great House and the ambassador and his wife as mere birds of passage. Just when I thought I was alone with my bride, I would find a member of the household staff lurking behind us. So we blocked two of the doors with cupboards. But it was not until our fifth year that we managed to create self-contained quarters, and this thanks to our security people, who insisted, after 9/11, that we have a reinforced area where, in the event of attack, we could take refuge until help arrived.

When they came to stay, my sons James and William did much to humanize the Great House. I once found James, aged twenty-two, riding a small bicycle along the upstairs corridor. William, six years younger, would skateboard all over the house and gardens, usually accompanied by a couple of school friends from England, all of whom had their hair dyed in lurid colours. We ourselves tried to lower the pomposity level by putting baseball caps on the Nollekens busts of William Pitt the Younger and Charles James Fox.

From the start we could not help taking the Great House almost for granted. I knew it well already from my first tour in Washington. Then, when Catherine and I arrived, we were immediately hurled into a maelstrom of activity. The house became part backdrop, part tool of the trade for our heavy schedule. My favourite moment of the day was to sit on the terrace, watching the sun rise over the bottom-left-hand corner of the gardens. I had the newspapers scattered around me and a steaming mug of leaf-brewed English breakfast tea in my hand. To get a head start on the day I liked to have gutted the *Washington Post*, *New York Times*, *Washington Times* and *Financial Times* by the time I arrived at the office. The *Wall Street Journal* had to wait until later in the day. The night before I would have taken advantage of the time difference to read the internet editions of the main British newspapers. The BBC News website became indispensable.

I would look across the gardens at the profusion of rose bushes, lovingly cultivated for over a generation by our New Zealand gardener, Kerry. There were trees of all shapes and sizes. In the spring we had cherry blossom to rival anything along the Potomac river, where the tourists flocked to see the riot of pinks. Between the trees, on the wide, sloping, grassy expanse, there were squirrels, the occasional raccoon, turkey vultures (a kind of hideous giant crow), deer in the autumn, and, in the summer, Jemima the duck, who came every year to hatch her chicks in a tree box. I used to say to myself time without number: Remember this, enjoy this; you will miss it when it is gone.

As time passed and routine increasingly dominated our lives, it took the pleasure and wonder of those who were visiting the Great House for the first time to remind us of our privileged existence. From time to time I was asked why Britain needed a residence of this scale and grandeur. The question came sometimes from MPs, sometimes from Jonathan Powell, the Prime Minister's chief of staff, sometimes from officials in the Foreign Office itself. Would it not be more appropriate, they suggested, to have something in keeping with modern Britain – a smart, practical apartment, say, in down-town Washington or in the leafy suburb of Bethesda? This would, they went on to say, approximate more closely to life in Bromley, Kent, the Foreign Office benchmark for the calculation of our overseas allowances.

No disrespect to Bromley, as they say on *Match of the Day*, but the name of the game in Washington for an ambassador is access and influence. It is who you know and who you can get to. It is putting your country and yourself on the map. It is promoting every kind of British excellence. It is making the British embassy the place to which the powerful and influential want to be invited. It is using the residence as a tool to create that network of influence which allows you to achieve the multiple objectives set by the government. It is providing neutral ground where senior Repub-licans and Democrats can meet, debate and overcome the partisan divide, which increasingly vitiates political discourse in Washington. It is providing the right setting for the droves of visiting British ministers and officials to meet their counterparts. It is being a good neighbour to, and participant in the life of, the Washington community. As the bureaucrats say, the Great House is ideally 'fit for purpose'.

Every year Catherine and I welcomed between twelve and four-teen thousand people. After five and a half years that is the equival-ent of a sizeable town. Only the Great House could handle the traffic: the breakfasts, lunches, dinners, seminars, receptions, teas –

not to mention the two hundred-odd official overnight visitors, mainly British ministers and their staff.

You do not have to spend long in the US to realize that it is not what sells in Bromley that matters, but what sells in Washington, the capital of the most powerful nation on earth. Understatement – still seen, however mythically, as one of the great British virtues – has never enjoyed the same success in the US. The British interest gains nothing from being sold short: whether it is the crabbed post-modernist vision of contemporary Britain, devoid of a sense of history and dismissive of British power; or whether it is talk of our 'punching above our weight'. The challenge for Britain is to punch *at* its weight in world affairs, as the world's fourth-largest economy, a nuclear power, a permanent member of the UN Security Council, and one of the handful of nations capable of projecting serious military power beyond its borders. We are no longer an imperial power and we are not a superpower; but Britain is a great power and requires a great house in Washington that reflects its status. Americans expect no less and would think the worse of us if we were to trade down.

If there was one thing that Catherine and I did not regret about leaving the Great House, it was the need to shake several hundred hands several times a week. Before a reception we would take up position at a point where the entrance hall debouched into the ballroom. I would welcome each guest and introduce him or her to Catherine. By our third year, after about thirty minutes in the receiving line, I started to become deranged. I would forget Catherine's name. Strange reflexes seized me. I have introduced Catherine by my ex-mother-in-law's name or even more bizarrely as 'Christopher'. I have said 'goodbye' to people when I meant to say 'hello'. I have just stopped myself from kissing a man, after greeting a sequence of women. In other people's houses I have gone up to complete strangers and welcomed them to the British embassy.

The vast number of guests also took its toll on the Great House. When we arrived it was starting to look a bit knocked about inside. It had the faded elegance of a Brighton hotel. Major renovation had last been done twenty years previously. Lutyens's bold, clean lines had disappeared in a jungle of Laura Ashley fabrics. Carpets had been nailed into the marble surrounds of the library floor. Foreign Office issue reproduction furniture spread like fungi through the public rooms. Some of the bathrooms and most of the plumbing remained untouched since 1930, when the Great House was completed.

With all the enthusiasm of a newcomer Catherine threw herself into restoring the house to something like its pristine glory. She has a natural talent for design, decoration and colour. She was discouraged and resisted at every turn. There was almost no money in the embassy budget. London said that they had little to spare. Taking her cue from the way the US government often financed the upkeep of its embassies, she suggested some kind of private–public partnership for restoring the residence. This was shot from the skies in London like a grouse in August. Things only worsened when the *Sunday Times* ran a cock-and-bull story suggesting that Catherine intended to spend a million pounds with the Mulberry company. That was the final nail in her novel suggestion for a special Millennium bond issue.

It was a tiring, disillusioning experience for someone of Catherine's energy and enthusiasm, who wanted to show Britain at its best. She even had to put up with a pompous rebuke from one of our more elderly predecessors, who was responsible for an earlier and now worn-out renovation. There was a strong whiff of who did this chit of a girl think she was?

In the end, through sheer perseverance and good luck, Catherine was able to renovate and redecorate the entire guest floor, including the ambassador's apartment, and, downstairs, the library, dining room and drawing room. The ballroom had to await our successors. This labour of love and hard slog took almost our entire five and a half years. It meant our enduring drilling, banging, dust, and asbestos removal. It also meant floods, thanks to the contractors' incompetence. The newly redecorated drawing room was ruined when the ceiling collapsed under the weight of water leaking from a recently installed but faulty pipe in the bathroom above. One evening we gave a black-tie dinner in honour of Placido Domingo, the great Spanish tenor, who was director of the Washington Opera. He had just been given an honorary knighthood. As Colin Powell and his wife Alma arrived and greeted us, Catherine and I noticed, to our horror, a fat drop of water fall from the ceiling onto the General's shoulder. A large damp patch was spreading above us. I prayed that the attendant photographers would not notice. They didn't. We were just able to shut off the water main in time before the ceiling came crashing down.

Two things did the trick in getting funds from London. The 1930s lead pipes had become so furred that there was imminent danger of a sewage back-up. I could see the diary pieces in British newspapers and, more to the point, so could the Foreign Office: 'Britain's Deputy Prime Minister was in deeper s—t than usual this week, when while shaving in an Embassy bathroom . . .' We replaced all the bathrooms and old pipes. Then Stephen Hawking came to dinner and rightly criticized wheelchair access. This led to our being able to replace the rickety guest lift and sordid guest cloakrooms, which, at least on the men's side, looked to have been modelled on the urinals at a 1940s British railway station.

My personal obsession was to replace the miserable embassy offices with a building of which we could be proud. The need for new offices had been recognized in the early nineties. The central-heating and air-conditioning systems were increasingly unreliable. Black soot would fall in great gobs from the ceiling heating vents in my office. Sewage back-up was already a regular occurrence in my lavatory. The staff worked like monks and nuns in a warren of cell-like offices and corridors, which appeared deliberately designed to discourage team spirit. Mysterious holes appeared in my office curtains. When they were replaced, great nests of cockroaches came tumbling to the ground. I suggested a millennium architectural competition for a new building. This idea was given the shortest of shrift by the Foreign Office, who asserted shortage of funds (they were already building incredibly expensive new embassies in Moscow and Berlin) and, fantastically, that our clapped-out offices had plenty of life in them yet. I even tried to persuade our good friend Tony Williams, the Mayor of DC, to condemn the building as an eyesore on Massachusetts Avenue. It was only as I retired from Washington that I detected the first stirrings of awareness in London that our building was on its last legs and would have to be replaced sooner rather than later.

10

Sir Winston Churchill's Ghost

The *lares* and *penates* of the Great House had been for long accustomed to seeing the good, the bad and the ugly pass through its portals. Our time in Washington was no different. Even more in America than in Germany, as ambassador you get to meet people that no other job, besides monarch or prime minister, makes possible. The house was constantly filled with politicos, business people, journalists, students, soldiers, spies, Shakespearean actors, diplomats, policemen, musicians, academics, dancers, churchmen, bureaucrats, movie stars – and 'ordinary people', including friends and family.

Private life was squeezed into the outer margins of our existence. It was over two years before we were able to have a honeymoon. A free weekend was a rarity to be savoured. Mostly, we just collapsed inside the Great House. Sometimes we would fly to New York or Florida. Occasionally we went up the road from Washington and took the South-West Airlines flight from Baltimore to Las Vegas. This was not because we were gambling addicts. Since Vegas was as remote from reality as an Earth colony on Mars, it allowed us to decompress rapidly after the stresses and strains of DC. But it was all worth it. The stimulation of holding the best job in the Diplomatic Service trumped the attrition.

In early November 1997, in our very first week, Lady Thatcher and her husband, the late Sir Denis Thatcher, came to stay. I had the civil servant's terror of her. I had seen a good deal of Margaret Thatcher in the 1980s, when she was at the height of her powers as Prime Minister. My then boss was Geoffrey Howe, the Foreign Secretary. He would travel with her to the great international meetings: European councils, economic summits and Commonwealth conferences. As his press secretary, I always accompanied Geoffrey. Margaret Thatcher's press secretary was the great Sir Bernard

Ingham, perhaps the most accomplished government spokesman of all time. At these international meetings it was Bernard's and my responsibility jointly to brief the media. This meant that, before Bernard and I went into battle, we were sometimes ushered into her presence to get our marching orders. I would conceal myself as best I could behind Bernard in the hope that the glittering eye would not fall upon me.

Among Margaret Thatcher's formidable assets was a strong loyalty to those who worked for her. Almost inadvertently I had provoked a storm at the Vancouver Commonwealth Conference in 1987, when I pointed out to the press that Canada, one of the severest critics of our policy towards South Africa, had seen an enormous leap in its trade with the apartheid regime. This touched a very raw nerve. Bernard and I came under sustained attack from a raft of Commonwealth leaders, who called a special press conference to denounce us. The Canadian Prime Minister, Brian Mulroney, was enraged. That was a bit rich, since we were told that he was personally responsible for much of the anti-British press briefing. The issue dominated the conference. I had consulted absolutely no one about using the Canadian trade figures. But I was sick and tired of sanctimonious criticism from the Canadian press, fed by the Canadian government. What infuriated our critics was the accuracy of our figures. They came from an impeccable source, the International Monetary Fund – though, to be fair to the Canadians, the increase in trade was from a very low base. When Margaret Thatcher was taxed with all this at her final press conference, she swatted aside our critics and gave staunch support to Bernard and me.

We gave a dinner, our first ever in Washington, for the Thatchers. We were nervous. It was a great honour to have them under our roof. When I had travelled with her and Geoffrey Howe around the world, she had made me proud to be British. She had the measure of every foreign politician she ever met.

The guests that evening were a mixture of the Thatchers' friends and politicians. Margaret Thatcher still had huge drawing power in the US. She was apparently making a lot of money on the speech circuit.

'Will you say a few words?' I asked her at dinner.

'What can I say that will interest people? Denis and I are has-beens now, you know,' she replied, a tad disingenuously.

'No, no,' I countered. 'People will be very disappointed if they leave without hearing you. Why don't you talk a bit about Russia?'

She sprang to her feet and delivered a barn-storming, twenty-minute speech about how she and 'Ron' Reagan had defeated communism and worked with Mikhail Gorbachev. This prompted Senator John Kerry, who was to lose to George W. Bush in the 2004 presidential election, to respond with a paean of praise for Lady Thatcher and Britain. I always liked Kerry. In private he was personable and well informed on foreign affairs. Teresa Heinz Kerry, on a later occasion, offered to invite us to dinner and make a typical English dish. It was, I think to be either a queen's pudding or a shepherd's pie. Unfortunately, the invitation never materialized.

We were just about to break up at the end of dinner when one of the guests – Henry Catto, a former American ambassador in London – asked, almost as an aside, what Margaret Thatcher thought about recent developments in Europe. This was like a spark to dry tinder. In a flash she was on her feet again, to deliver a caustic indictment of European integration. Eyes blazing, she began to bang on a bit. Suddenly, from next to Catherine, a voice rang out: 'Enough, woman, enough. Sit down.'

It was Denis Thatcher. His wife meekly obeyed.

After dinner, when the guests had left, Denis Thatcher passed out on the ballroom floor, with a terrible crash. The sheer ghastliness of the moment was matched only by the time when, as a young third secretary in the embassy in Madrid, I had run over the ambassador's two Ethiopian hounds as they lay sleeping in the residence driveway. Denis, like the hounds, survived the mishap; but for a moment it looked serious. Catherine and I were horrified by the face-down, prostrate figure. What a way to begin our assignment in Washington! Suddenly an apparition hove into view, clad in a flowing nightie. It was the Thatchers' faithful assistant, Crawfie, a bundle of formidable, rotund determination. Between them, Margaret and Crawfie got a somewhat groggy and bloody Denis to his feet. He had a nasty gash above his eye. He and Margaret brushed it aside, refusing to go to hospital. It was not until the following morning that he was stitched up.

It was at moments like these that I would say to myself again, Can this really be happening to me? It was a sensation I never shook off in the whole five and a half years.

When I was a small boy I spent years living with my maternal grandmother, just outside Brighton. After my father was killed in action in 1944, a week before I was born – I finally got to see his grave in 2004, in the Commonwealth War Cemetery just outside Athens – my mother returned to the WRAF, where she had spent most of the war, to pursue a career and make ends meet. This meant her spending long periods away from home. So I went to live with my grandmother. She loved the music hall and cinema. Thanks to her, I must have seen live at the Brighton Hippodrome every top-ranking comedian of the 1950s. I remember the Crazy Gang, Arthur English, Monsewer Eddie Gray, Wilson, Keppel and Betty, Peter Brough and Archie Andrews, Jimmy Jewel and Ben Warriss and a very young Max Bygraves ('I've arrived and to prove it I'm 'ere'). We always used to see the touring shows like the *Fol de Rols* and *Twinkle*, with Clarkson Rose and Olive. Dickie Valentine was my first introduction to live pop music.

My grandmother loved Bob Hope as well and took me to all his films. This was the era when, all over Britain, there were 'news theatres'. These were small cinemas that showed the weekly Pathé newsreel, with an hour's programme of, say, Disney cartoons, Three Stooges shorts, and a Western serial, usually starring Roy Rogers, Gene Autry or Audie Murphy. Bob Hope entertained me more than any of them. What really made me laugh was the way he flared his nostrils. I used to stand in front of the mirror and try to do the same. I was not very good at it; but, I discovered one day, when my face was contorted with effort, that I could wiggle my ears, a trick that used to reduce my own children to hysterics.

All this came flooding back when it was decided to give Bob Hope an honorary knighthood in 1999. He had been born in Eltham, south London. Throughout his long life he had never forgotten his origins and had always generously supported a charity there.

Every year the Queen, usually on the advice of the embassy, would confer 'honorary' honours on Americans – honorary because they were not the Queen's subjects. As Her Majesty's representative, I would present the insignia to the recipient. When it was a knighthood, the ceremony would follow a formal dinner. In this way a parade of American notables passed through the Great House. I presided over the presentation of insignia of knighthood to, among others, General Wesley Clark, the Supreme Allied Commander of NATO during the Kosovo campaign; to Steven Spielberg for his support of the British film industry when he was making *Band of Brothers*; and Lou Gerstner, the former head of IBM, for his help in bringing information technology to British schools.

Bob Hope, with his wife Dolores and a large number of family members, arrived one fine spring evening. Hope was sadly reduced from his prime. He was in a wheelchair, silent, and appeared not to comprehend his surroundings. By contrast, Dolores was a live wire, who took close, personal care of her husband. After dinner I made a short speech in which I recounted the nostrils story, before coming to the formal part of the ceremony. The insignia of an honorary knighthood include an ornate cross attached to a ribbon, which is worn around the neck. There is also an even more ornate star, which is pinned to the breast. I used to hang the ribbon around the recipient's neck at the climax to the ceremony. For this I was rebuked by someone in London, who told me that I should only hand over, not hang, the cross and ribbon. I turned a blind eye, because no American would leave the Great House without being photographed in the full monty with me.

Dolores Hope pushed Bob towards me in his wheelchair. It was a long way from the news theatre in North Street, Brighton, *circa* 1950. I wondered if he had any idea what was going on. I picked up the ribbon with the cross hanging from it. Suddenly I saw a blaze of light enter Bob's eyes. For a moment there was the star of *Paleface*. Looking at the cross, Hope exclaimed with a clear, strong voice: 'I'll have one of those!'

Dolores helped him to his feet, I put the ribbon around his neck, and then he was lowered gently into the wheelchair. He seemed at once to fall back into his catatonic state, except that for the rest of the evening a smile played on his lips.

I had in my office a photograph of Winston Churchill standing on the terrace of the Great House at some point during the Second World War. He is addressing embassy staff, some in uniform, who are gathered around him on the steps. Their faces are suffused with hope and affection. Beside him stands the tall, stooping figure of Lord Halifax, British ambassador for most of the war.

I would often place myself on what I calculated was the exact spot where Winston had stood. I wondered how many other spots there were in the Great House that had been sanctified by his presence; probably not many, because when he visited Washington during the war, he usually stayed at the White House and then, incredibly to our modern sensibilities, for weeks at a time. During one of Churchill's visits, Roosevelt went home to his house at Hyde Park on the Hudson River, giving Churchill the run of the White House until he returned. Now that is what I call allies!

There is a thesis to be written about the damage done to international relations by the failure of today's leaders to spend significant time with each other, like Churchill and Roosevelt. Twenty-first-century politicians take a macho pride in having breakfast in one country, lunch in another, and dinner in a third. This is no way to get to understand a political ally or rival. Why the hurry? The excuse is usually urgent business back home and the 'twenty-four-hour news cycle'. Churchill was fighting a war for Britain's survival, which is about as urgent as it gets; and when did a day not have twenty-four hours?

I always fancied that Winston Churchill's spirit hovered over the Great House and its terrace. What would he have thought? Whenever I see grainy newsreel of yesterday's political leaders, they always look more solid and substantial figures than most of today's crop. Is this the distorting vision of the rear-view mirror; is it a case of a civil servant in regular close contact with cabinet ministers allowing familiarity to breed a smidgeon of contempt; or are today's politicians second-raters compared with those of a generation or more ago?

I suspect that, like human nature, politicians do not change much, and that Churchill's verdict on New Labour's crop would have been no harsher than on those with whom he worked over his long political life. For Catherine and me, visits by New Labour ministers and the occasional Tory opposition figure offered endless variety and stimulation. There was a minority of capable ministers, who stood out like Masai warriors in a crowd of pygmies. Several women were among them. The late Mo Mowlam (Northern Ireland Secretary) and Clare Short (International Development Secretary) – whose political careers came to grief – were, at the height of their powers, formidable operators who enjoyed the respect of their American counterparts. Mo's talents were intuitive and political; Clare had some of the same qualities, married to a firm grasp of her brief. Both were admirably blunt and direct. They were also good company and liked a tipple at the end of a full working day. Margaret Beckett (Environment, Farming and Rural Affairs – Agriculture to you and me), in her understated, underestimated way, quietly impressed well beyond her reputation and was a vast improvement on the hesitant and almost inaudible Nick Brown.

One problem that became immediately clear was lack of government experience. It does the British democratic system no favours when the main Opposition party is out of office for nearly twenty years, as was the case with Labour. It means a prime minister, a cabinet and a cadre of junior ministers who have almost no experience of governing at all. It is hardly surprising that Labour in power have found it so difficult to change habits formed in opposition. It explains why, to the detriment of the Cabinet's authority, Tony Blair relied for so long on the coterie of personal advisers who had accompanied him in the storming of the Labour Party heights.

It may explain the hesitancy and nervousness of some ministers on business in Washington. It took Jack Straw, someone more to be liked than admired, a long time to find his feet, in sharp contrast to Robin Cook. On a visit in 1999, as Home Secretary, he was mystifyingly tongue-tied in the unthreatening presence of Janet Reno, the Attorney General, and Louis Freeh, the Director of the FBI. He was not much better in his early days as Foreign Secretary, though, as he himself was the first to admit, his appointment after the 2001 election had come as a complete surprise, catching him unprepared. After a press briefing by an amiable but stumbling Jack on his first visit to Washington, an American journalist came up to me and said: 'I never thought I would say it – but bring back Robin Cook!' With the acquisition of experience, Straw was to develop into a solid and competent Foreign Secretary, though, as the French say, he did not invent gunpowder.

Straw's uncertain touch was as nothing compared with poor old John Prescott. I really liked Prescott, though I know that the feeling was never mutual. The only time when Prescott and I seemed to find real common ground was when I helped him choose eight recordings for the New Zealand equivalent of *Desert Island Discs*, over which he was much exercised. It was a shame. Somebody said to me that he thought me a pin-striped toff, determined to belittle him. Each time Prescott arrived at the embassy he was like a mastiff

Wedding day. Chelsea Town Hall, 30 October 1997. We had made it,
the day before leaving for the United States.

A winter's view of the Great House showing its 'ante-bellum' façade
with grand portico, terrace and staircase.

The drawing room of the Great House as redecorated by my wife Catherine.

Right: Catherine.

Below right: One of my mentors: Geoffrey Howe as Foreign Secretary. I was his spokesman from 1984 to 1988.

Below: Sir Henry Wotton (1568–1639), one of the founders of modern British diplomacy.

President Bill Clinton beginning the 'upper arm rub'.

Catherine and I with President Clinton and his wife Hillary in the White House.

The Chairman of the Federal Reserve, Dr Alan Greenspan, dancing with his wife, Andrea Mitchell, the television journalist, at the Great House.

Vernon Jordan on the Great House dance floor with Mrs Bill Cash.

With Madeleine Albright at the State Department.
With Mayor Rudy Giuliani of New York, 1997.

Meeting President George Bush in the White House during HM The Queen's visit to Washington, 1991.

Our very good friends Ben Bradlee and Sally Quinn.

Mo Mowlam with Bill Clinton, a just visible David Trimble, and me at the Speaker's St Patrick Day's lunch, March 1998.

with his hackles up, just waiting to be 'dissed'. In fact, I thought he had a sharp political brain and that it would be folly to underestimate him; but, somehow or other, we got off on the wrong foot from the beginning. I learnt later that he had complained in London about my reading the morning's telegraphic reports from the Foreign Office and our overseas posts on overnight developments across the world while he held forth to his staff over breakfast. We were about to call on Vice-President Gore. It was indispensable for Prescott and me to be fully briefed beforehand as I knew Gore and his staff would be.

Prescott took his status as Deputy Prime Minister very seriously, insisting always on seeing the Vice-President and on discussing the full range of foreign policy issues of the moment. The problem with this was that he never appeared to be sufficiently up on these issues and he always seemed nervous. I would will him on as he sank lower in his chair and talked faster and faster. During the Kosovo campaign Prescott got into a terrible tangle with a senator, to whom he talked about war in the 'Balklands' and 'Kovosa'. The senator, who knew something about military matters, was surprised to hear from the Deputy Prime Minister that British Harriers were bombing from fifteen feet. On another occasion, with Vice-President Gore, the two subjects for discussion – transatlantic air services and the environment – melded indistinguishably into each other under the pressure of Prescott's syntax and verbal velocity. A member of Gore's staff called afterwards to 'clarify' the discussion. Though Prescott raised a few eyebrows – Vice-President Cheney and his staff were a study in poker faces and twitching eyebrows when he saw them in 2002 – Americans on the whole took to him and he had good friends on Capitol Hill.

There were others who assumed their ministerial roles as to the manner born: Gordon Brown, the late Robin Cook, Peter Mandelson, John Reid, Paul Murphy, Dennis McShane, the late Donald Dewar. They handled themselves with skill and self-confidence in a city which can intimidate.

The performance of the lamented Dewar, Scotland's first First Minister after Devolution, was a *tour de force* of intellectual brilliance, incisive negotiation and humour. His amiably uncharismatic successor, Henry McLeish, was struck nearly dumb with shock when to his astonishment (and mine, to be frank) a chance remark that I had made to the White House about his visiting Washington led to an invitation to meet President Bush. As poor Henry twitched and stuttered in the Oval Office, George W. Bush, accompanied by the then National Security Adviser, Condoleezza Rice, genially recounted stories of his time in Scotland as a boy.

After Henry McLeish's *coup* the sound of spitting from envious Westminster politicians became audible in Washington. It caused me all kinds of problems with those who wanted me to deliver something similar for them. There are few things harder to handle than a government minister who expects access in Washington way above his or her pay grade. One minister threw a tantrum and cancelled her visit, because her unreasonable demands for access could not be met.

Then there was the case of Michael Levy – Lord Levy – New Labour's fund-raiser, Blair's special envoy to the Middle East, and, so he was described by those close to him, the intimate friend and tennis partner of the Prime Minister. At some point in 2001 he announced his intention to come to Washington. This was the kind of news that chilled to the marrow even the hardiest ambassador. Levy, I was told, wanted to be seen as a latter-day Kissinger of the Middle East peace process. He shuttled around Israel and the Arab countries, giving birth to voluminous reports to London in which he played a prominent role. But as I reported to Jack Straw, I was myself warned on separate occasions by members of the Saudi and Jordanian royal families that Levy was not terribly welcome in their countries; and that he was received only out of friendship for Tony Blair.

I had been hearing for some time from the Foreign Office that Levy was keen to break out of the Middle East and extend his activities to the US. We had already had to advise against his coming to Washington during the Bush/Gore campaign of 2000 for fear this would translate in American eyes into a signal of support from Blair for Gore. But there was no stopping his coming to Washington in the following year.

At first his ambitions were reasonable in scale. He had got to know Rich Armitage, the Deputy Secretary of State, somewhere in the private sector and quite understandably wanted to see him. He had others on his list, who were senior, influential people appropriate to his status. It was too good to last. Not long before he was due to arrive Levy called me to say that he now wanted to see Condi Rice, Colin Powell and others of Cabinet rank; and that this had Blair's backing. I told Levy that this was unrealistically ambitious, if only for protocol reasons. I phoned Jonathan Powell, who confirmed that I was not to waste capital in trying to secure access for Levy at this level. I implored Powell to tell Levy this before he arrived.

Levy duly arrived at the residence. He immediately asked to speak to me in private. I deduced that Jonathan Powell had not spoken to him. I told Levy that, to be frank, the top echelon of the US Administration was out of his reach. If Colin Powell were in his office when we went to see Armitage, it was possible that we would be taken in to see him. For the rest, he had a very good programme. Levy was not to be consoled. He told me that humiliation awaited him in London if these meetings did not materialize.

The programme went ahead as originally planned. Levy met senior and influential Americans. He had good meetings. To be fair, he was quite interesting and informative on Israeli politics (if I remember rightly, his son is, or used to be, chief of staff to the Israeli politician Yossi Beilin). Before he departed, Levy said what a good job I was doing as ambassador and how much the Prime Minister appreciated me. But a little bird later told me that, on returning to London, Levy had complained in No. 10 about the way I had organized his visit.

There was some fortuitous extra needle in the visit, for reasons that had nothing to do with foreign affairs. By chance, the record producer Mickie Most and his wife Chrissie were staying with us (Mickie died in 2003). Mickie had discovered and recorded some of the biggest pop acts of the sixties and seventies: the Animals, Herman's Hermits, Donovan, Hot Chocolate, Lulu, Mud, Suzi Quatro, among others. Mickie had known Michael Levy when the latter had been a humble and, according to Mickie, unloved accountant in the music industry. Levy's main claim to fame was to have managed seventies glam rocker Alvin Stardust (aka Shane Fenton, for those who remember Brian Matthew's *Saturday Club* on the BBC Light Programme). There was no love lost between Mickie Most and Levy.

So much happened on that terrace where Churchill had stood: our social secretary, Amanda Downes, rushing out to tell us and John Major, on a sparkling September morning, that an aircraft had crashed into the World Trade Center. The night before, 10 September 2001, Condoleezza Rice, her deputy Steve Hadley, David Manning, Blair's new foreign policy adviser, and myself dining quietly together, discussing the world. Michael Douglas courting Catherine Zeta-Jones after a dinner in 1999 at which Hillary Clinton had fallen asleep during a narcoleptic speech from Chris Smith, Secretary for Culture, Media and Sport. Seamus Mallon, Deputy First Minister of Northern Ireland – very prickly, very decent – and Catherine, sharing cigarettes, with long exhalations of relief. A group of women from Northern Ireland, all whom had lost menfolk to terrorism, recounting how they had refused to tell the White House who was Protestant, who Catholic. A drunken Scottish MP looking at me and asking loudly, 'Who's that f—ing p—k?' Catherine in earnest conversation with Alan Greenspan, the usually taciturn Chairman of the Federal Reserve, about commodities and financial futures (the other keys to a lively conversation with Alan were jazz – he played professional clarinet and saxophone as a young man – and the novels of Ayn Rand). Robin Cook in earnest pursuit over the phone of his bride-to-be, Gaynor. John Sununu, chief of staff to President Bush the elder, commenting to a departing ambassador and his wife that the farewell parties given in their honour would be 'as nothing to the parties they will be giving once you're gone'.

11

Like Brothers

Our first weeks in Washington at the end of 1997 are a chaotic kaleidoscope of memories. Leave aside that Catherine and I were learning to get used to each other as man and wife, we were confronted with *le tout* Washington. Invitations to dinner, lunch, drinks, the opera, the ballet rained down on us like a summer storm. Everyone wants to meet a new British ambassador and his wife. The word quickly spread that Catherine was different: outspoken, half-French, half-Russian, very pretty, short skirts and the legs to match. We were as excited as schoolchildren as we whizzed from one event to another in the back of the ambassador's Rolls-Royce. People fawned on us as if we were royalty – though the deference shown could not rival Germany's, where more than once a woman curtseyed to me.

It was the greatest fun. But it was also business. We had to be hard-headed and selective in deciding which invitations to accept. This was not a social whirl for its own sake. It was a means of meeting as many movers and shakers as possible, as rapidly as possible. The higher the quality of your contacts – your network – the more effectively you can operate in Washington. We made mistakes along the way, finding ourselves trapped at occasions which were as unenjoyable as they were useless; but by the end of the year our network had begun to take shape. More important, friendships of enduring quality were beginning to blossom.

Torpor, meantime, afflicted the political class of Washington. It reminded me of 1989, when the veteran American journalist David Brinkley had written in the *Washington Post* that the town was becoming so boring it had lost all interest to foreign journalists. This is the kind of comment which invites history's retribution. Similarly, somebody of very great standing in Washington society told me that I had come to the US at precisely the wrong time. It was going to be so boring: Clinton was comfortably into his second term, budget surpluses stretched ahead as far as the eye could see, the President would spend his time playing a lot of golf. A wistful Mike McCurry, the White House spokesman, told me later that it was such a golden scenario that he had changed his mind about resigning and going into the private sector.

My own experience had already suggested something different. On our first weekend in Washington, before we had had a chance to unpack, I took a call from Tom Pickering, Under-Secretary for Political Affairs in the State Department. This was nominally the number three position in State. I soon discovered that this veteran diplomat had the energy of a twenty-year-old and was State's driving force. The very best American diplomats are pound for pound as good as any you will find anywhere, and often better. Tom was up there among the best.

He wanted me to call on him on my first Monday morning and talk about Iraq. Saddam Hussein was playing worrying games with the UN weapons inspectors. The dictator sensed weakening unity and resolve in the UN Security Council. At every turn he sought to hamper the ability of the inspectors to do their job. He claimed that he was in full compliance with all UN Resolutions passed since the 1991 war and that sanctions against him should be lifted.

The Americans were worried. In reality Saddam was still in breach of the terms of the ceasefire which had ended the Gulf War of 1991 (as indeed he was at the outset of the Second Gulf War in 2003). A significant quantity of agents and substances that could be used to make chemical and biological weapons was unaccounted for. At the United Nations in New York, France and Russia, with large economic stakes in Iraq and dubious links with Saddam Hussein himself, took a more relaxed view. They wanted to offer Iraq a road map to the early lifting of sanctions. Here already, in embryo, was the rift that in 2003 was to split the Security Council and the Atlantic Alliance at the time of the second Iraq war.

Even the British were not fully aligned with the US. We argued that, subject to the fulfilment of rigorous conditions (which we believed Saddam would never honour), the theoretical possibility of lifting sanctions should be offered Iraq in a new UN resolution. This was the so-called 'light at the end of the tunnel'. The Americans made plain that, for political reasons, they could never acquiesce, even hypothetically, in the removal of sanctions while Saddam was in power, even though 'regime change' was not yet declared American policy. It would become so in the following year, fully five years before the Second Gulf War and the arrival of George W. Bush on the scene.

All this was a harbinger of great events to come; but in autumn 1997, as we settled into Washington, Iraq was for most people no more than a storm the size of a man's fist on the horizon. It took Monica Lewinsky to catapult the nation's capital out of its Southern lethargy and ruin the golden promise of Clinton's second term.

The Monica Lewinsky affair burst into the open in January 1998, a few days before we gave our first big black-tie dinner. We had been in Washington for three months. The time had come to repay hospitality and make our mark. We told people that the dinner was to celebrate three things: our arrival, our marriage and Catherine's birthday. About a hundred and twenty guests accepted the invitation. We seated them at round tables of ten in the grand ballroom, with its mirror-lined walls and nineteenth-century Austrian chandeliers. We rapidly discovered an old Washington habit: people sneaked into the ballroom before dinner and tried to switch the place cards to a seating they found more congenial or advantageous.

The guests were quite a mixture: big cheeses from Washington and New York, old friends from Britain, and our parents. Though it was a formal affair, we decided to loosen things up a bit. We hired a black soul band called Curtis Pope and the Midnight Movers. We wanted people to stay late and enjoy themselves. Washingtonians were notorious for leaving a party immediately after dinner. The convention was that if you had an important job, you had to be up at 5 a.m. and at work by 6.30. Anyone who stayed late at parties was considered not to have an important job. This was a living death for the socially ambitious.

We discovered another Washington phenomenon: the impossibility of moving people with any speed to their tables once dinner was called. At large parties, Washingtonians fell upon each other as if long-lost friends. In fact, most of them had probably seen each other the night before at one occasion or another. Small groups of guests gathered, dissolved and re-formed in new permutations. The noise of conversation was deafening. Our guests were trading the most highly prized commodity of all: political gossip. To drag them away and move them into dinner was, as the Americans say, like herding cats. We learnt to allow half an hour for this arduous manoeuvre. If it was the annual St Patrick's Day lunch, with over a hundred Irish-Americans and Ulster politicians of every stripe, you were talking a good forty-five minutes. The Irish also insisted on standing up and working the room between courses, so turning these occasions (I loved them) into marathons of food and drink.

On that first evening a large number of our guests stayed well beyond midnight. But it was not Curtis Pope's music or the colour of our eyes or the fact that it was Saturday night. It was Monica. There was an excitement like electricity in the air. As we welcomed our guests, everyone had a comment to make on Clinton's alleged dalliance. It was striking how many seasoned hands thought his resignation inevitable in a matter of days. That evening there was no other topic of conversation. The air hummed and twanged with speculation and gossip. The Secretary of State, Madeleine Albright, who was our guest of honour, told me that she just could not believe that the President had enjoyed sex with a White House intern. A top Washington lawyer put another view: 'Hell, if you can't have sex with a pretty young woman, what's the point of being President?'

Dinners like these comprised in large part the so-called 'A' list of the most influential and socially desirable denizens of the nation's capital. The list was solemnly compiled every year by a local magazine, with a Top Ten in which the British ambassador and his wife featured virtually by right. In our time the only other ambassador permanently admitted to this apex of exclusivity was the French. At an A-list dinner there was always a man or woman of the moment, enjoying fifteen minutes of mega-fame, towards whom all others gravitated. That night at our embassy it was the tall, handsome and urbane Vernon Jordan, Clinton's close friend and golfing partner, and probably the best-known African-American in Washington. I had got to know Vernon during my first incarnation in Washington in the early nineties. He was a highly successful lawyer and businessman, who had come up the hard way from humble roots in Georgia and then through the civil rights movement. He was, and remains, a major power in the Democratic Party. If Senator John Kerry had won the presidential election in 2004, I would have put a lot of money on Vernon, with his wife Ann, becoming US ambassador to the Court of St James.

It had already become known that, at Clinton's request, Vernon had tried to get Lewinsky a job in New York. Everyone assumed that Vernon had the inside track on what in fact had taken place between the President and the intern. We had a lot of big media figures at the dinner – the late Kay Graham, owner of the *Washington Post*; Barbara Walters, at the height of her powers as presenter of ABC's *20/20* programme; Jim Lehrer of public television's *Lehrer Newshour* and moderator of presidential election debates; Johnny Apple of the *New York Times*, and so on. With all his charm and persuasiveness, Vernon cruised among them in the embassy reception rooms, making sure that they fully grasped his side of the story. That done, he then, with equal charm and persuasiveness, took to the dance floor with the better-looking women among our guests. He was especially solicitous towards Biddy Cash, the stunning wife of Bill Cash, Tory MP, Eurosceptic extraordinaire, and doughty supporter of Catherine in her struggle to gain access to her children.

The party made an unusually big splash for an embassy event. This was for reasons largely beyond our control. The following day, in Sunday's *New York Times*, Johnny Apple wrote a big front-page story on the Lewinsky scandal. As background, our party was mentioned 'above the fold' – that is, in the top half of the paper. *New York Times*, front page, above the fold – 'Hey!' said Washington's insiders admiringly. They traded their grandmothers for this kind of publicity.

The Lewinsky story broke in the final stages of preparing Tony Blair's first official visit to Washington. Downing Street were worried that Clinton would be too distracted. Briefly, postponement was considered; but the White House wanted the visit to go ahead and so did I. By the time Blair arrived, Lewinsky fever had started to cool just a little.

Blair performed brilliantly during the visit. He was still in the full splendour of his election victory. Something had changed since the happy-go-lucky band of brothers and sisters that had visited Bonn the previous year. Blair arrived with a large retinue, which included his wife Cherie and three ministers: Alan Milburn, Helen Liddle and Jack Straw, stars of the New Labour firmament. There were large numbers of minor courtiers and logistics people. The Blairs and the VIPs were lodged at Blair (pure coincidence) House, the grand American residence for state visits. There was more than a whiff of imperial progress.

The whole No. 10 team, from the PM downwards, pulsed with ill-suppressed excitement. Washington. Bill Clinton. Third Way. World Stage. This was the Big One. This was what really mattered. The Foreign Office never stood a chance. Nor did Europe, for that matter. It was always going to be a lesser magnet. America belonged to Downing Street.

Blair had several starring performances: his expression of personal loyalty and friendship towards an embattled Clinton, which defused a potentially awkward White House press conference; a moving toast at the state dinner, which had several Americans in tears; a persuasive exposition of his Northern Ireland policy to senators and congressmen, which had long-term benefits for Britain; a speech of similar strength at a big breakfast hosted by Al Gore, the Vice-President. Blair faltered only at a dinner to discuss world economic trends. The guests included mega-stars like Alan Greenspan, Chairman of the Federal Reserve, and Jim Wolfensohn, President of the World Bank. Blair was under-briefed and out of his depth. He shared Margaret Thatcher's propensity to invest rhetoric with moral philosophy. But he seemed to have little of her appetite for detail.

The Clintons pulled out all the stops. The state dinner at the White House was a grand and glittering affair. It was littered with Hollywood stars. For the first time I noticed that Harrison Ford wore an earring. We talked to a bored Barbra Streisand, whose eyes flickered around the room like a chameleon's tongue. A marquee had been pitched in the White House grounds for after-dinner musical entertainment by Elton John and Stevie Wonder. They took turns to play. Stevie Wonder's virtuosity made Elton John sound like a pub pianist. Wonder wrapped up the evening singing 'My Cherie Amour'. Cherie herself looked star-struck, almost over-whelmed, by the glamour of the occasion.

I ran into the combination of Stevie Wonder and Bill Clinton once more in Washington. It was several years later. I received an urgent summons from the White House to attend a ceremony, at which some of America's most distinguished scientists were to receive awards. I walked into one of the White House reception rooms, to see a row of white men with white hair and grey suits. The only exceptions were two black men. One was Stevie Wonder, the other his assistant. Wonder told me that he was the guest of one of the scientists, who had invented a keyboard enabling blind musicians to use an electronic Braille system for composition. Clinton entered the room and moved down the line, shaking hands formally and rather stiffly with each of the scientists. Then he reached Stevie Wonder. His face relaxed into a broad grin. 'Hey, man, how y'all doin'?' enquired the forty-second President of the United States, giving Wonder a hug and pat on the back. I marvelled at the way Clinton had slipped effortlessly out of formal American into that mixture of Hot Springs, Arkansas and African-American vernacular he did so well. Clinton turned to me and asked Wonder, 'Do you know this man?' I then got a different kind of greeting: a firm handshake and a grip on the elbow.

The elbow manoeuvre, which betokened a degree of familiarity, showed that I had made modest progress up the ladder of presidential salutations. Before Clinton left office, I graduated to the upper-arm rub. This involved having your hand vigorously shaken, then dropped, to be replaced by a rubbing of the upper right arm, while a conversation took place. This signalled a greater intimacy than the elbow grip. I mentioned this to a friend in the White House, saying that I was touched by this gesture of friendship. My friend, disillusioned by the Lewinsky business, commented, sardonically, 'Friendship, hell! He was just wiping his hand.'

The handshake and its variations occupy a minor but interesting niche in the rituals of American politics. For the full inventory, I commend the opening frames of the 1998 film version of Joe Klein's *Primary Colors*.

On this first visit, Clinton took the Prime Minister to Blair (again no connection) High School in Maryland. The entire school – in the thousands – was gathered in the sports hall. The noise was thunderous. The High School band was playing at full volume. Clinton and Blair waited in the wings to address the students: two trim, tall, youngish figures in blue suits. I remembered a remark of Peter Mandelson's: 'When you see them together, they are like brothers.'

They went out on stage. It was President and Prime Minister as rock stars. Give them black pork-pie hats and shades and it would have been the Blues Brothers. The screaming was deafening, the adulation total. 'How,' I thought to myself, 'how can you do this and not let it turn your head?'

The visit was a great success for Blair's status in Washington and his relationship with Clinton. Nothing terribly concrete was agreed but that did not matter. Catherine struck up a good relationship with Cherie and her chief of staff Fiona Millar. This was to be very important for Catherine's charitable work in the future.

As ambassador I basked in the reflected glory. A success for the Prime Minister is a success for the ambassador. Jonathan Powell had said to me before I left for Washington the previous year that he would ensure that the White House understood I was Tony Blair's personal choice. The only evidence I ever received that this undertaking was made good came from Peter Mandelson. Whenever he visited Washington in our first year, he went out of his way to tell Americans that I was the Prime Minister's personal appointment. I was grateful. Americans need to be told this. Their major embassies are part of the political spoils system. This means that US ambassadors can be appointed, including to Britain, who have no knowledge or experience of foreign policy. They are often regarded by their own administration as simply ceremonial figures unequipped to do policy. The British government's expectations of its ambassador in Washington are the polar opposite. No. 10's appetite for our reporting was voracious from the start. The challenge for the embassy was to add value to what London could obtain from the press and their own links with Washington. The answer to that was to secure contacts and sources of information that trumped anything available to London. The key was access to those who mattered in Washington; and the key to access was credibility.

In February 1998 our credibility in Washington was high: thanks to the Blair visit, thanks to Peter Mandelson, and thanks to our own efforts. But there was already a worm in the apple. During the February visit there were the first signs of a 'them and us' relationship between embassy and Downing Street staff – the beginnings on their side of a churlish, chippy arrogance, which came to characterize too many of the support staff and minor courtiers. A female voice was heard to ask sourly in the corridors of the embassy, 'Is there anyone here who hasn't been to public school?' To which the answer was, 99 per cent of the embassy staff, unlike, of course, the British Prime Minister himself.

Blair was the sixth Prime Minister in my career and I had known nothing like this before. As the years passed, things got worse. There were times when I felt that No. 10 regarded the embassy as a competitor in dealing with the Americans. I detected a resentment at the close contacts we built with the Bush administration, contacts whose only rationale was to serve the interests of Her Majesty's Government. By the time I retired in February 2003, almost exactly five years after this first visit, I had reached the unhappy conclusion that what I had achieved as ambassador had been as much in spite of Downing Street as because of it.

Immediately after the Blair visit, Catherine and I left for Texas. We were picking up signals that the Governor, George W. Bush, son of former President Bush, would run for the Presidency in 2000. We needed to take a look at him.

12

Sex

Blair did not return to Washington for over a year. During most of that period Clinton was tortured on the rack of the Monica Lewinsky and Paula Jones affairs. Lewinsky was apparently blow jobs in the Oval Office with a touch of phone sex in the night. Jones was an allegation against Clinton, when Governor of Arkansas, of indecent exposure in a hotel room, accompanied by an invitation to fellatio. Throughout 1998 there were other 'bimbo eruptions', as women of varying credibility sought to insert themselves into the Lewinsky/Jones slipstream. According to people I spoke to who knew Clinton well, this was part of a pattern of sexual behaviour that went back years.

There were moments in 1998 when Clinton looked done for, when his presidency tottered. But despite the implausible fellatio-free definition of what constituted sex, he survived. This came as a shock to many in Britain. A British politician in a similar situation would not have lasted five minutes. Early resignation would have been the only option. This was yet another measure of how the political cultures of our two countries have diverged over the years.

The key to Clinton's survival was that he never lost the support of a majority of the American people. They liked the prosperity and full employment that he brought. They did not like him particularly, but that was another matter. Clinton never seriously risked a visit by the American equivalent of men in grey suits telling him to resign. He retained the unwavering support of powerful Democratic constituencies, in whom he had made an enormous political invest-ment: women's rights groups, ethnic minorities, organized labour. His political base stayed solid; and Hillary Clinton, bruised and bloodied though she was, stood by her man.

There was also a whiff of entrapment. Hillary Clinton was much derided at the time for talking of a 'right-wing conspiracy' against her husband. Clinton's sexual recklessness had, of course, handed a sword to his enemies; but those who seized the hilt included a cabal of right-wing lawyers allegedly close to Kenneth Starr, the independent counsel charged with investigating the Lewinsky affair. Some of them were involved in the Paula Jones case. Starr himself overreached by producing a report in the autumn of 1998 highly graphic in its sexual detail. Far from torpedoing Clinton, it went down badly in the country at large. Nothing more underlined the gulf between the fevered, poisoned, polarized politics of Washington, and the calm prosperity of the rest of the United States.

No. 10 were desperately concerned about Clinton's fate. Most of the time my reports said that, absent fresh evidence against him, he was likely to survive. I added that his position was bedevilled by the tension between his political and legal advisers. The former argued that a sinner come to repentance was the most powerful card Clinton could play. They advised a major act of contrition and 'fessin' up'. Knowing Clinton's histrionic skills, he would probably have done this to perfection, earning the forgiveness of the American people and gaining a few points at the polls into the bargain. But the lawyers always won the day, and Clinton is himself a lawyer. Their concern was that too much confession in public would lead either to impeachment as President or arrest on leaving office. These were risks Clinton could not afford to run. They explain a lot of his weasel words in public.

Towards the end of August 1998 Catherine and I were staying with our friends Claudine and Dennis Ward near Ste Maxime in the south of France. We watched Sky News every day. The reporting from Washington was increasingly strident and alarming. Sky said that Starr's report was imminent and it could well force Clinton out of office. Catherine and I decided that we could not risk being in France if Clinton resigned. We returned early to Washington.

On arriving in the States, we discovered that things were not as bad for Clinton as the British media were reporting. Starr's report had just been published. I said to London that Clinton's position was precarious and unpredictable; but it looked to me that Starr had given it his best shot and this had not been enough to land a knockout blow. On the really serious charges – suborning perjury, witness tampering, obstruction of justice – I thought the evidence produced by Starr was no better than circumstantial.

This assessment stood the test of time. Even though the impeachment process had not yet begun, and Clinton had several alarums and excursions in the months to come, it was the high-water mark of the threat to his presidency. But we did not know that at the time. A few days later, the Republican-dominated Judiciary Committee of the House of Representatives voted to release the videotape of testimony Clinton had given on the Lewinsky business to a Grand Jury in the summer. It would be broadcast on 21 September, the day Tony Blair was coming to New York for the annual opening of the UN General Assembly. This was a calculated partisan move intended to drive Clinton from office. I told Blair that his visit would coincide with a day of high drama for the United States.

There was much anxiety in the White House and among Democrats. Rahm Emanuel, one of Clinton's closest advisers and now a Chicago congressman, told me that he just did not know what the country's reaction would be to the videotape. One of my best friends on the Hill, the late Bob Matsui, an astute Japanese-American Democratic congressman from California, called me to say he had just seen the tape. 'It's horrible,' he said. I checked around further. The Democrats were in deep despair. The Republicans (but not those who cared for the reputation of their country) had their tails up.

Both Clinton and Blair were due to speak at the UN opening ceremony. The White House and No. 10 decided to take advantage of this to organize later in the day a Third Way meeting at the law library of New York University. Other participants were to include the unlikely combination of Peter Stoyanov, President of Bulgaria, and Romano Prodi, then Prime Minister of Italy. As these Third Way meetings reached out to embrace an ever wider circle of political leaders who laid claim to vague social-democratic leanings, I could not get out of my head that song by the Bonzo Dog Doo-Dah Band, in which Vivian Stanshall recites an endless litany of world figures, dead and alive.

On the Monday morning I ran into the White House team at the UN in New York. They were nervous as cats. I called Catherine in Washington, who was watching Clinton's interrogation on television. 'He's doing pretty well,' she said; 'if it goes on like this, he will be fine.' She was right. Clinton's testimony was not the nail in his coffin that the Republicans had hoped it would be. On the contrary, most Americans took a dimmer view of Republican partisan vengefulness than they did of Clinton's priapism. A few days later a poll came out, registering the overwhelming disapproval of the American people at the release of the videotape. In due course the Republicans would be punished in the November mid-term congressional elections.

Catherine's reaction and that of the embassy were very similar. I passed this to the No. 10 and White House people. They valued an outside opinion. Long faces lightened a bit. By lunch time everybody knew the crisis had passed and that Clinton would survive.

The Third Way meeting went ahead in an atmosphere of euphoric relief and windy generalization. It was a packed crowd at the NYU Law Library, including the high priesthood of New Democracy and Hillary Clinton. The discussion added up to very little, though the air was thick with mutual congratulation afterwards. Stoyanov was rather impressive in a self-deprecating way, Prodi eccentric when he was comprehensible, and Clinton and Blair too glib and practised. The rhetoric was fine; but there simply was not enough political ballast. As I sat there, fighting off sleep in the conspicuous front row, it became ever clearer that the Third Way was less a coherent philosophy of government, more a tactic for election-winning: how to hold your base and reach out to the centre ground at the same time. It is as old as the hills. When I did European politics at school, it was called 'Giolittismo' after an early twentieth-century Italian Prime Minister, Giovanni Giolitti, who used to steal the opposition's clothes.

Afterwards, the British and American teams went off to a room for a drink. It was a celebration. The Americans were almost light-headed after surviving yet another near-death experience. The Clintons and Blairs huddled together in a corner of the library, the two couples intimate and alone.

That evening, I accompanied Tony Blair to Kennedy Airport in the official limo. To my astonishment Blair asked, 'What exactly is the charge against Clinton? I mean, what is he supposed to have done?' 'Bloody hell,' I thought to myself, 'have you read nothing of what I've sent you?' (I had been instructed by Downing Street to send as much as possible on Clinton's fate, because of the Prime Minister's intense interest.)

So I began once again to explain the dreary litany of charges against Clinton, his rebuttals, the risk of impeachment, when is sex not sex, and so on. I tried to keep the sordid tale short and simple. But I could see that the Prime Minister had lost interest well before I had finished.

13

Blair for President

At the end of 1998 I reported to London that the issue was less whether Clinton would survive impeachment – I thought he would – but what kind of president he would prove to be afterwards. He would be damaged, but to what degree? There were fears that for the rest of his term he would be politically crippled. I was not sure about this. I thought it underestimated the institutional power of the presidency, Clinton's resilience and his political skills.

I remembered Clinton's State of the Union speech earlier in the year, only a week or so after the Lewinsky scandal had broken. This is a major event in the political calendar, when the President reports on the nation's health. He sets out his prospectus for the next twelve months to a joint session of Congress – that is, to the Senate and the House of Representatives sitting together, in the presence of the diplomatic corps and several hundred spectators in the galleries.

Clinton was then in deep political trouble, the worst since President Richard Nixon and the Watergate affair. He was a sitting target for the Republicans. Yet, standing on the floor of the chamber, I sensed that what was important for congressmen on both sides of the party line was the reputation of their country and of the institution of the presidency; and that this far transcended the behaviour of one office-holder. So there was a kind of rallying around that evening. Of course, to put it mildly, not everything that Clinton said was greeted with rapture by the Republicans; but if you had not known already, it would have been hard to detect from the proceedings that Clinton's presidency was at severe risk.

Clinton had his moments before he left office in January 2001. Two of the Republican ringleaders of the attempt to unseat him – Congressmen Newt Gingrich and Bob Livingston, successive Speakers of the House – were, irony of ironies, forced to resign towards the end of 1998 when allegations of sexual misconduct broke surface. Clinton continued to outwit the Republicans on the annual setting of the budget. At the end of 1998, Clinton's *annus horribilis*, he was like Muhammad Ali in his epic contest with Joe Frazier, bobbing, weaving and ducking, taking terrible punishment on the ropes, but finally administering the knockout blow to his adversaries. It was not for nothing that he was known as 'Slick Willy' or the 'Comeback Kid'. Impeachment proceedings in the following year petered out in a political humiliation to those who had instigated them.

All of this, while paying tribute to Clinton's phenomenal resilience, in the end knocked much of the stuffing out of him and his administration. Caution became the order of the day. Blair learnt this to his cost over Kosovo. It provoked a major dispute with Clinton.

At the beginning of 1999 the Serbs, under Slobodan Milosevic, embarked on a policy of ethnically cleansing the Albanian enclave of Kosovo. This was the latest in a series of atrocities which the Serbs had perpetrated on the non-Serb populations of what had once been Yugoslavia. Serious Balkan violence had gathered momentum in the early nineties. This coincided with John Major's government and Bill Clinton's first administration. In the beginning, the performance of the international community in putting a stop to this violence had been lumbering and feeble. The European Union had confidently declared through the improbable medium of the Luxembourg Prime Minister that the 'hour of Europe' was nigh and it would handle the Balkans, thank you very much. The EU then went on to demonstrate that it could barely boil an egg, still less contain the murderous instincts of the southern Slavs. Meantime the US, which did not at first want to get involved, could not desist from back-seat driving, so infuriating the Europeans. Bosnia, like Kosovo a few years later, was a source of intense transatlantic irritation.

John Major and Bill Clinton were not soul brothers at the best of times. The 'special relationship' did not look special at all. Handling Bosnia only added to the friction. The well had been poisoned, when the British Conservative government was judged by the Democrats to have tried to help President Bush defeat Clinton in the 1992 election. This was because (so the Democrats told me) Douglas Hurd, the British Foreign Secretary, had sent a good luck message to Jim Baker, the former Secretary of State, whom Bush had brought back to the White House to try to salvage the campaign. Even worse, according to the Democrats, was the British government's search of its records at White House request, to see whether Bill Clinton had applied for a British passport to dodge the Vietnam draft. I was pretty sure that the latter charge was baloney. The journalist who first wrote the story – a reporter at the London *Evening Standard* – told me that it had nothing to do with government conspiracy. He had simply asked the Home Office press office, on the off chance, whether Clinton had ever requested a British passport. To his astonishment – he was not used to getting a helpful response – the press officer had looked up the records, found no trace of Bill Clinton, and reported back accordingly.

I had made two trips to the US, in 1994 and 1995, with John Major. They were strained affairs. On the first of these Clinton invited Major to Pittsburgh, where one of the Prime Minister's forebears had worked in the Carnegie steelworks in the early twentieth century. The Americans had thought, not unreasonably, that this well-meaning gesture would be appreciated in No. 10 and would counter rumours of bad blood between President and Prime Minister. But John Major hated the exposure to public scrutiny of his family history.

Clinton also did John Major the special favour of flying him from Pittsburgh to Washington in Air Force One and putting him up for the night in the White House. But the two of them never clicked like Clinton and Blair or Major and Bush senior. On a subsequent visit the Prime Minister and his team had dinner one evening at Georgia Brown's, a restaurant in downtown Washington which specializes in Southern cooking. It was one of the very few upmarket places where you could see whites and blacks in almost equal numbers. Clinton had chosen it for us and said that he would come by for coffee and dessert.

We knew Clinton was on his way when the diners around us turned into Secret Service men and women talking into their tiepins. A jovial Clinton took his place next to Major. The two of them were seated side by side on a banquette facing the rest of us. It was a pleasant enough evening; Georgia Brown's was to become one of my favourite haunts when I returned as ambassador. I recall a quite interesting conversation. But the two men barely looked at each other, or exchanged a direct word, addressing instead the rest of us around the table.

Typically, it was only when the Americans got fully stuck in that a peace deal was imposed on the Serbs and Bosnian Muslims. The Europeans had shown themselves completely incapable of doing the job themselves. When the Serbs moved on Kosovo in early 1999 the Americans again called the shots. They decided that the Serbs would be brought to heel through a NATO operation, which depended heavily on air power, most of it provided by the US Air Force. Because of, mainly, Russian objections – Moscow saw the Balkans as its traditional sphere of influence – the entire war against Milosevic was waged without benefit of an authorizing UN Resolution. This would have required Russian acquiescence in the UN Security Council.

The air campaign was in full swing when Tony Blair returned to Washington in April 1999 for a grand NATO summit. There were big issues for discussion. NATO was agonizing – it still is – over its role in a world from which the Soviet Union and the Warsaw Pact had vanished. Reams of words had been drafted to construct a new post-Cold War strategy. Formulations of Byzantine complexity had been put together to permit the development of an 'autonomous' European defence force, inside NATO, but able to operate without the involvement of the US, if the latter so wished. The French wanted a separate European force which had as little to do with the Americans as possible. The Americans wanted the Europeans to assume more of the defence burden, but not to such a degree that NATO's cohesion under American leadership was prejudiced – 'separable, not separate' was their motto. Reconciling these two positions tested diplomacy's skills to the outer limits.

As usual a compromise was reached which allowed each side to interpret the documents as it wished. Not for the first time, or the last, Britain found itself in the uncomfortable position of trying to straddle the two positions. The whole thing was a charade anyway. The Europeans were as unwilling then as they are today to increase their defence budgets. Their pretensions were worth little more than the mounds of paper on which these solemn, but hollow, commitments were registered.

Besides, the real issue in the conference room was the war going on in the skies over Serbia and Kosovo. This did not seem to be doing very well. Targets were selected by cumbersome NATO Committee. The bombing did not look much of a deterrent to Milosevic. There was a suspicion that, thanks to NATO's leakiness, the Serbs often knew in advance what was going to be hit. Albanian Kosovars were still being massacred and driven from their homes. NATO's press briefing operation was a shambles that had to be retooled and reordered by Alastair Campbell. In Washington the pundits and armchair generals were out in force, questioning the effectiveness of the air campaign.

In London the British government had taken an aggressive position and sought to occupy the moral high ground. The tone was set by Blair. The challenge, he said, was to stop genocide. The international community had to rise to the occasion. British newspapers were briefed belligerently. This fed into the American press. With a five-hour time difference, British ministers were all over US television screens as Americans were having their breakfast. On the eve of the NATO summit, there were signs of irritation in Washington that Blair was articulating the NATO case better than Clinton.

The worry for Blair and his military planners was what would happen if the air campaign failed to bring Milosevic to heel. NATO and the international community could not afford to let Milosevic win: the humiliation would be overwhelming. There had to be a contingency plan for putting ground troops into Kosovo to dislodge the Serbs. Because the snows arrived in Kosovo in the autumn, any ground campaign would have to be successfully concluded by then. This in turn meant that serious planning would have to start no later than June – that is, not long after the NATO summit. A lot of this thinking started to appear in British newspapers on the eve of the summit.

I had already warned London that the administration was setting its face against calls for the use of ground troops. Blair arrived therefore in Washington out on a limb. The last thing that the White House wanted was for the issue to hijack the summit, so putting the spotlight on administration hesitations. It was decided that Blair should meet Clinton immediately after arrival, and try to bridge the gap.

Blair and his team flew in on Wednesday evening, 21 April, to Andrews Air Force Base. The plan was: a session that same evening with Clinton at the White House; a visit to Capitol Hill the next morning; off to Chicago to make a major speech; back to Washington that evening; then the summit on Friday and Saturday, followed by a Third Way meeting on Sunday, 25 April.

At the White House we were greeted by Clinton, his National Security Adviser Sandy Berger, Berger's deputy Jim Steinberg, and Secretary of State Madeleine Albright. Blair was accompanied by Jonathan Powell, Alastair Campbell, John Sawers, his foreign policy adviser, and me. Campbell opened by describing how he had shaken up the media operation at NATO. Then the Prime Minister went through the arguments for making contingency preparations for a land war in Kosovo. His most telling was that, to avoid the need to go to war on the ground, with possibly heavy casualties, you had to be seen by Milosevic to be preparing seriously for one.

We met in the small sitting room upstairs in the President's private quarters. The American team were not to be moved. Clinton did not say much. He sat there, chewing on an unlit cigar, while Berger and Steinberg deployed the counter-arguments. I do not recall Madeleine Albright saying a word. The American case rested on two propositions: that it would undermine the credibility of the air war if it became known that preparations were in hand for a ground war; and that a ground war would require calling up US reservists, which would not be good politically. After these sterile exchanges Clinton took Blair away for a private talk. It cannot have been a reassuring one. All the next day, as Tony Blair and I travelled around Chicago, he worried ceaselessly whether Clinton would abandon him on the end of his branch. I had little reassurance to offer. I had warned him.

By the end of this unusually long visit, some kind of deal was patched up that was supposed to result in private and deniable exchanges between No. 10 and the White House about contingency planning. But nothing came of it. The British newspapers continued to criticize Clinton for his caution, some of the time on the basis of unattributable briefing from government sources. Jim Steinberg, the deputy National Security Adviser, called me in high dudgeon. This was followed by Clinton himself in an explosive phone call to Blair, in which he accused Alastair Campbell of briefing against him.

The episode fascinated me. Blair should have known before arriving that planning for a ground war in Kosovo was going to be a tough sell. Yet Clinton's refusal to buy seemed to have come as a shock. Blair's anxiety was otherwise inexplicable in its intensity. I began to wonder to what extent his bold, admirable stance on Kosovo and genocide had been thought through.

Bill Clinton skates over this episode in his memoirs. In the end, several weeks later, Clinton was on the verge of serious discussion with his military advisers about preparing for a land war in Kosovo, when the Russians saved him the trouble. The former Russian Prime Minister Viktor Chernomyrdin told Milosevic that he could expect no help from Moscow if it came to all-out war. Milosevic promptly folded his hand. Since the collapse of the Soviet Empire, the Russians have learnt fast how to punch above their weight in international affairs.

It must have been a nerve-wrecking visit for Blair; but it allowed him an ego-boosting insight into his already enormous popularity and pulling power in the US.

My wife had been, in the 1980s, one of the few women to break successfully into the hitherto all-male bastions of commodities broking and financial futures markets. Catherine's mentor had been Leo Melamed, the founder of the Chicago Mercantile Exchange and one of the inventors, with Milton Friedman, of financial futures. She resumed contact with him after we arrived in the US. He urged us to bring Tony Blair to Chicago. No sitting British Prime Minister had ever come. He could guarantee a huge audience under the auspices of the Economic Club. I sold this excellent idea to No. 10.

Blair delivered a speech of some significance. It completely blindsided the Foreign Office. Against the background of Kosovo he promulgated a doctrine of international community and humanitarian intervention, almost pre-emption: that it was justified to violate the frontiers and sovereignty of a state if within its borders genocide was about to be, or was being, carried out. This was not a million miles from one of the main arguments used to justify the attack on Iraq in 2003. They say, though I could not corroborate this myself, that the ideas underpinning the speech were borrowed from the foreign policy analyst and academic Lawrence Freedman.

The speech made a lot of people sit up. Some even went as far as to say that the basic principles of the modern nation-state, established after the Thirty Years War in the Treaty of Westphalia of 1648, had been overturned. In fact, it was not that radical. The right to intervene on human-rights grounds in the internal affairs of another country had, to all intents and purposes, been ceded in the 1975 Helsinki Final Act, the grand bargain between the Western and Communist halves of Europe, which became one of the pillars of *détente*.

The speech, eloquently delivered in Blair's evangelical style, was received with a thunderous standing ovation from the hundreds of Chicagoans who filled the cavernous ballroom of one of the city's largest hotels. It was standing room only. There was a packed overspill room with a sound feed. Around the auditorium the cry went up: 'Blair for President.' What a superb American politician he would have made, I thought. Blair's gifts work even better in the US than they do in the UK.

This was the high point. It was followed by bathos in the shape of a Sunday morning Third Way meeting in Washington. The proceedings were no more enlightening than those of the New York meeting the previous autumn. Clinton and Blair joined an even wider cast of characters. These included the Italian Prime Minister D'Alema (a communist), the German Chancellor Schröder, and the Dutch Prime Minister Kok. A number of American politicians joined in, including the African-American Mayor of Denver, Wellington Webb, and the Lieutenant Governor of Maryland, Kathleen Kennedy Townsend. It was a bouillabaisse of random political musings. There were better ways to spend a Sunday morning.

14

'Up Yours, King!'

I did my apprenticeship on Northern Ireland as John Major's press secretary. I must have travelled with him to Ulster half a dozen times in 1994 and 1995. He made real progress. When we first visited, we travelled everywhere by military helicopter because of the threat of IRA terrorism. Then, on one visit, I suddenly became aware that we were travelling by road. That was a measure of the improvement in security.

The hatreds and rivalries between Catholics and Protestants were so deep, you did not know where to start. Thirty years ago when the civil rights marches began? Or a thousand years ago, when the Norman kings began to settle Ireland? I once called on the Democratic Unionist Party (DUP), the hard-line Protestant party, led by Dr Ian Paisley. I should be grateful, I said, to be brought up to date on events over the last six months. 'It's not that simple,' said the people on the other side of the table, smiling at me pityingly. 'If you really want to understand,' they said, 'you must go back to the Celtic migrations in the fourth century BC.'

In the end John Major's efforts to bring peace to Northern Ireland ran into the sand. By 1995 his slim majority in the House of Commons had been pared to the bone by death, desertion and rebellion in his own ranks. Major became unhealthily dependent for his survival on the small group of Protestant Unionist MPs, who could normally be relied on to support the Conservatives. They understood perfectly their leverage over No. 10. This made it politically impossible for Major to demand of them the flexibility necessary to enable negotiations with the Nationalists and Republicans to advance further. It is to Tony Blair's credit that, soon after his election victory of 1997, he picked up Major's baton and invested a large chunk of his political capital in the cause of peace in Northern Ireland.

In the US not everything melts in the melting pot. The history of the US is a history of successive surges of immigration. In a generation's time a majority of Americans may have Spanish as their first language, as wave upon wave of immigrants from Central and South America settle there. Beneath the genuine and intensely felt patriotism of many Americans, there is a powerful, tribal allegiance to ethnic origin.

It can be a shock to discover the tribalism of American politics. Catholic Irish America is one of the great tribes. The Irish immigrations into nineteenth-century America often triggered violent confrontation with other ethnic groups who had preceded them. The Irish response was to organize themselves politically in the great northern cities like New York, Chicago and Boston. There was a time when almost every New York policeman seemed to be Irish. Firemen in Boston still have shamrocks on their helmets.

In the US the dominant Irish voice is Catholic and nationalist. The Protestant Irish from Ulster, known in the US as Scotch-Irish, may have reached America first and in large numbers; but they never acquired the same tribal identity or clout. Catholic nationalist Ireland is powerfully represented in both houses of Congress. In my time Senator Edward Kennedy of Massachusetts – JFK's younger brother – was the doyen, flanked by Senators Chris Dodd of Connecticut and Pat Leahy of Vermont, big political beasts. In the House of Representatives, congressmen had formed a committee on Ireland. It overwhelmingly comprised those who favoured unification under the Dublin government. Their sympathies lay with Sinn Fein. Many of them were of Irish ancestry; many came from the north-east, where large Irish-American communities are still to be found. They were kept regularly supplied with Sinn Fein propaganda. This concentrated relentlessly on accusations of bad faith by the British government, or on human-rights abuses by the Royal Ulster Constabulary and the British Army.

Such was the place of Irish America in US politics that on St Patrick's Day each year the Speaker of the House of Representatives would give a lunch at which the Irish Prime Minister would present the President of the United States with a shamrock. The occasion was the envy of the Greeks, Italians, Scots, Spaniards, Armenians, Chinese, Portuguese – I could go on and on – all of whom could claim to have made a comparable contribution to American life and history. Only Jewish America had a tighter grip on American politics.

For years the British embassy in Washington had had appalling relations with the Irish lobby. Mutual hostility ruled. It was very difficult to have Britain's case heard. The embassy and our consulates ran a fire-brigade service – pretty successfully, it has to be said – racing from state capital to state capital to stop the passage of legislation that would make US investment in Northern Ireland conditional on giving advantages to the Catholic workforce.

Things started to get better as Major and Blair put their backs into sorting out Northern Ireland. Meantime, under Bill Clinton, the celebration in Washington of St Patrick's Day had developed into an unstoppable juggernaut of receptions, meals and parties. My predecessor, John Kerr, had decided that the British embassy could not stand aloof. He created the instant tradition of a lunch at the British embassy on the eve of St Patrick's. This was very good politics.

Catherine and I arrived in Washington as Marjorie 'Mo' Mowlam reached the zenith of her powers as Tony Blair's first Secretary of State for Northern Ireland. She was an inspired choice. Mo had her detractors in London and Belfast. But in 1997 nobody could have been better suited to the task of winning a fair hearing in Washington for what Tony Blair was trying to do. The challenge was twofold: to convince that Britain was negotiating in good faith; and to get accepted that in any new dispensation for Northern Ireland the rights of the Protestant majority could not go by default.

Mo was quite a sight. She had been treated for a brain tumour. It had left her bald. She wore a wig. She had the disconcerting habit of adjusting it or taking it off, when you least expected it. I went to see her before leaving for Washington. The first thing she did was to test me either by doing the wig number or belching, I forget which. It was clear what was going through her mind: 'Is this a pin-striped twit or what?' We got on quite well at that first meeting; and got on even better as time passed and she was a familiar visitor to Washington. We became good friends, and Catherine and I were saddened by her untimely death.

With his unerring political instinct, Clinton made the Irish cause his own. Under pressure from Senator Kennedy and Irish-

Americans, Clinton had in 1994 ignored the advice of almost his whole administration, and the vigorous protests of the British government, to give Gerry Adams, the most powerful figure in Sinn Fein, a visa to visit the US. The IRA had not yet declared a ceasefire. For London this was a reward for terrorism and a boost to the funds of NORAID, the Irish-American organization that collected money for the IRA. John Major was enraged and, while travelling in the Middle East, was in no hurry to take a call from Clinton, who wanted to explain his decision.

Given the subsequent course of events, leading to the Good Friday agreement of 1998, President Clinton is wont to assert the prescient wisdom of his decision. There is some merit in this, but less than he claims. Adams had already concluded that the Sinn Fein/IRA goal of a united Ireland could never be achieved by force of arms alone. A long-term political strategy was also needed. The heart of this was to have Sinn Fein accepted as a mainstream political party, capable of winning elections north and south of the border. The strategy needed American backing, if only to raise money and put pressure on the British government and the Unionists. Many of Adams's American supporters were disappointed, after so much effort to get him a visa, that there was no announcement of an IRA ceasefire during his visit to the US. On his return to Ireland this gave Adams a compelling argument to put to the IRA. A ceasefire followed not long afterwards.

Since then Sinn Fein have, with consummate skill, sold and resold the ceasefire in the interminable negotiations to implement the Good Friday agreement. This led to a situation several years later, in which, while the British government had discharged all its obligations under the agreement, the IRA remained in existence; had not disarmed; continued to kill and maim people, though not soldiers and police; and engaged in widespread criminal activity, including the biggest bank robbery ever, anywhere. Even now it remains to be seen whether their most recent declaration in August 2005 marks the end of the IRA.

By 1998 Britain, Ireland and the US were jointly committed to an end to terrorism in Northern Ireland and its replacement by democratic politics, in which Protestants and Catholics would have full equality of rights. The question of whether Ulster should remain British or pass under the sovereignty of the Irish Republic would be left to the democratic choice of the people of Northern Ireland. These were admirable principles. But, then, as now, the devil was in the detail. London, Dublin and Washington – in the last case through the stoic, patient figure of Clinton's representative Senator George Mitchell – encouraged, cajoled and kicked the political parties of Northern Ireland into a common understanding of its future governance. But, with hindsight, getting to the Good Friday agreement in 1998 was the easy part.

Our role in Washington at the embassy was to counterbalance the natural tilt of the White House and Congress towards Irish nationalism: to demonstrate that the British government was acting even-handedly and not, as Sinn Fein repeatedly claimed when they were not getting what they wanted in the negotiations, as a stooge of the Unionists. The State Department and the FBI were pretty much in the British camp. But they were marginal players. The key influences were at either end of Pennsylvania Avenue, in the White House and on Capitol Hill. Besides Clinton himself, the most important figure in the White House was the deputy National Security Adviser, Jim Steinberg, a brilliant, forceful character, of unnaturally youthful looks. He had once been on Senator Ted Kennedy's staff.

Every time the Northern Ireland Secretary came to Washington, there was no escaping a day on Capitol Hill in meetings with senators and congressmen. It was essential to rebut the latest crop of Sinn Fein allegations against us and explain in detail how we saw the next steps in the 'peace process'. These were never easy visits. The senators and congressmen would be primed by Sinn Fein. If not on top of all the detail themselves, they had staff, whispering in their ears, who were. Mo handled this well. Her combination of candour, lack of pomposity, and tough talking earned her respect and credibility on the Hill and in the administration. It helped also to be a woman in a wig. Her skills were instinctive and political. At one point in a particularly vigorous exchange with the House Committee on Ireland, she addressed Congressman Peter King, one of Sinn Fein's closest supporters, with 'Up yours, King!' and a V-sign. A moment's stunned silence was followed by chuckles and grins. King later invited Mowlam to join him on a visit to his Long Island district.

Mo could 'speak' American. Europeans divide into those who

can 'speak' American and those who cannot. This is not a narrow linguistic point. It means having the ability to slip naturally into the American idiom. Peter Mandelson, Mo's successor as Northern Ireland Secretary, could never do it, for all his intellectual brilliance. He managed profoundly to irritate the Irish-Americans of Capitol Hill, who are ultra-sensitive to any hint of being patronized by snooty Brits. The feeling was mutual. Handling the rough and tumble of debate with Irish-Americans was not among Peter's armoury of formidable political skills.

I spent a good deal of time myself on the Hill, especially in debate with the likes of Ted Kennedy, Chris Dodd and the members of the Ireland Committee. These meetings were always bracing. I enjoyed the cut and thrust. Most of the time they kept on the right side of acrimony. My staff also stayed very close to congressional staff, who were exceptionally influential in shaping the views of senators and congressmen (and not just on Ireland). 'Staffers' are among Washington's best and brightest. Many go on to brilliant careers in politics or the government.

Catherine and I started inviting to the Great House some of those who were Britain's most implacable critics. They accepted, and the debate continued around the dinner table. Our goal was always the same: to persuade them to accept Britain's good faith in the peace negotiations, the need for the IRA to abandon violence for ever, and that there could be no change to the status of Northern Ireland without the freely expressed consent of the democratic majority. After a while a few chunks of the pro-Sinn Fein glacier began to melt.

Some of the personalities became good friends. Senator Pat Leahy of Vermont and Congressman Ben Gilman, the veteran chairman of the Ireland Committee, became strong supporters of Catherine's efforts against parental child abduction across frontiers. (This, incidentally, is one example among many of the huge contribution that an energetic and savvy wife can make. Her Majesty's Government owe Catherine a great deal.) Congressman Peter King and his wife Rosemary became regular figures at our table. He was of Irish descent, a conduit to Gerry Adams, and a Republican. I admired his fierce integrity. He wrote novels and put a character based on me in one of them. One day he found himself at the Great House, drinking a toast to the Earl and Countess of Wessex on the occasion of their marriage. He said that he could hear his father and grand-father turning in their graves.

Under President Clinton the festivities to mark St Patrick's Day paralysed political Washington for two days. It cannot have done much for public administration in the island of Ireland either. Almost every politician, great and small, from north and south of the border, appeared to make the pilgrimage to Washington. To secure invitations to the events there would be a sudden inflation in the number of Americans laying claim to Irish ancestry. The whole colourful, babbling cast of characters moved from one event to another like a flock of migrating penguins.

On the eve of St Patrick's there was our lunch at the embassy; dinner with a cast of hundreds organized by the America–Ireland Fund, a philanthropic organization which did a lot of good in Ulster; on the day itself the smaller, more select lunch given by the Speaker of the House of Representatives, with the President, the Irish Prime Minister and Foreign Minister, the Northern Ireland Secretary, the leaders of all the Northern Ireland parties, Irish-American senators and congressmen, the Cardinal-Archbishop of Washington, and the British and Irish Ambassadors; that evening a huge reception for hundreds at the White House; and, finally, the Dionysian climax of a late-evening party at the Irish embassy, where unconsciousness settled on those whose stamina had finally worn out. Despite a significant Protestant, Unionist presence at all of this, the tone was unrelentingly that of the South: shamrocks, step dancing, John Hume singing 'Danny Boy' at the White House, and the constant invocation of southern Irish roots.

The St Patrick's Day lunch at the British embassy was the largest seated meal we ever gave. We allowed for about 130 guests, but were never quite sure how many would come. An invitation to the lunch was one of the hottest tickets in town. People lobbied for invitations. People complained if they had not been invited. Gate-crashers tried to get in. Some probably succeeded. Drawing up the seating plan based on twelve and fourteen round tables in the ballroom would have challenged Machiavelli. The political sens-itivities were exquisite.

In 1998, at our first St Patrick's lunch, there was much excitement in the air. The Good Friday agreement was not far distant. Mo was a big draw as the guest of honour. It was one of those symbolic turning points in Irish affairs. For the first time ever, every single Northern Ireland political leader, with the exception of John Hume, who was represented by his wife, attended.

Catherine and I were apprehensive. We knew that we had entered multiple minefields. A lot of people, in Britain and in the embassy, quite understandably did not like the idea of Gerry Adams under our roof. I wondered what Adams himself would think of the huge portraits of English kings and queens flanking the main staircase, as he entered a British embassy for the first time in his life. I worried about the potentially combustible proximity of Adams to David Trimble, the leader of the Ulster Unionists, not to mention David Ervine and Gary McMichael, leaders of the two small parties with allegedly close political links to Loyalist (Protestant) paramilitary groups. McMichael complained immediately before lunch about being seated too near to Adams. If I remember rightly, the only place that we could find for him was between two fervent American supporters of Irish republicanism. I looked up during lunch and saw the three of them laughing uproariously.

In the event the lunch went off without a hitch. Mo spoke to roaring applause. It was heady stuff. She was fêted by all. Clinton paid her particular attention the next day at the Speaker's lunch. At the White House reception that evening we ran into Michael Flatley, who was at the height of his *Riverdance* fame. One of Mo's staff had a camera. Flatley assumed that she would want to be photographed with him. To his mystification she handed him the camera and asked him to take a photo of our group. Flatley did so. Mo took back the camera, thanked him, and walked off, leaving Flatley mouthing like a goldfish.

There was, as ever, a dark side to all this good humour and backslapping. Washington's spring sunshine appeared to dissolve the enmities and lack of trust between the two communities of Northern Ireland. But the disease was only in temporary remission. As soon as the Irish politicians returned home, it was back, as virulent as ever. All that effort by the Americans, by Clinton himself in giving face-time to the Northern Ireland leaders, by the Irish and by ourselves, did not seem to add up to much under Ulster's leaden skies. I began to detect after the third such celebration of St Patrick – the most grandiose of all in Clinton's last year as President – resentment in the White House at Ulster's politicians: so ready to take the lavish hospitality offered them, so ready to return to the ancient feuds, once they were home.

I also saw, behind the masks of *bonhomie*, the single-mindedness of Gerry Adams and Martin McGuinness in pursuit of political advantage. They moved through Washington as smoothly as sharks in warm water. Whatever else they were, or had been, they were politicians to their fingertips, wholly at ease in their surroundings. It helped, of course, to have powerful friends at court. By contrast, there was something terribly awkward and admirable about the likes of Trimble, Mallon, Allardyce and the others who were Sinn Fein's political opponents. After the Speaker's lunch in March 2001, the first to be attended by President Bush, I stood at the top of the Capitol steps with the other guests to bid farewell to the President. As Bush headed down the steps to get into his car, I saw that Adams had somehow managed to insert himself into the small knot of American politicians who were escorting the President. He had a brief, smiling exchange with Bush. Cameras were flashing and rolling. What a photo opportunity for Adams and Sinn Fein! What a coup! I whispered to the other Northern Ireland party leaders, standing gauche and uncomfortable alongside me: 'For Christ's sake, get down the bloody steps before it's too late!' It was too late.

Mo blazed like a comet across the firmament, her light as brilliant as it was transitory. Along the way she became an honorary member of the most exclusive women's club in Washington: totally private and unadvertised, comprising Hillary Clinton, Madeleine Albright, Health Secretary Donna Shalala, and Hillary's chief of staff the excellent Melanne Verveer. When Mo came to DC, they would get together over supper or a drink. Men were excluded. I went over to the White House once to pick up Mo. As I waited outside the room where they were gathered, I heard peal upon peal of laughter. I asked Mo what had been so funny. 'Hillary told a dirty joke,' said Mo, grinning.

Mo mentioned to me later in the year that her poll ratings were higher than Blair's. His reference to her in his party conference speech that October gave Mo a standing ovation. 'This spells trouble for her,' Catherine and I said to each other. It did. In truth her star was already burning out. The writing had been on the wall ever since No. 10 had seized the reins of Northern Ireland negotiation at the end of 1997. There was briefing against her in British newspapers. She suspected the hand of Downing Street. She may have been right. President Clinton never again gave her the same level of attention. Her visit to Washington for the 1999 St Patrick's Day celebrations was not a happy affair. It is a cruel city for those perceived to be in political decline.

I thanked God that I knew something about Northern Ireland from my time with Major. Until the Good Friday agreement it was the top issue in British–American relations. After Blair's first official visit to Washington in February 1998, when he had given such strong public support to a Lewinsky-embattled Clinton, Jim Steinberg came up to me and said, 'We owe you big time.' London asked me how we should cash the cheque. I said that we had three priorities: 'Northern Ireland, Northern Ireland, and Northern Ireland.' Clinton certainly helped us towards the Good Friday agreement; but his debt was never repaid in full, in part because Blair never pressed him hard enough. As a result, the innate tilt of the White House towards Irish-America, and No. 10's inability or unwillingness to match the implacability of the Sinn Fein negotiators, contributed to a peace deal which posed almost as many questions as it was meant to answer.

There is a postscript. I ran into Pete King at the White House in late 2001. With tears in his eyes he thanked me for the British government's support for America in its hour of need after 9/11. A little later I received a letter addressed to Tony Blair, signed by a raft of US congressmen, expressing a similar sentiment. Among the names was almost every member of the Ireland Committee. From then on, until I left Washington over a year later, I never heard another word of criticism from anywhere on Capitol Hill of British policy in Northern Ireland. One senior member of the Ireland Committee admitted to me that he had been mistaken in the support that he had given Sinn Fein/IRA. I realized that, without forfeiting America's sympathies, it was now impossible for the IRA to return to terrorism.

15

The Great Banana War

Europe and the United States managed regularly to get themselves into trade disputes that made the Theatre of the Absurd look rational. One such was the Great Banana War. This involved a fruit grown neither in mainland Europe nor in mainland America.

It was all about subsidies given by the European Union to certain Third World banana-growing countries, mainly African and Caribbean. This meant that their banana exports entered Europe at preferential prices. The Americans claimed that these arrangements put the banana-growing countries of Central and South America at an unfair disadvantage, violating the rules of international trade. Many of the plantations in these countries were, as might be imagined, owned by American corporations, notably Chiquita. Their produce was transported in American ships through American ports.

It was a contest between the smaller, curlier and, some would say, sweeter 'European' banana and the larger, straighter and, some would say, coarser 'American' banana. This is as good a metaphor for differences between America and Europe as 'hard' and 'soft' power or Mars and Venus.

The Americans made a formal complaint to the World Trade Organization (WTO), which found in their favour. The EU was told to reform its discriminatory banana regime. The Europeans dragged their feet. This was largely at French instigation, since the countries which benefited from the regime included former French colonies. The United States got fed up and decided to retaliate, which it was entitled to do under WTO rules. This meant increasing tariffs on certain European imports.

The government department in Washington responsible for handling trade disputes is the Office of the US Trade Representative. Unlike other departments of the US administration, the Office of the Trade Representative is small and bureaucratically part of the White House. Sometimes the Trade Representative – known as the USTR – is in the Cabinet, sometimes not, depending on the whim of the President. Either way, it is a position of considerable influence, since, apart from the Secretary of State, no one else in the US administration spends more time negotiating with foreigners.

I knew many USTRs over the years and none was a shrinking violet: Carla Hills, under the elder Bush; Mickey Cantor and Charlene Barshefsky, under Clinton; and Bob Zoellick, under the younger Bush. Bob is now Deputy Secretary of State. All came from the hardball school of negotiation. I knew Bob particularly well; but I liked and respected all of them. I got more black eyes and bruises from bracing meetings with USTRs than from any other members of the US administration. I hope that they got a few from me as well.

Trade policy was one of the few areas where the UK found itself regularly at odds with the United States. It offered excellent lessons in how to negotiate. It also illuminated with great clarity the impact of US domestic politics on US external policy.

The problem for a British ambassador in Washington is that the UK, like all the member states of the European Union, has handed 'competence' in external trade matters to the European Commission in Brussels. This means that while the Commission gets its negotiating instructions from a collective decision of the member states, it is the Commission alone that has responsibility for conducting trade negotiations. When we talk about handing sovereignty to Brussels, this is one of the ways in which it is done. So, when the bananas hit the fan, strictly speaking it was for the Commission's representative in Washington to handle the consequences.

The Commission's office in Washington is organized like an embassy and its head has the status of a Chief of Mission, that is, an ambassador. For most of my time the position was held by a German veteran of the Commission, Gunther Burghardt. He was – how can I put it? – the quintessential German bureaucrat: didactic, a master of detail, and utterly rigid in his defence of the Commission's prerogatives, as he saw them. By prerogatives he meant not only the right of the Commission to speak for all fifteen member states, but also that the member states should pipe down on policy issues that fell within the Commission's 'competence'. Burghardt brought to these matters a potent mix of messianic zeal and Teutonic dogged-ness. My good friend the French ambassador, François Bujon de l'Estang, was forever firing off letters of protest to Burghardt about some perceived encroachment on France's national sovereignty. This only provoked a lengthy and self-righteous response. My technique was to ignore Burghardt altogether.

François's letters were couched in terms that would make a British Eurosceptic beam with pleasure. Yet France, as a founder member of the European Union, had been far more willing than Britain to subsume its national independence of action in the common policies of the Union. At first sight it is baffling. France is a fiercely proud nation, whose millennium-long history as an independent sovereign state is matched in Europe only by Britain's. Why had France and Britain taken such divergent attitudes to European integration? The answer is pure *realpolitik*. For France it was fine so long as Paris was in the European Union driving seat and it could in the process ensure that the Germans did not get uppity again. The Germans were happy to acquiesce, so long as they were allowed to share the driving seat with the French. This Grand Bargain – the heart of Franco-German reconciliation after the Second World War, itself the heart until recently of the European Union – is today under unprecedented stress. A European Union, now enlarged to twenty-five states, has weakened the Franco-German grip. The evolution of French policy inside a Union that it can no longer control will be interesting.

Actually, I liked Burghardt. He was a decent, dedicated servant of Brussels. But he could not have been worse suited for his role. He seemed to rub Americans up the wrong way wherever he went. I could not allow my country's economic interests to depend on this arch-disciple of the Brillo pad school of diplomacy.

American retaliation against Europe over bananas moved things from cold- to hot-war status. In 1998 Washington published a list of imports into the United States from various European countries, on a number of which it threatened to double import duties. Among these were Scottish cashmere wool products. This was a deadly threat to the Scottish cashmere wool industry. It was centred in and around Hawick, from where the Minto side of my family came. The US market was vital to the industry's survival. A 100 per cent tariff would price it out. There would be cheaper Asian competitors ready to seize the American market. Once lost, the Scots rightly feared that they would never regain market share. Thousands of jobs were at stake.

Persuading the Americans not to punish the Scottish cashmere wool industry became one of my top priorities for 1998 and 1999. The effort also involved Tony Blair, Gordon Brown, Robin Cook, Peter Mandelson, the late Donald Dewar and David Miliband, among others. This underlines the importance of Scotland to a Labour government. It is in some contrast to the lesser and failed effort to protect the British steel industry from the deeply damaging and illegal US tariff increases of 2002.

By the autumn of 1999 it looked as if all was lost. Despite British efforts, the EU had failed to come up with a new, improved banana regime. American patience snapped. Charlene Barshefsky, the USTR, who could see that the UK was doing its best to get the EU to move, told me to prepare for the worst. The matter had become highly political. Decisions would be taken in the White House. The man to see was Gene Sperling, President Clinton's Economic Adviser. Just as matters were coming to a head, David Miliband, then one of Tony Blair's chief Downing Street advisers, happened to pay a visit to Washington. He wanted to see Sperling anyway. I warned David that we would have to do bananas before anything else. Our meeting with Sperling was in the event entirely dominated by the fruit.

'This is no way to treat an ally,' I said to Sperling. 'If there are job losses in Scotland, it will be politically toxic for Blair. It's crazy to punish the one member state which is making a real effort to get the banana regime reformed.'

'I don't know about that,' Sperling replied. 'There is a view in town, especially on the Hill, that the UK is not trying as hard as it could and that you want to have it both ways. People say that it would concentrate your minds wonderfully if tariffs were raised on Scottish cashmere wool.'

'That's daft,' I said. 'The threat of sanctions has already concentrated our minds wonderfully. But if you carry out the threat, the US can whistle for further British help on bananas.'

The meeting bought us time. It also led to the matter coming up in conversation between Blair and Clinton. I was subsequently rebuked for allowing such a bread-and-butter subject to intrude into the exalted exchanges between Prime Minister and President. This was the first time that I encountered a resistance in No. 10 to sweating the smaller stuff in British–American relations. I pointed out that, once an issue becomes political enough to be seized by the White House, with the President's signature hovering over an executive order that is going to hurt Britain, the Prime Minister needs personally to be part of the countervailing force.

Sperling was frank about where the pressure to whack the Scots was coming from. He said two words: 'Trent Lott'. This was not a name to be trifled with. Lott, a Republican, was the Senate majority leader. He was a huge political beast. He was no friend of Clinton. But, precisely because the Republican senators were in the majority, the President had no choice but to deal with Lott to get legislation through Congress. For the White House this had become a punishing process of deal-making and hard bargaining with one of Clinton's least forgiving political opponents. Lott was fiercely in favour of hitting the Europeans hard, including Britain. The White House, unsurprisingly, was not disposed to expend too much political capital on a few thousand Scottish wool workers, if this were to upset Lott. The Scots counted for little in political Washington. They cast no American votes. They made no campaign contributions. It reminded me of the lines in Eddie Cochran's song 'Summertime Blues': 'I went to see my congressman and he said, "Whoa! I'd like to help you, son, but you're too young to vote."'

Clinton suggested Blair deal direct with Lott, a cop-out if ever I heard one. I strongly advised the Prime Minister not to do this. The British Prime Minister should not bend the knee to a senator, however powerful. What was more, the senator would almost certainly rebuff Blair and that would be all round Washington within the day. The Prime Minister had registered his concern with the President: that was all that mattered for the moment. I said that I would have a go with Lott in the extra time that we had bought.

The only trouble was: Lott did not want to see me. Meantime the Sword of Damocles over Hawick hung by a delicate cashmere thread. Debate raged in the US administration about which products to penalize. I was on the phone almost daily to the USTR and White House. The US did not like the latest version of the banana regime emerging in Brussels from an equally difficult debate among the EU member states. I added another argument to my armoury. The US had a long-standing concern for stability and democracy among the tiny Caribbean states. Many of them depended economically on guaranteed access for their bananas into the European market. They did not have the economies of scale to compete with the US-owned mega-plantations of Central and South America. Did the US want to see banana cultivation replaced by the drugs trade?

In the end it was my wife, Catherine, who saved the Scottish cashmere wool industry (though I was told that some damage had already been done by customers switching their source of supply away from Scotland against the possibility of a tariff increase). It was through a long, winding and indirect route.

In the spring of 1998 the *Washington Post* finally wrote the story of Catherine and the loss of her children. It was a long and detailed piece, based on an interview with her. It had a major impact. Some in Washington thought that Catherine was quite wrong to have publicized such a personal story. But, as already described, the *Post* had got hold of it months earlier as the result of an inadvertent indiscretion by my mother-in-law. It was going to publish anyway. Catherine had to be sure that the paper got the facts right, especially as the German courts had a habit of criticizing her for 'going to the media'. She also had to be careful about the impact of publicity on her children.

Two things happened almost immediately. Catherine began to get letters from Americans who found themselves in a similar predicament. They had married Germans, the marriages had broken down, the estranged German spouses had taken the children to Germany, the left-behind parents could not get access to their children, the German courts and Youth Authority took the side of the German parents, and, in some cases, child support was demanded of the left-behind parents on pain of arrest if they set foot in Germany.

She was also contacted by Ernie Allen, President and CEO of a major non-profit organization called the National Center for Missing and Exploited Children (NCMEC), which was funded both by the US government and private donation. Ernie, a former district attorney from Kentucky, is a great American. Hundreds, maybe thousands, of parents and children owe their well-being, and in some cases their lives, to Ernie Allen and the work of the NCMEC. The organization dealt with all kinds of cases in which children went missing or were exploited. This included parental child abduction in the US. Ernie and Catherine met. They got on immediately. They agreed that parental child abduction across frontiers was a growing, but largely unknown, problem. The time had come to bring it out of the shadows and to lobby governments and parliaments to take action against it. From this was born the International Center for Missing and Exploited Children (ICMEC), co-founded by Ernie and Catherine, and launched by Hillary Clinton and Cherie Blair at the British embassy in Washington in April 1999.

Catherine threw herself into lobbying Congress and the US administration on ICMEC's behalf and that of the many American parents who were now in regular contact with her. It was an advantage to be the British ambassador's wife. Catherine did not hesitate to exploit it on behalf of her cause. One thing led to another because of her driving energy. A British branch of ICMEC was established to help British parents. Links were established with France and Italy. As her work rapidly expanded, it became clear to Catherine and Ernie that her organization could not remain just part of NCMEC/ICMEC, based in Alexandria, Virginia. So, PACT – Parents and Abducted Children Together – was created, a charity incorporated in the US and UK, which would continue to work closely with ICMEC as an associate organization. Catherine became Chair and Chief Executive. Laura Bush joined Cherie Blair and Hillary Clinton as a patron. Henry Kissinger offered his support, as did many others.

I was constantly anxious about the effect on Catherine of losing her children. She knew next to nothing about their welfare. To have a normal conversation with them on the phone was impossible, even if she managed to get through to them – which was rare. She had no idea whether her sons ever received the letters and presents that she regularly sent them. She was once sent a perfunctory and uninformative school report, despite the German judge having once agreed to her receiving regular school reports. I knew that the worry gnawed away at her all the time. There was never a night when she did not dream of her sons. But her strength of will was astonishing. She just would not buckle under the strain. She refused to give up her efforts to see her children again. Meantime she was not only performing the role of ambassador's wife superlatively, but also launching a charity. I knew that this heavy work load helped her cope. In the creation of ICMEC and PACT she was sustained and consoled by the knowledge that, out of her personal suffering, good could come to others.

It was thanks to the campaigning of Catherine, Ernie Allen and an intrepid band of American parents that the US State Department energetically took up the issue of parental child abduction across frontiers; that the US Congress unanimously passed three concurrent resolutions, that is, by the Senate and the House jointly, condemning parental child abduction and naming Germany and others as countries which violated their obligations under the 1980 Hague Convention on the Civil Aspects of International Child Abduction; that President Clinton raised Catherine's case among others when he saw Chancellor Schröder in 2000; and that President Bush did likewise in 2001. When I asked Bush how Schröder had replied, he said, 'With a load of legal bullshit.'

On the back of American support, Catherine and Ernie Allen succeeded in 2001 in persuading countries that had signed the Hague Convention to produce a guide of good practice to its implementation. The aim was to ensure that future generations of parents and children did not suffer from the abuse to which Catherine and many other parents had been subject in Germany and elsewhere.

Behind all this American activity, the British government followed cautiously, with the then Lord Chancellor's Department in the brake van. Cherie Blair and her chief of staff Fiona Millar were always staunch supporters. Tony Blair wrote to Schröder about Catherine's case and got a very unhelpful reply. As junior ministers at the Foreign Office, Keith Vaz, Valerie Amos and Dennis McShane did their best but, like Catherine, ran into legal objections to intervening with the German authorities from the Lord Chancellor's Department and in particular Baroness Scotland, another Foreign Office junior minister. A small group of MPs, notably John Stanley, Bill Cash and Kate Hoey, were stalwarts on Catherine's behalf, pressing the government inside and outside the House of Commons to be more active in defence of Catherine's rights.

Robin Cook let Catherine down badly. In the summer of 2000, at the annual meeting of senior ambassadors, Cook's then private secretary approached me with a proposition. Cook was having difficulty with a constituent who had a child abduction problem with the United States. If we could help on that, Cook would raise Catherine's case with the German Foreign Minister, Joschka Fischer. This was, Catherine and I thought, as ethical as a £7 note. But needs must when the devil drives. Catherine's latest application to the German courts for access to her children hung in the balance. Strong American pressure looked as though it might at last be having an effect, though Clinton had only a few months left in office. Supporting action from the British government at this vital stage could tip the balance in Catherine's favour. Despite German protestations to the contrary, we knew the justice system was amenable to political pressure.

It was not to be. I delivered my side of the bargain by giving Cook the ICMEC/NCMEC details and drawing the case to Ernie Allen's attention. Cook for his part asked our ambassador in Berlin, Paul Lever, to pursue it instead. Good man though Paul was – and for years he did his level best on Catherine's behalf – he did not carry the necessary political clout. We were told that Cook's retreat was largely the result of pressure from Baroness Scotland.

We will never know if an intervention with Fischer would have made a difference. It certainly could not have made matters worse. By the end of 2000 an entire year's legal efforts had gone down the drain. These included the commissioning at the court's request of a German psychological report, which stated unequivocally that the children needed their mother and fast; and an agreement in court that the children should spend a New Year skiing holiday with Catherine in Switzerland. The judgement said that her ex-husband would be fined if he obstructed the holiday. The children never turned up. The court refused to impose the fine. Its reasoning was the usual catch-22, German style. The fine could not be levied, because the period for the children's visit to Switzerland had expired. But, of course, Catherine could not make her complaint to the court until she could demonstrate at the end of the period that her children had not appeared.

The German court appointed yet another psychologist. He was more amenable to their point of view. He did not bother to interview Catherine. She did not just go back to square one. In early 2001 the court handed down a vicious decision, putting an indefinite ban on Catherine's having access to her children.

Around this time Catherine and I had a meeting with the German ambassador in Washington, Jürgen Chrobog. He remarked that the German authorities had not failed to notice the lesser importance that the British government appeared to attach to Catherine's case when compared with the American. 'That is strange,' he said. 'Catherine is not even American and if your own government is not wholeheartedly behind you ...' Tell me about it, I said under my breath.

Individual American senators and congressmen played a heroic role in helping Catherine and her American parents. The support was bipartisan: Jesse Helms, John Warner, Nick Lampson, Pat Leahy, Mike DeWine, Steve Chabot, among many. Sandy Berger, President Clinton's National Security Adviser, and Melanne Verveer, Hillary Clinton's Chief of Staff, were hugely supportive.

Jesse Helms, the then Republican Chairman of the Senate Foreign Relations Committee, took up Catherine's cause as if it were his own. He was immensely powerful. Administrations lived in fear and trembling of him. No ambassador could be appointed without his approval. The State Department was stymied if Helms objected to what it wanted to do. He was highly controversial and a figure of hate to many Democrats, who saw him as an unreconstructed right-winger. But he was unflinching in the kindness and support that he showed Catherine and the American parents; and we will never forget that. He gave visiting German politicians a horrible time over these cases. He and his wife Dot became frequent visitors to the Great House, where the four of us would dine quietly.

Senator Trent Lott also has a place of honour in this pantheon of Catherine's heroes. When Catherine was lobbying for a Senate resolution, she was told that she needed the support of Lott, the majority leader. By chance, Catherine found herself at the same lunch as Lott's wife Trish. They knew each other already from a charity event we had held at the residence, when Trish Lott had spoken. Catherine explained the issue. Trish Lott said that she would speak to her husband.

This conversation took place when I was trying in vain to see the senator about bananas. When I came home the following evening, I found Catherine on the phone.

'Who was that?' I asked.

'Senator Lott,' she replied. 'He was calling me from his car in Mississippi.' This was said with a little smile. Catherine knew that

I had been trying for ages to see the senator. He was notoriously impervious to the charms of foreign ambassadors. I heard the news with stupefaction. The senator had called Catherine? From his car? Within less than twenty-four hours after her conversation with Mrs Lott? And he had agreed to help get the resolution passed? Wow!

Catherine got her resolution and, thanks to her influence, I got to see the senator. I gave him my pitch on bananas. He was tough and blunt. The banana boats from South America unloaded their goods at the port of Pascagoula, Mississippi, his home state. 'I will not see unfair European competition ruin the trade, putting good men out of work at the docks and jeopardizing the survival of a great American company [Chiquita],' he said thunderously. I later discovered that Lott had begun his political career as Pascagoula's congressman. I also knew that Chiquita's boss, Carl Lindner, was a big contributor to the Republican Party, as well as to the senator's re-election campaigns. 'You British,' continued Lott, 'are just not doing enough. A tariff on your imports will encourage you to do better.'

We met again not long after this unforgiving conversation. Lott told me that he had Scottish blood through his mother, who was a Watson. He was very proud of this. He had been the moving spirit behind a Senate resolution naming April 6 Tartan Day. This was to commemorate the Declaration of Arbroath of 1320, when the Scottish barons had declared their independence from the English king. Lott wanted to turn Tartan Day into a proper ceremony at the Capitol, with representatives from Scotland's newly devolved executive and parliament. This would include an annual William Wallace award, named after the medieval Scottish hero who had defied the English and met a grisly end at their hands (Wallace was portrayed ludicrously by Mel 'Mad Max' Gibson in the execrable movie *Braveheart*). Would I help him organize this?

I said that I would be glad to help, but I was not wholly certain how many Scots would turn up on the day when it became known that the senator was the driving force behind the Scottish cashmere tariff. This produced a kind of rumbling explosion, with a nervous aide instructed to look into where matters rested on the tariff.

The rest is history. Scottish cashmere wool was never penalized. The Europeans and Americans finally settled the Banana War (but not before other European products were penalized). Tartan Day went ahead to great success. The senator and I became good colleagues. I learnt a thing or two about not only American, but Scottish, politics. In helping to prepare the first Tartan Day in 2001 I got caught in the crossfire between the Scottish National Party (SNP), who want an independent Scotland, and all the other Scottish political parties. I was falsely accused in the Scottish press of banning SNP members from the embassy's party for Tartan Day. But that is another story, though I better understand now why Scottish politicians all seem to hate each other.

I did two Tartan Days in successive years in sublime spring weather. The ceremony took place on the top of the steep Capitol steps. There was a podium for speeches and rows of chairs for the VIPs, which included a strong delegation from the Scottish executive and assembly. There was, of course, a piper. At the bottom of the steps were the audience and TV cameras. Three senators – John Warner of Virginia, Wayne Allard of Colorado, and Trent Lott – were sufficiently proud of their Scottish heritage to take their chances in kilts for the occasion. As we all assembled in Lott's office beforehand, there was a fair bit of nervous joshing about the kilts. The moment of crisis came when the senators took their seats at the top of the steps. They primly crossed their legs, as if in a suit. Unfortunately, this gave the cameras and audience below a fairly good idea of what lay beneath.

It took Sean Connery to show them what to do. He received the second William Wallace award. Since he is an SNP supporter, this caused much twittering in the official Scottish delegation. But that again is another story. Connery took his seat, opened his legs wide, and allowed kilt and sporran to fall naturally, so preserving his modesty. The Senators gingerly adjusted their dress, Connery-style.

16

The Road to Austin

Towards the end of August 1988 I had found myself driving on an American road for the first time in my life. It was an eight-lane highway, somewhere north of Boston, Massachusetts. My car was one of the great abominations of the American automobile industry, a Plymouth Horizon, the sorry marriage of a Japanese engine with what looked like a Simca body. The car was tomato-red, with an interior to match. I had bought it from my predecessor as Foreign Office Visiting Fellow to Harvard University. My older son became so ashamed of its deeply unfashionable looks that he insisted we park the car around the corner when we picked him up from school. I later sold the machine to the ambassador's social secretary in Washington, Amanda Downes. It immediately broke down on her, when its petrol tank clogged with sludge. She christened it Uriah Heep. When last spotted, it was proudly owned by a Mexican gardener.

I was in a state of extreme nervousness. As I kept carefully to the 55 m.p.h. speed limit, enormous American trucks – known to the natives as tractor-trailers – roared past me on either side. Sometimes these behemoths would bear down on the Horizon from behind, lights flashing and horns blaring like the Last Trump. It recalled a horror movie that I had once seen, when a driver was pursued across America by a malignant truck.

It was a day of suffocating humidity. The East Coast of America had been for months suffering an intolerable heat wave. The Horizon had air conditioning, but to turn it on was to debilitate still further the vehicle's pitiful powers of forward motion. Perspiration streamed down my face, while the children's complaints rose to a whining torture. It was, as they say, a zoo out there. There was no lane discipline. American drivers drifted from one lane to another, overtaking to left and right in vehicles that handled more like boats than cars. Sometimes they signalled and sometimes they did not. Fortunately they drove 15 to 20 m.p.h. slower than Europeans. Otherwise there would have been more wrecks than in *Ben Hur*'s chariot race.

We finally reached our destination. We were desperate to find a beach and get away from the stifling heat of the city. Someone had recommended a beauty spot about an hour north of Boston called Crane Beach. This was near the town of Ipswich on what had once been the estate of an early twentieth-century industrialist from Chicago. We were not disappointed. The shoreline was superb. The sand was golden and the sea blue. There were surprisingly few people on the beach. No one was swimming. How odd, I thought, as we installed ourselves near the water. The temperature had to be up in the 90s. We put on our bathing costumes and raced our sweaty, overheated bodies into the sea. I do not know which of us screamed the loudest in shock. The water was not just cold; it was glacial, intolerable. We raced out as fast as we had raced in. A number of friendly Americans watched us in amusement. It was explained to us that, no matter how warm the air, the sea never really heated up. The warming Gulf Stream ran up the American East Coast as far as Cape Cod, where it was deflected eastward across the Atlantic towards Britain. North of Cape Cod the sea had no currents to warm it. It was, they said, actually quite dangerous to swim in such cold waters.

We soon warmed up on the hot sands. The children engaged in the traditional pastimes of the Sussex seaside, building sand-castles and tunnels. It was a long way from Angmering, with its pebbles, seaweed and breakwaters. My younger son, William, aged four, was used to running around naked on the beach. He proceeded to do so. We were immediately warned by our American neighbours that this was considered 'inappropriate'. Someone even said that it was illegal. It was our first encounter with American prudishness.

That night, exhausted but happy, we returned home to our ram-shackle rented house in Gray Gardens East, just above Harvard Common. We turned on the kitchen lights. We heard a scrabbling sound that took us straight back to Moscow. It was cockroaches racing for cover. They were pouring down the sink plughole as fast as they could manage. I opened a cupboard to find the anti-roach spray and recoiled in horror at the sight. Columns of the largest ants that I had ever seen were tramping across the surface like a foraging army. These were the dreaded carpenter ants which, like the cockroaches, were to be our constant companions in the house.

So ended the Meyer family's first day in the United States of America. We all agreed that it felt strange. On the surface America looked pretty familiar and people had already been very kind and welcoming to us. But as I lay sleepless that first night, listening to the unfamiliar sounds of police cars and fire engines, I had a deeper sense of alienation than I had ever expected. It was the eternal paradox of America for someone from Britain: so familiar but so different. There was something else as well. I had taken my family to a far stranger place when we had spent two years in Moscow in the 1980s. But there we had had the cocoon of the embassy, which provided a support system and an off-the-peg social life. Here, apart from the distant attentions of our consulate-general in Boston, we were on our own, living off the land. I felt vulnerable for my family.

Looking back, after having spent a total of eleven years in America, it all seems rather absurd. But at the time I was sharply conscious of having uprooted my then wife and children from the comforting routines of friends, family and school – for what? So that I could take a career break and swan around Harvard? It took a while for these feelings to evaporate.

This was the start of my Harvard sabbatical, to which the Foreign Office had readily agreed. The biggest decision to be taken before departing – as for any overseas posting in the Diplomatic Service – was about the children's education. Leave them behind in a British boarding school or bring them with us? It took us no time to decide. I was already deeply allergic to boarding schools, having been sent to one at the age of seven. I had been very unhappy and run away. Even today, a half-century later, a summer's twilight with the singing of birds brings back the desperate pangs of homesickness. I often wonder what those three years of misery did to me. At the age of eight I climbed through the dormitory window during our after-lunch rest period and jumped over the school wall. I then walked the five miles from Seaford to Rottingdean in Sussex, where my grandmother lived. Apparently my father had done the same. I was returned the next morning and threatened with a caning from the headmaster if I did it again. He eventually got to cane me, but not because I ran away again. I broke a school rule about not playing with sticks.

I did not want to inflict any of this on my children, though physical punishment had long since vanished from British schools. Besides, we felt strongly that they should not miss the experience of being educated in America. So, James, aged ten, and the four-year-old William came with us. But we had to leave my teenage stepson Tom at boarding school in England because at his age to change schools would have badly disrupted his education.

The two boys went to a local school in Cambridge. This is the undistinguished Massachusetts town on the other side of the Charles River from Boston to which Harvard is appended. The school was called Buckingham, Brown and Nichols. At the time we applied for places we had no idea that American parents would crawl on their hands and knees to get their children into this prestigious, fee-paying school. James, William and the son of Steve Biko, the South African anti-apartheid activist killed in police custody, were the only foreign children admitted that year.

Being the parents of children at a local school was a better introduction to American life and values than worldly, sophisticated, cosmopolitan Harvard. I was gratified that my sons were taught English composition and grammar in the traditional fashion to which I had been accustomed at school. To my surprise Latin was on the curriculum. This seemed to me an affirmation of the old, vanishing British virtues in education.

But, in other ways BB&N, as the school was called, was an alien experience. Compared with Britain, the parents were expected to play an extraordinarily active role in the life of the school. We were summoned to turn up at all kinds of occasions which brought parents and teachers together. There was none of that sense you had in British schools sometimes that parents were a nuisance, who got in the way of the serious business of teaching.

At the beginning of the year the principal addressed all the parents, unashamedly lauding the school's achievements under his direction and its ambitious plans for the school year. The first of many calls was made on the parents' generosity. Fund-raising was an integral part of school life. The parents, already paying heavily in school fees, were expected to give generously (and tax-efficiently). Parents were publicly graded by the generosity of their donations. The school knew that, in return, the parents wanted evidence of value for money. We would attend evenings when our children's teachers would more advertise than introduce themselves.

An entire life and community revolved around the school. My boys rapidly adapted and within a month or two were bilingual – sounding like Americans with their friends but still English with their parents. They grew rapidly in confidence. They were expected to get up and speak in class, again in contrast to their British schools. It is rare to come across an American who is diffident about public speaking. But the American classroom was not a competitive place. No child was allowed to fail a test, for fear of damage to its self-esteem or complaint from its parents (who were maybe big donors). No child was allowed to have a birthday party without inviting the whole class. At the end of the year I asked my sons what the school was doing to mark Christmas. 'Dad,' they said, 'we're doing Christmas, Hanukah and Kwanza.' 'What's Kwanza?' I asked. It turned out to be an African-American festival, devised by a Californian academic. Carefully calibrated equal time was given to the celebration of each. We learned to say 'Happy Holidays' and not 'Happy Christmas'. All this was strange in 1988. But a lot of it has since crossed the Atlantic.

Harvard is one of the world's great centres of learning and research. As a visiting fellow the entire university was open to me. I was based at one of Harvard's post-graduate schools, the Center for International Affairs, since renamed the Weatherhead Center after a benefactor. There were no rigorous academic demands of the visiting fellows. We were given offices and phones; the Center's schedule of weekly seminars and meetings; the University's course book for the year, listing every class, lecture and seminar; and told to get on with it. We were then expected to approach professors and lecturers to seek permisssion to 'audit' their courses. This meant to attend, but not take tests and examinations. Some of the undergraduate classes were so large our alien presence was never noticed.

I read the course book in an agony of choice. It was like standing before a huge table, groaning with a cornucopia of delicious dishes from which you could take only a mere handful. Just when I thought

I had settled on what I wanted to audit, the visiting fellows were handed the course books for the Massachusetts Institute of Technology and Tufts University, both of which were nearby. We could audit their courses as well. The Americans, generous to a fault, swamped the visiting fellows with an intellectual tidal wave.

Some of my fellow fellows arrived in Harvard with a clear project in mind, like a book. Others wanted to refresh parts of their intellect which earlier education had failed to reach. Others still had little idea of what they wanted to do.

I fell into the last category. The academic year at Harvard is divided into two terms, or semesters. With vacations, this adds up to about ten months. In the first semester I dithered over what to do, tasting and rejecting several courses. I was a little lost after the comforting routines of bureaucratic life. I found it hard to structure my day. I found this unexpectedly stressful. I started by playing safe. I went to classes on international relations where the subject matter was familiar. This proved unsatisfactory. The undergraduate classes were good but, unsurprisingly, not sufficiently advanced. By contrast, the postgraduate seminars, while often interesting, tended to be too specialized for my purposes. In my own area of expertise, the Soviet Union, where I had half-baked ideas for doing research, I found the academic establishment unwelcoming to a so-called practitioner from the outside. The big Harvard figures who had made their reputations writing about the Soviet Union had been thrown into disarray by the arrival of Mikhail Gorbachev, with his policies of *glasnost* and *perestroika*. His imminent downfall was repeatedly predicted. This was not the Soviet Union they knew and loved.

I came to realize also that professors with tenure – that is, the job for life – were at the top of an elaborate academic tree. They were the gods of the academy. Many did not welcome contact with students, however mature. Figures like Professor Stanley Hoffman at the Center for European Studies were unusual in their accessibility.

I was in danger of frittering away the entire first semester; but then, thanks to the Kennedy School of Government, its Institute of Politics, and the presidential election of 1988, the penny dropped. I should not be at Harvard trying to learn about Russia. I should be at Harvard learning about America.

And thanks to Professor Roger Porter. He taught an undergraduate course on the US Presidency. He was a brilliant and engaging lecturer. He had worked in the White House under various Republican presidents. He was soon to leave Harvard on appointment to the White House as domestic adviser to President Bush senior. His course was famous for its anecdotes. Porter was a keen tennis player. He used to say that you could always judge character by how someone played tennis. He told his class that President Bush was one of the few senior players on the White House tennis court (a broiling cauldron, incidentally, in the summer, as Catherine and I were to discover) who did not cheat on line calls. He ignored the urgent pleadings of his students to reveal the identity of the cheats.

Porter came top in student polls for best lecturer. My then wife and I decided to try him out – and to learn something about the governance of this country in which we were living. He readily agreed to our auditing his lectures. The two of us sat there like Darby and Joan, behind rows of enormous football players and earnest Asians, who seemed to write down every word that Porter said. The class was a rich ethnic medley, among which African-Americans were few and far between.

The counterpoint between Porter's lectures and the presidential election campaign of autumn 1988 was near-perfect. We would come home from class and turn on the television. We would witness, day by day, the remorseless destruction of the Democratic candidate, Governor Michael Dukakis of Massachusetts. It was something to see, live on television, Dukakis's self-immolation, when he replied soullessly and bureaucratically to a question about how he would react if his wife Kitty were raped and murdered. Then there was the doe-like haplessness of Dan Quayle, the young Indiana senator, whom Bush had inexplicably chosen as running mate. It was a moment not to miss, when Dukakis's running mate, Senator Lloyd Bentsen of Texas, destroyed Quayle's hopeless attempt to identify himself with the late President Kennedy: 'I knew Jack Kennedy and you're no Kennedy,' said Bentsen to lethal effect. Quayle, for whom 'lightweight' did not get the measure of the man, never recovered from this exquisite thrust of the political dagger.

I found myself frequenting the Kennedy School. It was a university within a university, focusing its immense resources on all aspects of government and politics. It was a magnet to politicians and all those who inhabited the penumbral world of pundits, pollsters, and political consultants. From the red-brick building on Kennedy Street there emerged the buzz of constant discourse on the 1988 presidential campaign, heavily slanted to the Democratic cause. I watched Jesse Jackson, the most famous African-American politician of the time, mesmerize a packed, adoring audience at the School with the soaring cadence of a black-American preacher. The political substance was pretty thin; but the performance sent a shiver down the spine. Several times a week I would go to the Institute of Politics, housed inside the Kennedy School, to take part in 'brown bag' lunches (bring your own food) and suppers, where a dozen or so of us would engage a visitor in vigorous debate. From time to time great figures, like Kenneth Galbraith, would pass by like majestic ocean liners.

It was exhilarating – and I was learning stuff. It set me straight for the second semester. I took courses on American politics, history and jazz. I plunged myself into nineteenth-century American history and the antecedents of the Civil War. I was already a jazz-lover, but I knew little of its roots and musicology. The jazz class was huge, with at least a couple of hundred undergraduates. It was taught with great brilliance and rigour: history, social and cultural background, musical structure. It was another way of understanding America. I was taken aback by how ignorant young Americans were of their great heritage in jazz. Ever since black-American jazz musicians found Europe in the 1920s and 1930s a more congenial place than segregated America, the Old Continent had been a keeper of the flame.

When, later, I went to work in the British embassy in Washington, I found myself in one of the great jazz cities, the birthplace of Duke Ellington. It had several jazz clubs, notably Blues Alley, a haunt of both established and up-and-coming artists. I was relieved to find that musicians were returning to a more classical and accessible jazz, after the impenetrability of performers like Ornette Coleman. I just did not understand what they were trying to do. But someone like Roy Hargrove, the black Texan trumpet and flugelhorn player, a regular at Blues Alley, could make the hairs stand on the back of my neck like Louis Armstrong or Roy Eldridge.

At the start of the second semester in early 1989 I was reminded that my status as visiting fellow imposed one obligation. I was required to write a paper based on my studies during the year. This fertilized the egg of an idea. After four years as the Foreign Office spokesman and Geoffrey Howe's press secretary, I had acquired strong views on how a government department should handle the press. I had distilled these into ten commandments. Bouncing around in my head like a pinball was the thought that I should develop the commandments into something more substantial.

I was encouraged in this by Marvin Kalb, the former television journalist who was head of the Shorenstein Center for Press, Politics and Public Policy, also part of the Kennedy School. The Shorenstein Center was relatively new and still finding its feet. But I enjoyed its classes and visiting speakers. The press, in a democracy, is endlessly fascinating and controversial. I decided to kill two birds with a single stone. I wrote a paper for the Shorenstein Center, which would serve equally for the CFIA.

From this emerged a slight work called 'Hacks and Pin-striped Appeasers: How To Sell Foreign Policy To The Press'. The phrase 'pin-striped appeasers' originally issued from the acerbic pen of a journalist at the *Sun* newspaper called Ronnie Spark. He always had it in for the Foreign Office. He and I used to spar, amiably.

My paper had a distant relationship to academic research. I decided that I had at least to give it some of the outward appurtenances of the academy. So I stuck in some footnotes. I was, of course, rumbled. Those who judged the paper said that it was 'great fun', Harvard-speak for lightweight, if tolerably interesting. In fact, to my surprise, thanks to Martin Walker of the *Guardian*, who later dug it out of the Harvard archives, I wound up having a minor *succès d'estime* with the paper. From time to time the ten commandments are given an airing in the British media. I was told that they are pinned to the wall of the press department in a European foreign ministry.

When I told American friends that I had decided to devote my studies to America, they all reacted in much the same way. 'Harvard isn't America. Nor is Boston, nor even New England. You need to go west and south.' So I did.

Towards the end of 1988 I was contacted by an organization called the English-Speaking Union (ESU). They wanted me to go on a speaking tour. I would address their chapters in Tulsa and Oklahoma City in Oklahoma, in Dallas and Fort Worth in Texas, and in Monroe and Shreveport in Louisiana. I jumped at the invitation. I set off with a speech which, at the ESU's request, married remarks about Gorbachev with others about the EU's Single Market and Fortress Europe. By the end of the tour you could barely detect the joins between these disparate subjects.

The ESU had been founded after the First World War. Its purpose was to sustain the ties between English-speaking peoples of the then British Empire and North America. The ESU had chapters all over the United States. They were, and remain, the home of American anglophilia. In 1989, with the passing of the years, the ESU's predominantly white Anglo-Saxon membership had aged, with little replenishment from younger generations. Later, at the turn of the century, under a more dynamic leadership, the ESU was showing signs of revival. As ambassador I gave it all the support I could.

The speaking tour opened my eyes to a new universe. Where possible, an ESU speaker stays privately in members' homes rather than in hotels. In Oklahoma City I lodged with a wonderful elderly widow, called Mary Elizabeth Thach. She lived on a large compound with other houses belonging to her father's family, the Edwardses, an old Oklahoma clan. The compound had a scattering of 'nodding donkey' oil wells. Her guest book included the signature of a very young Douglas Hurd, when he was a British diplomat at the United Nations.

Mary Elizabeth had a deep sympathy for the Native American Indian. Oklahoma had the largest population of any American state of what I used to call as a child 'Red Indians'. She was surprised at how much I knew already about Native Americans. This, I explained, was thanks to the *Buffalo Bill Annual*, which I used to receive every Christmas as a child. She took me to an evening of Seminole music and culture. We were accompanied by her sister-in-law, Dottie, who wore an amazing hat, as if at a Buckingham Palace garden party. I learned about the Five Civilized Tribes and the 'Trail of Tears', along which the Cherokees and Seminoles, expelled from Florida in 1830, were with great hardship sent into exile in Oklahoma. In conversation with a state senator of Seminole descent, I realized how the suffering of the North American tribes was still a live, raw issue for some. He told me how difficult it was for him and others of Native American descent to participate in the celebrations to mark Oklahoma's centennial as a state. For them it was synonymous with the seizure of Indian lands. I also found out for the first time that Native Americans had owned African-American slaves. As Mary Elizabeth and I parted, she gave me a copy of Evan Connell's marvellous book, *Son of the Morning Star*, about Custer's last stand and the uprising of the Sioux nation in 1876.

In Dallas, Texas, my host Jim Lynn gave me the first in my collection of vivid Texan expressions when he said that something was 'enough to give the Pope a harelip'. His wife Nancy, who had been a Canadian 'Wren' in the Second World War, had worked at the code-breaking centre at Bletchley Park in England. I wondered if her path had crossed my mother's, who had done something similar in the war for the WRAF. In Fort Worth, Texas, I was lodged with a fiery Baptist priest and his wife, who had preached in the slums of British cities; in Monroe, Louisiana, with another kindly widow, Jibby Fox; and in Shreveport, Louisiana, with a federal marshal and his wife. By happy coincidence I timed my visit to Shreveport with the Mudbug Madness Festival, when Cajun-style boiled crawfish from the Red River are eaten in huge quantities.

The contrast with Harvard could not have been greater. The mere mention of the university's name elicited mocking comment. I was introduced with remarks like: 'Christopher Meyer is currently a visiting fellow at Harvard University, but we won't hold that against him!' (audience split their sides with laughter). 'You can always tell a Harvard man, but you can't tell him much!' (audience fall off chairs with mirth). Harvard was seen as permissive, Godless, and – the most damning epithet of all – liberal.

Almost by accident, I prefaced my remarks in Dallas by saying that it was a true pleasure to be in the 'real America'. This was greeted by roaring, stomping, whooping delight. When I became ambassador I used the phrase to introduce almost every speech I gave in the cities of the American heartland. It nearly always got the same enthusiastic reaction. It was only in Milwaukee that it failed to work. My jokes 'died' there as well. This was no doubt the result of a preponderant German influence in the local population. As Mark Twain once said: 'A German joke is no laughing matter.'

Almost as effective a rhetorical device was to paraphrase Samuel Johnson: 'He who is tired of Indianapolis/Kansas City/Louisville etc. etc. is tired of life.' In the states of the Deep South a joke at the expense of Massachusetts always raises a deeply appreciative laugh. I liked to quote Governor Bradford's description of seventeenth-century Massachusetts as 'full of wild beasts and wild men'.

Thanks to the ESU I discovered the American God. He was everywhere in a profusion of churches and denominations. I spoke in church halls in Fort Worth, Texas, and Monroe, Louisiana. In Monroe I was shown the Bible Museum, which housed, unsurprisingly, a collection of Bibles. Next door was a Coca-Cola and opera museum combined. The building had been the home of Joseph Biedenharn, the first man to bottle Coca-Cola in the United States. The display featured bottles of different shapes and sizes. As you went upstairs, Coca-Cola turned into opera. This was in memory of Biedenharn's daughter, Emy-Lou, who had been an aspiring opera singer. Her foundation financed the Bible Museum. Behind the house was the Elsong Garden. As you walked along its pleasant pathways, electronic beams triggered snatches of opera from concealed speakers.

I returned from the tour with a kaleidoscope of impressions. In the Gilcrease Museum outside Tulsa, Oklahoma, I ate buffalo chili for the first time and discovered Western art – that grandiose school of nineteenth-century painting which sought to capture on canvas the newly conquered natural glories of the American West. I saw the proliferation of casinos on the impoverished reservations of Native Americans. I was astonished by the geographic diversity of the land; by the sharp contrast in culture and politics with Massachusetts (and by extension with Britain); by the innate conservatism, religiosity and unabashed patriotism of almost all whom I met; by the near invisibility of African-Americans, except for waiters and valet parking attendants; and by the spontaneous hospitality and generosity of my many American hosts. I fell for America in a big way.

The speaking tour spurred me to explore further this vast mysterious country. I was unable to do this until I became ambassador almost a decade later. When I first told Catherine about my time on the road for the ESU, she was as eager as I to get travelling. By the time Catherine and I left America in 2003 we had visited forty-four states and about 120 cities.

A couple of months after our arrival in Washington, we started our American odyssey in southern California and Los Angeles. Very soon after that, in February 1998, we set out for Texas: Houston, Dallas and Austin – and an appointment with Governor George W. Bush.

17

Dubya

As soon as we arrived in Washington in late 1997, my thoughts turned to the presidential election of 2000. US presidential elections are one of the great tests for an ambassador and his staff. I knew from experience that the Washington embassy would have to gear itself up well in advance to track and analyse the campaign and, if possible, to predict its outcome. We would need to get close to the candidates and their main advisers long before one or other was elected.

Americans complain that the campaigning season gets ever longer and more expensive. They have a point. There is almost a permanent campaign for the office of President. But that was fine by Catherine and me. We happily feasted on American politics. They provide the richest political diet in the world. From the President down to the local fire chief via senators, congressmen, governors, mayors – you name it – competitive electoral politics are unceasing. As time passed I found myself increasingly exploring the obscurer recesses of the *Washington Post* where political sagas from the suburbs of Prince George's County and Fairfax County were told in elaborate detail.

Strictly speaking the presidential campaign season does not begin until the primary contests at the start of the electoral year. This is when the Republican and Democratic Parties hold elections state by state to nominate from a raft of hopefuls the candidate that each sends forward to challenge for the presidency in the autumn.

The primaries, though a prelude to the main event, are an unforgiving examination of character, stamina, political skills and the ability to raise money. The weaker candidates fall rapidly by the wayside, out of money and support. Money – huge amounts of it – is indispensable to political success, though on its own it will never compensate for an inept candidate or campaign. A candidate doing well with the voters attracts donations and financial backers. If the candidate can go on building political momentum, it creates a virtuous circle by which cash and voter support become mutually reinforcing. The candidates who withdraw from the race are those who have been trapped in a vicious circle of dwindling voter support and financial backing.

Hindsight often makes the outcome of these primary contests seem preordained; but in 2000 it was not inevitable that George W. Bush and Al Gore should emerge as the Republican and Democratic presidential candidates; or that Senator John Kerry should win the Democratic nomination in 2004. What enlivened these campaigns, and for a while put their outcome in doubt, was the arrival on stage of a familiar character in the theatre of American politics. This is the maverick outsider, who, running as a plain-speaker and straight-shooter, shakes the foundations of the favourite's campaign. Though usually an experienced political hand and product of the establishment, the maverick will position himself as anti-Washington and anti-establishment, authentically in touch with the concerns and aspirations of Middle America. This is a country mile from being left-wing in any European sense of the word. That is the kiss of death in American politics.

The maverick's tale can be compelling and carry him a long way. In 2000 Senator John McCain, a possible Republican contender in 2008, gave George W. Bush a near-death experience in the New Hampshire primary, while Senator Bill Bradley took Al Gore on a vigorous run for his money. In 2004 it looked for a while that Howard Dean, Governor of Vermont and a classic maverick, would have the beating of Senator John Kerry for the Democratic nomination. When I saw White House friends, including the President's chief political strategist Karl Rove, on a visit in October 2003, they saw Dean as the easiest contender for Bush to demolish.

In the end the mavericks, with not quite enough money or seasoned advisers, tend to implode under the strain of campaigning. But two of the most politically astute Presidents of modern times – George W. Bush and Bill Clinton – captured the presidency with campaign messages strong in anti-Washington, anti-politics-as-usual content.

Halfway through a President's four years in office, mid-term elections take place to all the seats in the House of Representatives, some of the seats in the Senate and some of the governorships. Once these are out of the way, the political searchlight swivels immediately to the primaries, though it is more than a year before they are due to take place. Speculation starts to run riot about those with presidential ambitions, many of whom will have been plotting, scheming and positioning themselves already.

In other words, even at this early stage, thoughts begin to turn increasingly to the next President of the United States and who this might be. It is at this point that a second-term President like George W. Bush, debarred by the Constitution from running for a third term, begins to feel his authority start to deflate. This is the phenomenon of the lame duck. In fact, such is the deference of Americans to the institution of the presidency and such the President's continuing control of the levers of power and patronage that the duck's lameness can be exaggerated; but on the whole, second-term presidents look to achieve their most ambitious projects in their first two years.

With the mid-terms only a year away when Catherine and I arrived in Washington, I felt that there was no time to lose to get the embassy's election machine in good working order.

The Washington embassy had a long tradition of successfully getting alongside Republican and Democratic campaign teams. The ambassador engaged with the candidates themselves and their most senior advisers, the political officer with the rest of the campaign staff, though the dividing line was not watertight. Over the years I had seen a succession of young and resourceful political officers insert themselves into campaign aircraft and buses, as they criss-crossed America with the candidates. Jonathan Powell, Tony Blair's chief of staff, cut some of his American teeth this way when he worked in the embassy in the 1990s. As ambassador I was blessed to have the thirty-two-year-old Matthew Rycroft in this role for the campaigns of 1999–2000. He was as good as, if not better than, his illustrious predecessors. He bet on Bush early in the game (as did Catherine), while I still had my doubts. Between us, Matthew and I ensured that in 2001 there was a ready-made network of the most senior Republican contacts, including the President himself, to pass to Downing Street and the Foreign Office.

If we had not been able to achieve this, the embassy might as well have gone out of the business of political analysis and reporting. The interpretation of American election campaigns is a competitive business. The market is crowded with highly paid pundits, pollsters,

Catherine with Lady Thatcher, 1998.

A warm autumn evening on the terrace of the Great House with two of my former bosses: Sir John Major and Lord Howe. I'm sitting next to Arabella Warburton, John's personal assistant.

Cherie Blair, Catherine and me at the launch of Catherine's charity at the Embassy, April 1999. William Pitt the Younger peeps over my left shoulder.

The Odd Couple. Al Gore and John Prescott at the Vice-President's Residence.

Alastair Campbell.

I tell a story while presenting a bust of Winston Churchill to President Bush in June 2001.

Left: Tony Blair, Condoleezza Rice, George W. Bush at Camp David, February 2001.

Bush and Blair meet for the first time after 9/11: the White House, 20 September 2001.

Colin Powell and assorted British and American aides at the White House before the Bush and Blair press conference, 20 September 2001.

White House press conference, 20 September 2001.

and consultants. From these spews a constant stream of comment and analysis, much of it regurgitated in the media. Conventional wisdoms emerge from this political Tower of Babel. The challenge for the embassy is to cut through it all; and to add value. That, of course, requires good political judgement. More than that, it demands the ability to acquire political intelligence directly from primary sources in the Republican and Democratic camps. We were able to do this better than most.

In late 1997 the state of our political intelligence was out of kilter. There were well established links between New Labour and the Democrats, which went back almost a decade. These included close ties between Downing Street and the White House. New Labour used Democratic political consultants like Bob Shrum and Stan Greenberg to advise them on elections in the UK. Peter Mandelson sought my advice on the wisdom of hiring Shrum for the 2001 election in Britain (not the kind of question a civil servant likes to answer). The Blairs and the Clintons were in the first flush of trying to convert the slogans of the Third Way into a coherent political philosophy. These links generated an enormous flow of political intelligence, some of it very valuable, most of it skewed to a Democratic interpretation of American politics.

Among Democrats it was probably Clinton himself who gave Blair the most clear-eyed view of what was going on. At the end of 2000, in the dying days of his presidency, he warned Democrats not to underestimate Bush. He gave similar advice to Blair – as did we from the embassy. It took a politician's politician like Clinton to recognize similar attributes in Bush.

But for New Labour the Republican Party was *terra incognita*. In some parts of No. 10, there was such ideological hostility to the Republicans that it blinded them to the possibility that Bush could beat Gore in 2000. When the embassy began to advise London that Bush might win, I heard that some of those closest to the Prime Minister were accusing us in the embassy of pro-Bush bias.

One of my first tasks was to bring our intelligence back into balance against the possibility of a Republican victory in 2000. Serious doubts about Al Gore's electoral appeal already existed and added urgency to the task. We sniffed the wind. It came from Texas and carried the name of Governor George W. Bush.

We knew very little about Bush. My predecessor, John Kerr, had met him and had been impressed. Barbara Bush once told me that, of her sons, her expectation had been that George W.'s younger brother Jeb would be the first to move into big-time politics; but Jeb failed at the first attempt to secure the governorship of Florida. In contrast, to the surprise of some, George W. unseated the well-regarded incumbent Democratic Governor of Texas, Ann Richards, at his first try in 1994. It was Governor Richards who had once remarked of George Bush senior that he had been born with a silver foot in his mouth – this a reference to both his mangling of vocabulary and aristocratic lineage. Since Jeb Bush did not win Florida until 1998, if any Bush were to run for President in 2000, it would have to be George W.

I called our well-connected and politically astute consul-general in Houston, Texas, Peter Bacon. Again carrying on a long tradition, Peter and his wife Valerie had got to know everyone worth knowing in the Lone Star State.

'Peter,' I said, 'Catherine and I are coming to Texas. We want to meet the Governor. The rumour in Washington is that he is going to run for President. Can you fix this?'

'Sure,' said Peter. 'My information is that Bush is giving serious thought to running, but nothing is decided. There should be no problem getting an appointment. I'll have a word with Al Gonzalez, whom I know well.'

'Who's Gonzalez?' I asked.

'His official title is Secretary of State. He handles visits by ambassadors. He's the gatekeeper.' Al Gonzalez subsequently travelled with Bush to the White House, was his general counsel for the first term (i.e. legal adviser), and is now Attorney-General of the United States.

Peter went on: 'You can't come to Houston without paying your respects to President and Barbara Bush. I also think you should go and see this political consultant called Karl Rove. He was Governor Bush's campaign manager. If Bush runs for President, Karl will be at his side again.'

Catherine and I set off for Texas in February 1998, just after Tony Blair's first official visit to Washington. We established a pattern for these visits around the United States. The local consul-general did the logistics and fixed the appointments. We called on the Governor if we were in the state capital, the local mayor, leading politicians, the editorial board of the local newspaper, and businesses which were either British-owned, investors in the UK, or whose investment we wanted to secure. I did interviews for local TV and radio. I gave a speech or two, either to business groups or those interested in foreign affairs. Increasingly I spoke to students at universities. I liked doing this because they challenged your assumptions from first principles.

I did about thirty of these speeches a year. I wrote them myself because I have never been able to speak words crafted by someone else. This is probably an allergic reaction to having been a speech-writer in the 1970s. I wrote for three Labour Foreign Secretaries: Jim Callaghan, Anthony Crosland and David Owen. Owen at first was the most difficult. He commented on the first draft speech I gave him that it was as useful to him as 'a dead fish'. He then proceeded to give it almost word-for-word, telling me afterwards that he had had to redraft it. It was no good my protesting. I soon learned the wisdom of Justinian's adage that 'what pleases the Prince has the force of law'. Later we got on very well.

After a while Catherine became an established speaker in her own right, addressing lawyers, women's groups and universities on children's issues. She attracted huge audiences, the largest being a thousand Mormon students and faculty at Brigham Young University in Provo, Utah. Sometimes we would do a double act, usually at universities, where I would speak to one department and she to another. At Vanderbilt in Nashville, Tennessee, I was taken by the university authorities to be her bodyguard. This was testimony to a blue suit which was a tad too sharp, with a bulging wallet (of one-dollar bills). I did not disabuse them until the last possible minute.

Our core message was always the same. We banged the drum for Britain. We never let typical British understatement get in the way. We celebrated British excellence in science, technology, the arts and education. We advertised Britain as a dependable, candid ally, a strong economy and the best place in Europe to invest. We did not hesitate to draw favourable comparisons with France and Germany, with their inflexible labour markets and over-regulated economies. Any joke at the expense of the French brought the house down.

In Texas we did a three-city tour. We started in Houston, went on to Dallas, and finished in the state capital, Austin, where we had our appointment with Governor Bush.

In Houston our main business meeting was with Enron, at the time the largest energy corporation in the world. Enron was at the height of its glory. No one I know of suspected that it was rotten at its core. Its chairman, Ken Lay, bestrode American business like a colossus. He counted the Bush family among his friends. You did not pass through Houston without doffing your cap to Ken Lay.

I had a particular reason for going to see him. Enron's expertise in energy and power generation was of great interest to the British Government. They wanted to attract Enron's investment to the UK. But there was a problem. Enron wanted to build gas-fired power stations. The Labour Government had introduced a moratorium on building power stations that were not coal-fired. This was a bow to the miners, a rapidly declining force in the British economy, but one that could still tug Labour's heartstrings. Lay said that either he or one of his senior executives wanted to go to London and make the case to British ministers for lifting the moratorium. When I returned to Washington, I strongly advised the Government to see him, if they wanted Enron's investment.

Enron's offices were housed in a vast building of palatial magnificence. It was an awe-inspiring, marble-clad temple to American capitalism. The Union Jack was flying over the main entrance in our honour. We ascended heaven knows how many floors. We were ushered into an office with a view of Houston that took the breath. Lay impressed me. There is a certain type of American, usually in business, who exudes power and ease at using it. The only other place where I found something similar was in the top echelons of German banks. But as we left, Catherine turned to me and said in a phrase all of her own: 'My nose does not smell that right.'

I asked her to explain.

'It's hard to put into words. It's my intuition more than anything. It was all too perfect. It did not feel like a working office. There's too much opulence. The secretaries were beautiful like the "Stepford Wives".'

I dismissed Catherine's suspicions. That was a mistake, as we now know. I learnt to respect Catherine's nose. It is more sensitive than early-warning radar. She proved far better than I at spotting the rotten apples among the thousands of people we met. It was her nose, as well as her brain, that had once made her a top commodities broker, one of the first women to break into a male-dominated world. The nose has also some mystical, probably Russian, affinity to numbers. This explains a remarkable record of success at the roulette table.

In Houston we had a drink with the former President Bush and his wife Barbara. It became a practice, whenever we were in Houston, to pay our respects to '41'. Catherine had always thought him the best-looking man in the United States. It came as a shock to see their comfortable, unpretentious home guarded by a full Secret Service detail; but former American Presidents enjoy a high level of protection for the rest of their lives.

The Bushes received us with great warmth and hospitality. Barbara Bush always showed a sympathetic interest in the story of Catherine and her children. But at that first meeting the conversation soon turned to whether their son, George, would offer himself for the Republican nomination. I was a bit hesitant to ask, not wanting to abuse their hospitality; but they seemed keen enough to talk about it. The former President said that his son had a tough decision to take. He had to think hard about the impact on family life of continuous exposure to the national spotlight: on his wife Laura and on his twin teenage daughters Jenna and Barbara. Mrs Bush's comments were grittier. The twins were already used to the spotlight. They would adapt to the national stage. 'She wants George W. to run,' Catherine and I said to each other afterwards.

After picking up a pair of cowboy boots in Dallas thanks to the genial hospitality of its impressive African-American mayor, Ron Kirk, our next stop was Karl Rove in Austin. Karl has become one of the most powerful men in the United States: the architect of the President's two election victories and his principal political adviser. In 1998 he ran his consultancy out of modest, nondescript premises, which belied his political influence in Texas. His own office was an untidy mass of papers and books. From behind the haphazard piles emerged a jovial, round-faced man, with receding, swept-back sandy hair. His eyes seemed permanently to twinkle from behind rimless glasses. His accent was strongly Southern.

This was the start of a friendship with Karl and, later, his wife Darby which endures to this day. When in 2003 Catherine put herself forward – in vain – to replace Michael Portillo as the Conservative candidate for the seat of Kensington and Chelsea, she got a little email advice from the other side of the Atlantic. Karl was in turn the recipient of Catherine's pungently hostile views on the European Constitutional Treaty.

I wanted to know as much as possible about Bush's intentions. Karl stuck to the party line that the Governor had taken no decision to run for President. But the body language and a remark here and there told a different story. Catherine and I concluded afterwards that Karl fully expected Bush to enter the race and that he would be by the Governor's side.

Karl went out of his way to emphasize that George W. Bush was more like his mother than his father. At one level this was an observation on the Governor's temperament and character. He would be tougher and more single-minded than his father. At another it was a clear political message, intended to dispel doubts among the Republican faithful about the Bush dynasty. If he won the presidency, George W. would, unlike his father, have the right stuff to win a second term.

In the election campaign of 2000 Bush ran explicitly as the anti-Clinton candidate. Implicitly he also ran against his father's presidential model. In hard political terms it meant that George W. had no intention of losing the support of the Christian Right as his father had done. That had allowed Ross Perot, the ultra-conservative Texas businessman, standing as an independent, to split the Republican vote and hand the presidency to Bill Clinton. Even as we spoke, a similar threat from another ultra-conservative billionaire, Steve Forbes, the publisher and businessman, was emerging on the horizon. The Bushites feared his money – he had an immense personal fortune to spend on his campaign – and his populist appeal, which included a proposal for a low flat tax. But George W. and Karl saw him off in 2000 by never allowing Forbes to outflank them on the Right. This is one reason why tax cuts were in the Bush political armoury from the beginning.

Karl Rove's success has led his envious political enemies to invest him with demonic qualities. To us he was always friendly, helpful and accessible. There was also, at least at the outset of the Bush presidency, some Washington snobbery and condescension about a campaign which had been run out of Texas by a Texan for a Texan. It did not help that Washington is a Democratic town which in 2001 thought that Bush had stolen the election from Al Gore. But the people from Arkansas who accompanied Bill Clinton to Washington made a similar complaint about snobbish Washingtonians.

Washington is the capital city of American political consultants. It stuck in the craw of some of them that Bush had not sought political advisers from among their number. This fed the notion that the Bush people were parochial Texans who knew and cared little of the outside world. When Catherine and I saw Bush later that day, he was the first to admit that he had travelled only modestly outside the US. But Karl Rove knew Europe from his days as Chairman of the College Republicans, an organization of right-wing students set up in the sixties to counter the influence of left-wing politics in American universities. Most of George W.'s foreign policy advisers had extensive experience of Europe.

Rove had made his name largely in Southern politics. He had supported the Republican Party since his teen years; had known the Bush family since the seventies; and had been hired by George W. in 1993 to handle his successful run for the governorship of Texas. When Catherine and I visited Mississippi and Alabama in 2002, we found traces of him still. We stayed in Greenville, Mississippi, with Scott and Judy Reed, the parents of an old friend, Julia Reed the journalist. Scott was credited with having masterminded the capture of Mississippi by the Republican Party. Greenville is in the middle of the old Blues country and calls itself the 'Heart and Soul' of the Mississippi Delta. We travelled Highway 61, made famous by Bob Dylan's 1965 album, passing the crossroads which Robert Johnson, the greatest of all bluesmen, used to sing about in the 1920s and 1930s. We ate barbecue in an old juke-joint in a cotton field and dined massively at Doe's Eat Place in Greenville itself. I believe that there is still a photo of Catherine and me on the wall of Doe's.

As Catherine had to return to Washington, I headed alone to Alabama and its state capital, Montgomery. As the *Michelin Guide* would put it, Montgomery *vaut un détour*. It was the epicentre of the Civil Rights movement in the sixties. You will find there the Rosa Parks Museum, dedicated to the African-American woman who sparked the boycott of segregated buses; the Dexter Avenue Baptist Church, where Martin Luther King started out as a preacher; and, for lovers of country music, the Hank Williams Museum.

In the Governor's absence I went to see his deputy, Lieutenant-Governor Steve Windom. In his waiting room I found something that I had never come across before. It was full of people, milling around. I was accustomed to quiet, orderly ante-rooms before seeing governors or big-city mayors. The crowd looked at me enviously as I passed without waiting into the Lieutenant-Governor's office.

Windom asked me to say a few words to the Alabama Senate, who were in session. As we made our way to the chamber, the crowd in the waiting room surged forward, with individuals breaking out of it to seek favours from the Lieutenant-Governor. It was like petitioners at the court of a medieval king. Windom had a few murmured words for each of them.

I talked to the Alabama Senate about Britain standing four-square with America in the struggle with terrorism. Some of the senators wept.

Just as you are beginning to succumb to the clichés and stereotypes of the Deep South, something snaps you back into the twenty-first century. Thirty minutes outside Montgomery is Tallassee, where you will find a factory owned by GKN, the British engineering company, which manufactures the most sophisticated composite materials for high-performance aircraft (I now sit on the board of GKN as a non-executive director). On the drive there I passed the pens where catfish, the traditional Southern staple, are farmed. I was told that the farms were under threat from imports of a cheaper Vietnamese fish from the waters of the Mekong Delta. *O tempora, O mores!*

The office of the Governor of Texas is in a fine, domed building in the state capital, Austin. It also houses the Texas legislature, which meets every other year. For better or worse, depending on your point of view, this is a striking example of government keeping off the backs of its citizens. Texas has a population of 22 million, larger than most sovereign states. I can think of no democracy in the world which would content itself with a parliament's meeting in alternate years only.

In Texas, in contrast to other states, the Governor's powers are limited. The office is akin to that of a constitutional monarch. It is the deputy, the Lieutenant-Governor, who is the chief executive officer. Of course, this tells you only so much about the Governor's influence. It is exercised as much through networks, where friendships, family connections and business relationships are as important as formal channels or party allegiance.

When we arrived in Austin, Bush had acquired a reputation for consensus politics and working across party lines. This, and his 'compassionate conservative' rhetoric during the 2000 campaign, when he proclaimed his credentials as a 'uniter, not a divider', led many to think that he would bring a similar approach to national politics. This proved wrong. As President, Bush drew a sharp line between those who were with him and those who were against him. It helped keep the Right happy.

Texas politics seemed to march to a more relaxed beat. Party differences were less marked. Almost everyone was a conservative. It was easier to reach across the party line without getting snagged on ideological barbed wire.

After paying a visit to the US, Clement Attlee, the first Labour Prime Minister after the Second World War, was reputed to have reported to his Cabinet colleagues in something like the following terms: 'Gentlemen, I have just visited the USA and very interesting it was too. In many ways America is like Britain. For example, they have two main political parties. One is called the Republican Party and it is a bit like our Conservative Party. Then they have the Democratic Party – and it is a bit like our Conservative Party.'

True or not about American politics at the national level – and it is truer than many Republicans or Democrats would care to admit – it is certainly true about Texas politics.

Al Gonzalez met us in the Governor's outer office and took us in to meet him. Catherine and I liked him from the first handshake. The more we met him over the next five years, the more we liked him – and his wife Laura. It was not just the easy affability and charm. There was a complete lack of pretentiousness or standing on dignity. His office was modest.

Among the scores of politicians that we had met over the years, Bush was one of the very few to have the confidence to admit to what he did not know. Bush said that he knew Mexico, Texas' southern neighbour, pretty well. He spoke some Spanish. He had visited the Middle East and Italy with his father. He had spent holidays in Scotland as a child with family friends, the Gammells. He had been to London. But that was about it.

Bush was formally non-committal about running for President. But he too went out of his way to tell us that he was more like his mother than his father. Again, afterwards, we felt strongly that we had been signalled that he had decided to run. We revisited him in Austin almost exactly a year later in 1999. By then the clamour within the Republican Party for him to declare his candidacy had grown deafening. Delegations of Republicans from all over the US were making pilgrimages to Austin to urge him to stand. Again he would not confirm to us in terms that he would do so. But by then it was obvious that once the biennial session of the Texas legislature had wound up, Bush would declare.

On this second visit his manner had changed. Bush was thinking seriously about what a run for the presidency would entail. There was a more purposeful edge to his remarks on foreign policy. He repeated that there was a lot that he did not know about abroad; but, he said, he was a quick learner. If he ran for the presidency, he would surround himself with good people, experts, who would teach him. The previous day, in Houston, the Governor's father had virtually confirmed to us that his son would run. The elder Bush mentioned Condoleezza Rice and Paul Wolfowitz as two good people who could advise his son. In due course Rice and Wolfowitz were to run George W.'s team of foreign policy advisers, known collectively as the 'Vulcans'. Condi Rice is now, of course, Secretary of State, while Paul Wolfowitz runs the World Bank after four years as deputy Secretary for Defense.

On this second visit, Bush said that he wanted to try something on us. He gave a little speech, no more than a couple of minutes long, which set out principles for American foreign policy. He talked of America's mission to be a champion of democracy and freedom around the world, not only to make it a better place but also to ensure the security of all peace-loving people. What did we think of it? Bush asked.

I was a little lost for words. Who could object to what I thought at the time was just motherhood and apple pie? I made ritual noises of approval. I could tell from his shrewd, humorous eyes that he had detected my scepticism. With the benefit of hindsight, I now know that the little speech was the precursor of an entire foreign policy that was to lead to the toppling of Saddam Hussein. It was almost word-for-word identical to what Bush has repeatedly said since becoming President about America's vocation in the wider world.

This came home to me most vividly three years later, when Tony

Blair and George W. met at Camp David in September 2002. It was the end of the meeting. A small group of us was standing around, waiting for the Prime Minister, before the British contingent embarked on helicopters to return to Washington. The group comprised the President and a handful of American and British officials, including myself. Bush suddenly said that sending young Americans into harm's way was the greatest responsibility of all for an American President. But if the result was a victory for liberty and democracy, future generations would thank us. As he said this, Bush became quite emotional.

Bush told us at our second meeting in 1999 that, if he became President, he would seek to re-establish good personal relationships with foreign leaders. Loyalty was all-important. You had to be able to depend on people, and they on you. Clinton had damaged these relationships. He and his father had been told by Egyptians that Clinton got in touch only when he wanted something. Bush would change that.

At our first meeting in 1998 Bush said that he had heard through his Scottish friends, the Gammells, that Tony Blair was a good man. But he did not know much about other British politicians. There was this fellow from the British parliament – what was his name? – 'Jim Hague', who was coming to see him next week. Did I know him?

'Governor,' I said, 'I think you mean William Hague, the leader of the Conservative Party. You will like him. He's inexperienced, but clever and amusing. You'll like his wife too.'

At the time the Tories were trumpeting a close relationship with the Governor and possible future President. When William and Ffion passed through Washington en route to Texas, we did not have the heart to tell them that Bush hardly knew who they were.

Two things emerged from these meetings with Governor Bush in 1998 and 1999. Firstly, he was as smart as a whip. Secondly, he would view events, countries and people in black and white: good and bad, friendly and hostile, loyal and unreliable. It was not difficult to tell London, repeatedly, that, verbal stumbles notwithstanding, this was someone not be underestimated. He was after all the only Texas Governor to be elected to consecutive four-year terms. This was not a message everyone at home wanted to hear. But Tony Blair, another politician's politician, got it in one.

On one of our walls, in pride of place, there hang two framed documents conferring on Catherine and me honorary citizenship of Texas, signed by Governor Bush. We have always felt an affinity – dare I say it, a special relationship – with Texas, where we have many friends. But then it was the first woman Governor of Texas, Ma Ferguson, who said at some point in the 1920s, 'If the King's English was good enough for Jesus Christ, it's good enough for Texas.'

18

Republicans at the Gates

On 11 December 2000 I found myself sitting on a hard wooden bench at the US Supreme Court. The grand, high-ceilinged chamber was packed with Washington's political elite. There was the buzz of excited conversation. The air crackled with electricity. To my left, along the bench, sat the high command of the Gore campaign. Fatigue and anxiety were etched in equal measure on their faces. This was the climax to over a month of intense legal and political struggle. At stake was the presidency of the United States.

It was a moment of high, historic drama. The nine Justices of the Supreme Court were about to hear arguments from Republican and Democratic counsel on the vexed question of how votes cast in Florida should be counted. The Justices' ruling would decide whether Bush or Gore became the forty-third President.

I had decided to do something well-nigh unprecedented, so that I could be witness to the moment. The hearing coincided with President Bill Clinton's farewell visit to Britain. An ambassador is expected to return to London for a presidential visit. It is not just a matter of protocol. It is enormously useful to take part in talks between Prime Minister and President. But on this occasion I thought the Supreme Court hearing more important than a visit by a President in the final weeks of his term.

The presidential election had taken place just over a month previously, on 7 November. It was extraordinarily close. As the night wore on, with Catherine and I and some friends glued to the television, Florida emerged as the decisive state. At one point Gore was on the verge of conceding the race on the basis of television network projections of the Florida result. Then it looked as if he might have won after all. When the final count came in, Bush had more votes than Gore. But the margin of victory was less than half of one per cent. Under Florida law that triggered a recount.

The American electoral system is very different from the British. The President is not directly elected by the people. He is chosen by the majority of members of a body called the Electoral College. The College as such does not exist. It is the collective noun for 538 Electors who are drawn from each state of the Union. Their origins go back to the foundation of the Republic at the end of the eighteenth century, the term 'Elector' coming into general use at some point in the early 1800s. A presidential candidate needs the votes of at least 270 Electors to win.

The number of Electors sent by each state is determined by the state's quota of senators (always two) and of members of the House of Representatives. The latter is a fluctuating figure, which varies according to population as recorded by each census. Florida, being a big state, had twenty-five Electors in 2000. That figure has now risen to twenty-seven as a result of the 2000 census.

The political affiliation of the group of Electors sent by each state is determined by whichever presidential candidate has won the state. In an age when the American electorate is pretty evenly split between the two parties, the way a single state, especially a big one, votes can decide the election. That is why, when the dispute erupted over vote-counting in Florida, the stakes were so high and the outcome of the 2000 presidential election had to be put on hold.

The struggle for Florida went through innumerable twists and turns, as the matter bounced from one court to another like a pinball. The appetite in No. 10 for the embassy's reporting was insatiable. My sense was that we were witnessing a drama. It was not yet a crisis. But if the impasse went on much longer, for example causing Florida to miss the December deadline for choosing its Electors, the US could be in dangerous, uncharted waters, where politicians might try to seize the helm from the courts. All manner of horrible but possible scenarios then loomed. One of the most extravagant was that neither Bush nor Gore would be able to occupy the Oval Office, the presidency passing *faute de mieux* to the oldest senator, the ninety-eight-year-old Republican Strom Thurmond of North Carolina.

Thurmond had, to put it delicately, a controversial past in the politics of the South, where he had fought long and hard against civil rights legislation. He was, by all accounts, an energetic ladies' man. Catherine once found herself sitting next to him at a dinner.

While she was talking to her other dinner partner, the elderly Thurmond scribbled her a note on the back of his place card: 'Lady Catherine, you are a very lovely woman.' Catherine turned to talk to him; but he was as deaf as a post.

After the first recount Gore still trailed Bush by several hundred votes. By this time the deficiencies of some of the voting machines and ballot papers had become a blazing issue. The Democrats could not understand how, in Palm Beach County, a strongly Democratic bastion, 19,000 ballot papers had apparently been declared void and 3,000 given to the right-wing maverick Pat Buchanan. Voters were supposed to use punch-card machines, into which they put their ballot paper and made a hole against the candidate of their choice. The papers were then counted automatically. The Democrats claimed that some of the punch-card machines had failed to drive a clean hole in the ballot papers, so causing the counting machines to void them. Gore demanded manual recounts in four counties where he believed the Democratic vote to have been heavily undercounted. From this flowed the saga of the dimpled and hanging chads, as election officials peered at the ballot papers to gauge whether mechanical inadequacy had deprived people of their vote.

The Republicans resisted manual recounts. Florida was flooded by armies of Republican and Democratic lawyers as the courts were asked to intervene. Sub-plots erupted alleging the confusing layout of ballot papers, the disenfranchising of African-American voters, and the manipulation of postal votes.

In the end, it all boiled down to the US Supreme Court overruling the Florida Supreme Court. The latter had shown itself consistently favourable to Gore's arguments for manual recounts. On 8 December the Florida Supreme Court ruled that additional recounts should go ahead, even though the state had already formally announced that Bush had beaten Gore by just over 500 votes. Bush went to the US Supreme Court to try to overturn the ruling of the Florida Supreme Court. This was the hearing that I attended. It would lead to the crucial decision.

Passes for the hearing were as valuable as gold dust. I managed to get one thanks to one of our friends among the Justices, Stephen Breyer. For an hour or so Counsel for the Republicans and Democrats made their opposing arguments to Chief Justice Rehnquist and his eight colleagues, who flanked him on a raised dais.

I was glad that it was not I having to make a case in these intimidating surroundings. Ted Olson for the Republicans and David Boies for the Democrats were at the top of their game. Olson, whose wife was to perish in one of the aircraft crashed by the 9/11 hijackers, went on to become Bush's Solicitor-General. He was blunt and workmanlike, but no less effective for that. Boies, with a reputation as one of the foremost court-room lawyers in the United States, was more theatrical and eloquent. I found it impossible to tell which of them had 'won'.

The tension was almost unbearable for an audience split evenly between Republicans and Democrats. A mildly humorous exchange at one point made everyone laugh with exaggerated heartiness. From the corner of my eye I observed the Democrats on the bench to my left. It was like being in the stands at a Chelsea–Arsenal game. When Olson made a telling point, faces fell and shoulders hunched. When Boies did likewise, faces lightened, torsos straightened, fists punched the air. The hearing was punctuated with sighs, groans, grunts, and the occasional whispered 'yeah!' I did not have a dog in the fight; but I left the Supreme Court drained. I headed for the nearest Starbuck's for a massive injection of caffeine.

Thirty-six hours later, on a five to four ruling, the Supreme Court handed the presidency to George W. Bush. The Justices ruled that further manual recounts would be unconstitutional. There was, they said, no uniform standard for judging the intent of the ballot papers. Therefore not all votes would be treated equally as the Constitution demanded. Gore had little choice but to concede. He did so with a graceful speech, one of his best of the long campaign.

The ruling of the Supreme Court was deeply controversial and provoked bitter recriminations from the Democrats. Everything in Washington is seen through a political prism. People divided the nine Justices into a conservative (i.e. Republican-leaning) majority of five and a liberal (i.e. Democrat-leaning) minority of four. Many Democrats charged the majority on the Court with having handed down a politically biased decision which unfairly delivered the Presidency to Bush. Gore had, they felt, been robbed.

A number of news organizations decided to do what the Supreme Court had refused: use the Freedom of Information Act to make a comprehensive count of all votes cast in Florida. There was a wide expectation in Washington that this would reveal a clear majority for Gore; but in the end these investigations brought no greater clarity. They too were defeated by the difficulty of establishing voter intent, where the vote-counting machines had failed to register a preference. One of the news organizations later claimed that on the basis of a hand count of all Florida counties Bush was the winner.

I said to London that the issue was less whether Gore had been robbed, more how he had allowed the race to get so close in the first place. A political consultant from the planet Mars would have said that Gore held most of the aces. America basked in prosperity, Gore was immensely experienced, and Bush, in his public appearances, was too often stumbling and tongue-tied. He was learning on the job and it showed. His political enemies questioned his fitness for the highest office.

Gore would probably have made a good President. As I said in one report, Gore 'is more comfortable with policy than politics, with governing than campaigning. A steady Vice-President, he is an insecure and inconsistent campaigner.' Like Senator John Kerry in 2004, Gore lacked the instinctive ability to connect with ordinary Americans.

On the campaign trail Gore often looked unhappy in his skin. In an attempt to overcome his innate woodenness, Gore's advisers submitted him to repeated personality transplants, to varying degrees of success. This fed the fatal notion that he, and the voter, did not know who he was or what he stood for. In the three televised presidential debates of the autumn, where the Martian observer would have expected easy Gore victories, Bush won on points. In each debate a different Gore was on display: aggressive, passive and something in between. Bush, despite lapses, stuck consistently and affably to a series of simple propositions.

Above all, Gore crippled himself by his reluctance to capitalize on the boom times of the Clinton years. He was entitled to a share of the credit; it should have been a trump card. But he was fearful of associating himself too closely with his political partner and President. He was so concerned to be seen as his own man that he even declared at the Democratic Convention in August that he would run on future intentions not past performance.

The relationship between Clinton and Gore was edgy and complicated. It was made more so by the Lewinsky business and the failed impeachment. Clinton staggered from the wreckage bloody and partly bowed. Gore was concerned not to be tainted by association, though his own personal life appeared impeccable. As a result he never laid full claim to his share of the Clinton legacy. His campaign team were divided over how, if at all, to make use of Clinton. This offended the Clintonistas. They tore their hair out at what they saw as the ineptitude of Al Gore's campaign.

Nor, incidentally, was Gore particularly close to Tony Blair. It was John Prescott who claimed a 'special' relationship with the Vice-President, forged in the negotiation of the ill-fated Kyoto Protocol on protecting the environment: an odd couple, it has to be said. I was struck how Gore was largely absent from the series of Clinton–Blair Third Way meetings. His people showed little interest in the project.

These weaknesses as good as neutralized Gore's in-built advantages over Bush. Once this happened, it meant that the election would be decided as much on perceptions of character, as on policies, promises and records. This played to Bush's strengths.

Bush was no natural orator. He has improved a lot since then; but in 2000 the more set-piece the occasion, the more leaden he tended to become. But he was good on the stump. He is an instinctive retail politician. He connects with Middle America. His campaign strategists made a virtue of necessity. They stripped his messages down to a series of simple, unchanging propositions: less tax, less government, returning integrity to the Presidency, a 'unifier not a divider'. This buttressed an image of affable constancy and plain speaking.

The Europeans scoffed at Bush's staccato utterances and mangling of vocabulary and syntax. It brought to mind their similar contempt for, and underestimation of, Ronald Reagan in 1980. Millions of Americans responded to Bush's simple, unadorned style. If he tripped over his words from time to time, Well, hell, I do so myself, said Middle America. There was more than a hint of Reagan about Bush. It worked again against John Kerry in 2004, despite a background of doubts about the Iraq war and policies where the Democratic option was often more popular. Character and values prevailed, reinforced by strong messages, both overt and subliminal, about decisiveness and fortitude that flowed from Bush's status as war leader.

Catherine and I had ringside seats at the political drama, sometimes literally. In the summer of 2000 we attended the two party conventions, finding ourselves temporary members of the Texan delegation at the Republican event in Philadelphia and, at the Democratic Convention in Los Angeles, part of a group of Illinois firemen and their wives.

In the old days, in the notorious smoke-filled rooms, the convention was the place where the deals were done to select the candidates for President and Vice-President. Nowadays, the party convention is a pre-packaged coronation, with the candidates already chosen. But conventions are stirring events, nonetheless: part political rally, part revivalist meeting, part pop concert. They are a networker's paradise, a hypermarket of politicians, political operators, and journalists. Every morning Catherine and I would cruise the corridors and sky-boxes of the great arenas in which the conventions were held, glad-handing, gossiping, and plucking political intelligence like ripe, low-hanging fruit.

Most weeks, through the spring and early summer of 2000, members of the Gore and Bush campaigns dropped by for lunch on the terrace overlooking the embassy gardens. I felt that they were happy to be on neutral ground – to have an hour or so's respite from the fiery furnace of electoral battle. They often wanted to unburden themselves: either to defend campaign tactics that looked to be going wrong, or to explain how they were going to outsmart the other side. Sometimes they even sought my advice!

For our part we wanted to keep close to those who we thought would play important roles in a Bush or Gore administration. In some cases this became inextricably entangled with real friendship. Condi Rice would drop by from time to time. Her equivalent on the Democratic side was Leon Fuerth, who would have been Gore's National Security Adviser. I had known him from the early days of the first Clinton administration in 1993. We saw a lot of him and his wife, Lynn. He could be rather severe and unbending; but at home, with his wise-cracking wife and irreverent daughters, it was another story. One of my abiding American memories is, with Catherine and my younger son, William, having Fourth of July dinner with the Fuerths and then lying on the beach of a nearby lake to watch the fireworks. It was a Norman Rockwell moment.

Colin Powell was another visitor to the house. He was always sceptical about belligerent notions for dealing with Saddam Hussein and the rationale for missile defences. With Rich Armitage, his deputy at the State Department, he was one of the very few senior members of the Bush administration who had experienced war at first hand. They had seen the horror of it all. Colin was ever the diplomat and loyal soldier. But Rich Armitage, one of the most impressive Americans I ever met, could not conceal his contempt for the bellicose civilians of the Pentagon, who had never seen combat.

Colin ran a charity called America's Promise. Its purpose was to help children pull themselves out of the ghetto by showing them what others had achieved. He sought to convince them that they too could succeed. For role models Colin drew on his enormous network of friends and contacts. Once a year he asked them to play host for a day to a couple of African-American children. One year he brought a small boy and girl to the embassy, shy and wide-eyed. They came to my office and then I showed them round the Great House. At the end of the visit Colin drove off with the children in one of his beloved old Volvos. Later he told me that what had most impressed the children were the red stair carpet in the grand entrance and the chandeliers in the ballroom, the like of which they had never seen before. At my suggestion he and Robin Cook, when Foreign Secretary, created an Anglo-American version of America's Promise, which provided for two British and two American youngsters to spend time in each other's countries.

As the American people waited in November and December 2000 to find out who would be their President, London was getting increasingly anxious. Gore was a relatively known quantity; Bush was not. The tension was getting to No. 10 too.

The Bush people had already set off one alarm. Shortly after dawn on 21 October, the anniversary of the Battle of Trafalgar and a few weeks before the election, I was sitting on the terrace in my dressing gown, with the usual mug of Twining's English Breakfast tea. I looked at the front page of the *New York Times* and shot bolt upright. In an interview Condi Rice appeared to say that a Bush administration would withdraw from the Balkans, where US troops were part of a NATO peacekeeping force which included the British. Bush felt that there should be a new division of labour in which the Balkans would be left to the Europeans.

I could hear the alarm bells ringing in London. The American presence was indispensable to the effectiveness of the NATO operation. If the US were to withdraw unilaterally and soon, the very integrity of NATO would be jeopardized. This sat awkwardly with the strong support for NATO which the Bush people repeatedly professed. If this were a harbinger of a Bush foreign policy, it was very worrying indeed.

I was about to hunt down Condi to find out what was going on when she called me. She had been misrepresented, she said. There was no question of precipitate, unilateral American withdrawal from the Balkans. Governor Bush would never leave America's allies in the lurch. I said that London would be relieved. Precipitate withdrawal would endanger everything we had achieved to bring peace to Bosnia. When we left, we should leave together, and only after full consultation within the Alliance and when the time was right.

No sooner had I put the phone down than a worried No. 10 came on the line in the shape of the Prime Minister's Foreign Policy Adviser, John Sawers. I cut him short.

'Condi's just called. She claims to have been misrepresented.' I went on to describe the rest of the conversation, which was reassuring as far as it went. 'Actually,' I continued, 'there's no smoke without fire. I think the Bushies really do want out from the Balkans. They are fed up that the Europeans can't handle it. But the last thing they need right now is to provoke a major crisis with their main European allies.'

In another conversation almost a year later, when she had become National Security Adviser, Condi confirmed that in an ideal world Bush wanted to get out of the Balkans. Peacekeeping was not what the American military were supposed to do. 'The 82nd Airborne is not trained to escort Serbian grandmothers across the road,' was her tart comment. Nor, indeed, Iraqi grandmothers.

This attitude was not just a Republican thing. It was widely held across Washington in both parties. The Americans were forever looking for gendarme-type forces which could take on peacekeeping and relieve the military of what they considered a burden unfit for warriors: Italian *carabinieri*, French CRS, Royal Ulster Constabulary and so on. In a conversation once with senior figures from the Clinton White House and Pentagon, I pointed out that these *gendarmeries* actually had a job to do at home in their own countries. Why on earth didn't the Americans train some military units in peacekeeping? I might as well have belched in church.

Rice and I had been saying to each other for some time that we needed to sit down and go through the full inventory of foreign policy issues. The Balkans embarrassment brought home the importance of doing this as soon as possible. We needed to find out where Bush and British foreign policies might clash. As far as I was concerned, we could not afford to await the outcome of the US presidential election, which, by December, was looking increasingly problematical. If Bush lost, so be it. If he won, it would be a timely investment. Here was a chance to influence Bush's foreign policy at source.

Condi and I agreed to have a private and confidential working breakfast on 8 December – so private and confidential that the excellent Carla Robbins of the *Wall Street Journal* knew about it in advance. Condi made plain that Governor Bush was aware of our meeting. I said that so was the Prime Minister and that I would be reflecting his personal views (I had been in close touch with John Sawers beforehand). Over fruit juice, scrambled eggs, bacon, tomato, black pudding, sausage, coffee and toast, we spent ninety minutes in the intimacy of the residence's small dining room, moving from one foreign policy issue to another.

We already knew quite a lot about Condi Rice's thinking. In an earlier contact with her in August 1999, when she was still Provost of California's Stanford University, she had emphasized that Bush would be an internationalist and free-trader; but a Bush foreign policy would be different from Clinton's.

Sometimes one felt in those early days that being the anti-Clinton was what animated the Bushies most. She was, she had said in the Stanford conversation, troubled by Clinton's promiscuous use of American force. The US military could not be the world's emergency service. She was worried by the concept of humanitarian intervention. Most humanitarian crises were at heart political and should above all be tackled politically. Clinton, she had claimed, had also got too involved in Russian domestic politics: too hooked to a narrow group of politicians, including Yeltsin. Bush would not want to do that. He would be tougher. If the Russians remained hostile to the development of defences against missile attack, too bad. America would test and deploy systems anyway. They had to be placed in a new and broader concept of deterrence, one which rested not only on the aggressor's fear of catastrophic retaliation, but also on his fear that his attack would fail. This, she had asserted, was actually in the Russian interest. It would help deter rogue states like Iraq and North Korea, both of which were in the business of developing missile technology and nuclear weapons. A Bush administration would seek to isolate them further. The policy focus for Iraq had to be weapons of mass destruction and getting the UN inspectors back as soon as possible.

A little later, at the beginning of 2000 in the magazine *Foreign Affairs*, Rice set out more formally the principles of a Bush foreign policy. She portrayed Iraq, Iran and North Korea as a triumvirate of dangerous rogue states. (Bush would later transform them into the Axis of Evil.) She exalted the national interest and the exercise of US power. She rejected the primacy of international community and humanitarian interests. 'America's pursuit of the national interest will create conditions that promote freedom, markets and peace ... multilateral agreements and institutions should not be ends in themselves ... the United States has a special role in the world ... American values are universal.'

This too was a repudiation of Clinton and his allegedly 'mushy' multilateralism. It was also, I noted with some alarm, on a collision course with some of Tony Blair's cherished notions about international community and humanitarian intervention. Nor did she and we seem to be on the same page about handling Russia.

At the start of our breakfast on Friday, 8 December 2000, I said that, unlike some Europeans, the Prime Minister did not think that George W. Bush was an isolationist. There was no more pro-American state in the European Union than Britain. We regarded our engagement in Europe and alliance with the United States as mutually reinforcing commitments. Condi said that she warmly welcomed this. It would be a great comfort to the Bush administration. She was glad the British did not consider Bush an isolationist. He believed strongly in international engagement. But he would be a different President from either Clinton or his father.

There goes that contrast with his father again, I thought to myself.

A similar breakfast today would have a very different set of issues and priorities. Then it was how long NATO should stay in the

Balkans; how Europe's military effectiveness could be strengthened without aiding and abetting the French ambition to weaken NATO; how to handle Putin, whose reflexive authoritarianism was already apparent; and how to reconcile Bush's determination to deploy defences against ballistic missiles without provoking a crisis with Russia and inside NATO. I recall no mention of international terrorism. The Middle East and Iraq were marked as subjects for later discussion between British and American experts. Condi said that Bush had no appetite to get as deeply involved as Clinton in the dispute between the Israelis and Palestinians.

She also hoped that we would have 'fixed' Northern Ireland by the time Bush was inaugurated. Again, there was little appetite to get as deeply involved in the affairs of Ulster as had Clinton. I doubted that anything would be fixed. From time to time we might well have to come to a Bush administration for a little help. We had made huge progress. But the main problem remained: to get the IRA to abandon violence for good and to honour its commitment to 'put weapons beyond use' (a euphemism as tortured as 'decommissioning') in a way that gave real confidence to the Protestant community. Of all the subjects we discussed, this was the only one where I would have said exactly the same thing in 2005 as I did in 2000. Bush later pledged to Blair that he would do what he could to help us in Northern Ireland. He has been as good as his word.

As Condoleezza Rice and I parted, we concluded that there had been no areas of obvious disgreement. But there were issues that were going to need careful handling and much further discussion, if they were not to become problems between us. We agreed that there should be contact as soon as possible between the Bush team and No. 10. As to a meeting between Bush and Blair, this might be pencilled in for March. The Prime Minister should be among the first, if not the first, to visit a President Bush.

All this was conditional on Bush winning the struggle for Florida. Later that day, the Florida Supreme Court ruled in Al Gore's favour by permitting additional recounts of the vote by hand. I wondered whether my conversation with Condi had been a waste of breath; but, of course, the US Supreme Court trumped its Florida colleagues and Bush became the forty-third President.

In May of 2000 Tony Blair had sent Bush a message of congratulation on securing the Republican nomination. He had said that if Bush was able to visit London, he would be delighted to see him. Blair encouraged Bush and his people to keep in close touch with me. The Prime Minister sent a further warm congratulatory message in December once Bush's victory was clear. It spoke of the special relationship, of common interests and shared values. The Prime Minister said how much he was looking forward to working with the new President. Downing Street were itching to get to grips with Bush. So was Robin Cook with Colin Powell. Cook and Powell had met in London earlier in the year and had got on surprisingly well.

Just before Christmas No. 10 asked me to try to bring forward the Prime Minister's visit to February instead of March. They wanted the visit to take place in the Parliamentary recess, which began on 18 February. That would be only a month after the President's Inauguration, a tall order at the best of times. Worse still, because of the Florida impasse, the Bush people had already lost five weeks of valuable preparation before taking the reins of power. February would be a tough month for them.

As much as No. 10, I wanted Tony Blair to be the first European leader to be invited to meet the new President. The great French diplomat, Talleyrand, used to urge *'pas trop de zèle'* on his profession. I had no qualms about ignoring the mighty Talleyrand and being extremely zealous to ensure my country got in first. It was sheer competitive spirit.

I got Downing Street's message as I was about to board a train with Catherine and my younger son, William, to go to New York to do some Christmas shopping. I made contact with Condi on my cellphone from the gloomy lobby of an ill-chosen and uncomfortable hotel in midtown Manhattan. I argued the case for a February visit. She listened but was noncommittal. A visit before March would be difficult. But she did not say no. She would consult the President and his chief of staff, Andy Card.

No. 10 had so little direct feel for a Republican administration that they began to get nervous about sending the Prime Minister in 'cold' to meet George W. Bush. Jonathan Powell, Blair's chief of staff, and John Sawers, his foreign policy adviser, proposed coming to Washington in the New Year to take the temperature of the administration-in-waiting. It was never clear to me whether this was a joint initiative; or a case of one of them deciding to come to Washington and the other, not wishing to be upstaged, jumping on the bandwagon.

Either way, I thought it a good idea – if we could persuade the Bush *capi* to see the No. 10 emissaries at this intensely busy period just before the Inauguration. Matthew Rycroft and I set to work.

The response from the Bush people exceeded our wildest ambition. Nothing underlined more the importance of early cultivation of a presidential candidate and his staff. By the time Powell and Sawers arrived, on 14 January 2001, we had a programme arranged which knocked their socks off. In the next forty-eight hours they would meet Dick Cheney, Colin Powell, Condoleezza Rice and her deputy-to-be Steve Hadley, Karl Rove, Andy Card, Card's two deputies Josh Bolten and Clay Johnson, Bob Zoellick (about to be appointed US Trade Representative) and a bunch of other Bushmen and women. Some of the meetings took place in the nondescript campaign headquarters in downtown Washington, others at the embassy.

Jonathan Powell and John Sawers returned to London with the pungent smells of the new team in their nostrils. They learned a lot about the new administration, its senior personalities, its view of Britain, and how it was going to organize itself. For a start, it was not going to be an administration for the faint-hearted. It was going to have a tough, hard-nosed approach to the American national interest. The foreign policy team of Cheney, Powell, Rice and Rumsfeld looked stronger and more experienced than anything we had seen since 1989 and the presidency of Bush's father. Cheney's enormous influence, possibly unique in the history of America Vice-Presidents, was already apparent. If anything, the Beasts were too Big and too many. Even then people were speculating about Powell's relations with Cheney and Rumsfeld, and whether Rice would be strong enough to control the jostling between them.

During the visit, Jonathan Powell spent a lot of energy telling all and sundry that we wanted as good a relationship with Bush as we had had with Clinton. He could have saved his breath. It was already an administration with a deep fund of goodwill towards Britain. 'The UK is our single most important bilateral relationship,' said Condi Rice. 'The UK is our closest friend,' said Andy Card. Colin Powell was no less fulsome, invoking yet again the special relationship. Some of this was telling us what we wanted to hear. A lot of it was heartfelt. After all the British had fought the first Gulf War with Cheney (then Secretary for Defense) and Powell (then Chairman of the Joint Chiefs of Staff) back in 1991.

But, goodwill, though always nice to receive, was not the main point. The challenge was, as ever, to turn it into influence and the effective defence of British national interests.

Unsurprisingly, in the foreign policy discussions with Sawers and Jonathan Powell, the issues were little different from those Rice and I had debated five weeks previously. But some new points emerged. Bush would take no decisions on developing missile defences that would be awkward for the British government before our elections planned later that year. That was a relief to us all. The last thing Tony Blair wanted was an early request from the Bush administration to use US bases and radar sites in Britain for his 'Son of Star Wars' project. There was markedly more American scepticism about Blair's initiative with the French to strengthen Europe's defence capability. The Bush people feared that it would both weaken NATO and in the end do little to sharpen Europe's military teeth (and so it has turned out).

On Iraq the focus was on 're-energizing' sanctions and making them 'smarter' – that is, making it harder for Saddam to smuggle out oil and to smuggle in components for chemical, biological and nuclear weapons. The Americans wanted the removal of Saddam – regime change – because it was official American policy and had been so since 1998 and Clinton's second administration; but discussion of this moved no further than a debate on the effectiveness of the Iraqi opposition, where the Americans were more optimistic than we.

A week or so after the Powell–Sawers visit, just after Bush's Inauguration, Condi called me to say that after all the President would like the Prime Minister to visit Camp David over 22–4 February. Blair would be the first European leader to receive such an invitation, though he had been pipped by the Mexican President, Vicente Fox, for the world title! President Chirac of France had also met Bush before Blair, but only because he happened to be in Washington for other reasons. Robin Cook was the first European foreign minister to pay an official visit to Washington to meet Secretary of State Colin Powell, shortly before the Prime Minister's own visit.

Twenty-four hours before Blair arrived I sent five diplomatic cables to help him prepare. Three of them dealt with policy issues, one gave an assessment of Bush's first month in office, and one was about Bush himself. I said that Bush was affable and easy-going most of the time, but he had his mother's steel. He was quick-witted, self-assured, a fast learner, a natural-born politician who had earned Bill Clinton's admiration. It would be a huge mistake to underestimate him. Bush would seek in international relations what had worked for him well as Governor of Texas: a network of personal relationships built on loyalty and mutual trust.

An easy, informal, results-oriented approach would be the key to the success of the Camp David meeting. How do you get from A to B? Bush, a natural conservative, was underpinned by strong and simple values: God, love of country, family. He admired Churchill. He did not like ceremony. He was a joker and a mimic. He gave people nicknames. He had not touched alcohol in fifteen years, though, by all accounts, including his own, he had been a heavy drinker before. He jogged most days. He was early to bed, early to rise. His presidential style was to pick good people, delegate, demand their absolute loyalty, hear their views, take a decision, and stick to it. His unassuming wife, Laura, was his tower of strength.

Over to you, Tony. We had done our job at the embassy. The baton had been passed. Now it was up to Blair, Cook and the rest of them to run with it.

19

Toothpaste

'I don't expect that they are looking forward to this any more than we are,' said Cherie Blair ominously, as she looked out of the helicopter window.

The Prime Minister said nothing. A pained expression fleetingly crossed his face.

Jesus Christ, I thought to myself as we prepared to get off the helicopter, this is going to be a disaster.

It was a crisp February morning in 2001: the twenty-second, to be exact, George Washington's birthday and my own. My predecessor, John Kerr, had also been born on 22 February. I used to tell people with as straight a face as I could muster that you could not be British ambassador to the United States unless you shared the birthday of the founder of the republic. A few believed me. Tony Blair had brought a birthday card from London, which he was supposed to give me over breakfast at the embassy. Alastair Campbell had issued him a reminder over the scrambled eggs and bacon by saying very loudly and slowly, 'Happy birthday, Chris!' But Blair was too distracted. My staff found the card afterwards among the debris of toast and marmalade.

A couple of large, dark-green Sikorsky helicopters of the presidential fleet had carried the Blairs, the No. 10 team and me north from Washington to Camp David in the Catoctin Mountains of Maryland. Blair was about to meet Bush for the first time. I had fluttering sensations in the stomach.

Camp David is the official presidential retreat, a bucolic encampment of plainly furnished log cabins set in thick woods, through which the Secret Service prowl like brown bears. It is only a forty-five-minute helicopter ride from the nation's capital. It is the place where the President can repair to escape the pressures of Washington. It is a mark of friendship or importance for a foreign leader to be invited to spend the weekend there.

To get away from it all, Bush prefers his ranch in Crawford, Texas. Just before the Blairs' visit he told me that, had renovation work on the ranch been complete, he would have invited them to the ranch. This was to happen just over a year later. An invitation to Crawford has become the ultimate symbol of a close relationship with the President of the United States.

There was a high degree of nervousness in the No. 10 team. They had neither wanted nor expected Bush to win. Others have recorded that, after visits to Washington in 2000, despite the Embassy's cautions, both Jonathan Powell and David Miliband (then a Blair adviser and now a cabinet minister) had returned to London with confident predictions of a Gore victory.

The well-connected American commentator Irwin Stelzer had also stoked No. 10's anxieties with an article in *The Times* of London, which appeared in January 2001 just before Bush's inauguration. Stelzer is a Republican who represents Rupert Murdoch in Washington. With a home in London as well as Washington, he had got to know Blair well and, as Murdoch's man, had easy access to No. 10. His article criticized Blair for being unprepared for a Bush victory. It urged him not to underestimate the new President. He was good enough to compliment the embassy on our contacts with the Republicans. If Blair wanted a good relationship with the new administration, said Stelzer, it had better be careful about cosying up to the French.

Irwin and his wife Cita became our firm friends and we still see them regularly. They invited us to dinner ten days before Tony Blair was due to arrive for his first meeting with George W. My report of this occasion further fanned Downing Street's worries. Catherine and I found ourselves in the company of Rupert Murdoch and salient members of the Republican Right. These included Richard Perle, the 'Prince of Darkness', a hawk who had been one of Bush's foreign policy advisers during the campaign. He then became chairman of a body called the Defense Advisory Board, whose job was to advise the Pentagon. He was a long-standing advocate of invading Iraq. Other guests included David Frum, a Bush speechwriter, who was to be a major contributor to the 'Axis of Evil' speech; and Larry Lindsey, just appointed Bush's chief economic adviser.

As frequently happened at American dinners, I was asked to sing for my supper. I was pressed to justify Britain's enthusiasm, inexplicable to this audience, for closer defence cooperation in Europe and, in particular, with France. There had recently been a European Council at Nice in which further decisions had been taken on European defence cooperation.

For the Republican Right Britain could commit no greater heresy. Even the Clinton administration had been suspicious of what Blair was up to with the French. In October 1999 I had sent a strong warning to No. 10 that Blair's initiative to strengthen European defence capabilities, launched with France, risked being seen in Washington as a French trap to break up NATO and detach Europe from America. In reality Blair wanted the opposite: to reinforce NATO by strengthening the military capacity of its European members. But the initiative had been poorly presented to the Americans by London. It had been appropriated by the Europhile enthusiasts of the Foreign Office, who were careless of American sensitivities. This was pretty dumb, given the UK's dependence on America for defence equipment and contracts. From then on I found it an uphill struggle to place our initiative in the context which Blair had intended.

I withstood a full-frontal assault from all concerned against our alleged sell-out to the French. A low rumbling sound issued from Murdoch, in which the word 'appeasement' could be identified. This was, I countered, an acute example of the mutual assured schizophrenia that had always afflicted transatlantic relations. On the American side this would take the form of complaining that the Europeans had failed to assume their rightful share of the military burden; and then complaining when we tried to do something about it. The equal and opposite phenomenon on the European side was to complain that America was not taking the lead, for example in breaking the deadlock between Israel and the Palestinians; and to complain when it did, for example in bringing Saddam Hussein to heel. As to the French, the exaggeration of their influence was daft.

This was all good sport – 'blood sport', muttered someone at the table – which managed to stay on the right side of rational. But then debate turned to political correctness and its allegedly growing grasp on British life. I felt constrained to point out that, like hamburgers, political correctness had been an American import. David Frum argued that America's national cohesion was built on core values inherited from Britain. Now we were allowing ourselves to be corrupted by political correctness and socialist Europe. We were, he said, drifting away from our traditional transatlantic loyalties – look at the threat to fox-hunting, for Pete's sake!

Some of this was barking mad. But lurking in there was a serious point. How could even Tony Blair, the most gifted performer of his generation in the circus of British politics, ride the American and European horses at the same time, without falling between two saddles?

The real answer was: with difficulty. At the Stelzer dinner I fell back on the holy mantra of British foreign policy. There was no choice to be made between Britain's European and Atlantic vocations. If we were strong and influential in Europe, this would strengthen our hand in the US. If we were close to the US, this would redound to our benefit in Europe.

'No, no!' the cry went up around the table, in an unconscious echo of General de Gaulle. 'Britain must choose.' To this audience of Manicheans I sounded feeble and temporizing, a typical product of the Foreign Office. Murdoch was rumbling away.

Catherine provided powerful flanking fire in support of my beleaguered position. She had a secret weapon. Yes, she was of French blood. But she was also ferociously Eurosceptic. This blew everyone's fuse. She made hay with Richard Perle's Francophobia, which appeared no bar to extensive sojourns in France to satisfy his gourmet's palate.

In due course the debate blew itself out. Attention turned to Larry Lindsey. Fuelled by an excellent dinner and some of the best claret in Washington, I happily took part in an unsparing examination of Larry's economic philosophy.

For some in London the realization that there had been regime change in Washington took an unconscionable time to sink in. At the start of Blair's visit I had to endure the finger-wagging self-importance of one of No. 10's minor functionaries, an odious species that seemed to infest the Blair entourage. She wanted me to know that Bush's victory had gone down very badly in Downing Street. Cherie was so upset. After all, hadn't Al Gore really won?

'Get over it,' I said. 'Bush is President and that's that.'

I prayed that Blair himself had not been infected by this childishness. Whatever No. 10 had wished for in private it had been good at maintaining strict public neutrality during the election campaign. It would be rank folly to spoil it all now. I need not have worried. Blair was too pragmatic and aware of the importance of the United States to let this happen. After all, he had ringing in his ears Clinton's advice to 'hug them close', as Peter Riddell says in his book of the same name.

I had done what I could to prepare the Prime Minister for this moment. I had returned to London at the end of 2000 to brief Blair. On the eve of his arrival I sent him further advice on how to approach the President and Vice-President. I drew pen portraits of both of them. I stressed that the Bush style would be informal, no frills, practical, direct. Chirac's grandiloquent, lecturing style was anathema to Bush, as Colin Powell once told me. The White House had taken a deliberate decision to open their European account with Britain. It was the Prime Minister's challenge to show that they had made the right judgement. I warned that there was a risk and an opportunity for us. 'The risk is to be seen as American bag-carriers, a story which the British press is already starting to write. The opportunity is to be able to influence American policy before it has formed.'

In December 2000, on the eve of Bill Clinton's farewell visit to London, Karl Rove came round for a drink at the embassy. I took the bull by the horns: 'Is Tony Blair's close relationship with Clinton going to be a problem for you? If so, the sooner we know, the better.'

'Absolutely not,' said Karl. Bush recognized the importance of close relationships. It was always good for Britain and America to be close. Bush hoped to establish a close relationship with the Prime Minister 'on its own merits'.

I took a cross-bearing separately with Condi Rice. She gave an almost identical answer.

I had reported these conversations, and the reassurance they conveyed, to London. But on the morning of 22 February, the confidence of Blair and his team took a knock from a meeting with Dick Cheney, just before we set off for Camp David. The Vice-President is not enormously demonstrative at the best of moments, especially when he meets someone for the first time. After that, if he likes you, he displays a kind of avuncular amiability. Catherine always found him good company at dinner. I thought that the meeting had been fine for a first outing. So did Scooter Libby, Cheney's chief of staff. True, it had a certain Soviet woodenness to it; and some of the No. 10 team were chagrined that, unlike so many others, the Veep (as the Vice-President is sometimes known) did not seem to have been instantly felled by the Prime Minister's fabled charm.

As the helicopter dropped to the pad at Camp David, we looked out of the window to see George and Laura Bush waiting to greet us. It was this that had prompted Cherie's sour remark.

With a minimum of ceremony we were whisked away in a fleet of golf buggies to our cabins, where we changed out of our suits for lunch. White House instructions were to be informal, but not too informal: chinos, but no jeans. Blair put on a pair of ball-crushingly tight dark-blue corduroys. I was later told that his wardrobe for the weekend had been the result of intensive debate within No. 10. If true, it was not wholly successful. Bush and Blair had a photo call later in the day, as they went for a walk in the woods. Bush looked pretty relaxed in what one assumed were his usual weekend clothes. By contrast, Blair looked uncomfortable, his efforts to appear similarly insouciant undermined by the inability to get his hands fully into pockets that appeared glued to the groin.

In my experience prime ministers have an unhappy relationship with clothes. For Tony Blair there was to be another awkward trouser moment a year later at the President's ranch in Texas. When I travelled with John Major to Moscow in 1994, the burning issue was his head and what to put on it. Major had, on arrival at the airport, to inspect a Russian guard of honour. We had been told that it was too chilly to do this without a hat. A large cardboard box full of fur hats in different styles was on board. Major tried them all and liked none of them. In desperation, I offered him my own hat, a robust, no-nonsense job, purchased in Moscow years before and a classic example of the Soviet style of men's winter millinery. He took it, wore it and was ridiculed in the British press. Unhappy comparisons were drawn with the aristocratic elegance of Harold Macmillan's fur hat on a visit to Moscow in 1959. Where did he get that hat? asked the Lobby. I never had the nerve to reveal that the hat was mine.

Laura Bush took Cherie off for lunch. The Prime Minister and the President were to have a separate, working lunch with their main advisers. This took place in one of the largest lodges, equipped with a conference room, dining room, large drawing room and the President's study. The style was anything but luxurious. It was comfortable, homely and just a little faded. I had the feeling that not a great deal had changed since President Eisenhower.

At the table, Bush was flanked by Colin Powell, the Secretary of State, and Condi Rice, the National Security Adviser. Also present were Andy Card, Bush's chief of staff; Condi's deputy, Steve Hadley; and Dan Fried, a senior member of the National Security Council. Blair had with him Jonathan Powell, Alastair Campbell, John Sawers (his foreign affairs adviser seconded from the Foreign Office) and me. To help take the record of the discussions I had brought Matthew Rycroft from my staff at the embassy. Matthew went on to become a member of the No. 10 foreign policy team and is now ambassador in Bosnia.

Matthew's presence gave rise to unpleasant and bizarre difficulties with some of the No. 10 staff. These came to plague the embassy's relations with Downing Street. My sources told me that this had enraged a junior member of the No. 10 logistics team. She apparently held me responsible for her expulsion from the inner circle where she thought, absurdly, that she, not Matthew, belonged. This was to have consequences, which in due course came to the attention of the President and First Lady.

The two teams faced each other across the table. The black waiters, old retainers who had been at Camp David for goodness knows how long, began to pour iced tea and water. This, I thought to myself, is the moment of truth.

Bush said: 'Welcome to Camp David, Tony – may I call you Tony? – it's great to have you here.'

Blair replied: 'Thanks, George – may I call you George? – it's great to be here.' And off they went.

I heard the rapid cracking of ice. Both were smiling, pretty laid back. I heaved a sigh of relief. You know immediately if the chemistry is going to work. This was going to work.

Without further ado, Blair and Bush got down to business. They agreed to begin with the Middle East. This, said Bush, would suit Colin Powell, who had to leave Camp David that afternoon. Bush then invited Powell to speak.

The chemistry on the American side of the table was fascinating. From the outset there was no doubting the President's authority or grasp on the proceedings. So much for what *Le Monde* had called the 'cretinization' of American foreign policy. Without a note in front of him, Bush chaired the meeting and led discussion with self-confidence and aplomb. There was no sign of the verbal stumbles that plagued his public speaking. He had obviously done a lot of homework on foreign policy; but, unlike several politicians I have known, he did not feel the need to dominate the conversation all the time. He was perfectly happy to let Powell do the talking on the Middle East; but I could see that there was no question of his being overawed by his illustrious Secretary of State. The deference shown to the President by his most senior advisers was in some contrast to the free-and-easy style of Blair and his entourage. Bush and Powell were a little stiff and formal with each other. Bush and Rice had an obviously more familiar relationship, which occasionally became teasing and playful. But I sensed that Condi had a clear red line in her head which she knew she would cross at her peril. Bush was the boss.

The Middle East discussion was dominated by the conflict between Israel and the Arabs. On Iraq the concern was to tighten sanctions, close down the smuggling of Iraqi oil and make the oil-for-food programme work better. That remained the British/American agenda for Iraq until 9/11.

Bush peppered Blair with questions on international issues, especially Russia, which was to become the leitmotiv of US foreign policy before 9/11. Blair clearly found this flattering. He had taken something of a gamble in cultivating Vladimir Putin very early on before he was elected President of Russia. By 2001 Blair had probably had more meetings with Putin than any Western leader. He had become a bit of an expert on Putin. Blair told Bush that the advent of Putin marked an historic opportunity to bind Russia to the West and to bury for good the old hostilities of the Cold War. Bush and Rice, an old Soviet expert, were interested. Bush thought Putin 'one cold dude'. That was a view which would change later in the year.

Today, Blair's historic opportunity, even if it existed, seems to have slipped through his and everyone else's fingers. Putin's priorities after the collapse of communism have been to restore the authority of the state and Russia's position in the world. Relations with the West matter to the Kremlin only in so far as they serve these strategic goals. The historic opportunity, as No. 10 saw it, for implanting democracy and Western values in Russia was for many Russians a moment of deep national humiliation.

But in any case, other than public exhortation there seemed to be no plan for turning this so-called opportunity into reality. From time to time records of meetings and conversations between Blair and Putin would pass across my desk in Washington. They were notably thin in content, with Putin apparently doing most of the talking. It had the look of a trophy relationship.

The White House had purposely allowed for a lot of 'face-time' between Bush, Blair and their wives. Laura and Cherie spent most of the afternoon together. After lunch, Bush and Blair did their walk in the woods, followed by the press conference. Then we all assembled for drinks before dinner. Good spirits abounded. Cherie looked happier. Laura Bush, unpretentious and humorous, is impossible to dislike. The unspoken thought was that a first, and crucial, hurdle had been jumped successfully. Relief added to the levity of this completely casual occasion. One group of us sprawled on chairs with the President. Bush was drinking a non-alcoholic beer from the bottle. I asked him about the rigours of campaigning. Didn't it drive him crazy to have to make the same speech several times a day, day-in, day-out? He explained the importance of always being on message, the need for discipline – you did what you had to do. The conversation brought home how much experience Bush had had as a campaigner, both nationally and at the state level. I looked up and saw, in the centre of a group, Tony Blair and Condi in animated conversation.

In the evening the Blairs and Bushes dined alone. The advisers from both sides ate together. Jonathan Powell and Alastair Campbell were still sniffing around the Bush people like wary dogs. They had got so used to dealing with Democrats. Here was a new and unfamiliar political animal. Conversation did not always flow quite as easily as it should have done.

Towards the end of dinner word was brought that we were invited to see a film with the Bushes and Blairs. This was a true mark of hospitality. It was already known that Bush liked to go to bed early. The movie would take him way past his bedtime.

The film was the comedy hit *Meet the Parents* with Ben Stiller and Robert de Niro. We watched it from the comfort of armchairs and sofas in the Camp David cinema. I found it very funny. So did Bush. We laughed at the same places. This bothered me a bit. I sounded like an obsequious courtier. When it was revealed that the character played by Stiller was called Gay Focker, the President split his sides. Condi slept through it all.

The next morning, after a convivial brunch, made more so by the ebullient presence of George Tenet, the Director of National Security (he had come to give the President his daily intelligence brief), the British team left for Washington. There was a feeling all round that this was a visit that had gone very well. I gave the President a copy of the penultimate draft of the Atlantic Charter, with Churchill's manuscript amendments.

The previous afternoon Blair and Bush had given a press conference which did not really do justice to the weekend. Neither looked entirely comfortable. There was a stilted quality to their performance. Bush is now highly practised; but he has never liked press conferences, and it showed. At one point Bush was asked what he had in common with Blair. There was a pause, which was a shade too long to be comfortable. Then Bush said that he and the Prime Minister shared the same toothpaste. A *frisson* passed through the British press party (and, it looked to me, through Blair as well). What could this mean? Was the 'special relationship' now so special that the American President and the British Prime Minister shared the same bathroom or, God forbid, slept together?

Much journalistic ink and hot air were expended on divining the riddle of the toothpaste. As usual, the answer was banal and straightforward. All the Camp David log cabins were furnished with tubes of Colgate toothpaste. Bush has a tendency to be flippant in public. This was a quip which misfired a little. That did not stop Colgate from using it in their advertising. Catherine has hung a copy of the advertisement in our bathroom.

As Condi Rice had said to me before the visit, bonding would be as important to the President as business. To keep that balance Condi and I agreed that there should be a short joint statement to issue from the meeting. This would be largely prepared in advance and would deal with the key issues of substance. It would also discourage the press and others from trying to pick apart what the two men said at the press conference. John Sawers and she negotiated the final draft of the text at Camp David itself.

There were two issues which dominated and which both sides wanted to neutralize as irritants in the relationship. The first was the one that had given me such grief at Irwin Stelzer's dinner: European plans to enhance defence capabilities. The second – neuralgic for the British and continental Europeans – was American plans to create missile defences and to withdraw from the Anti-Ballistic Missile Treaty, one of the cornerstones of the old US–Soviet *détente* policy of the Cold War years. Condi agreed with me that there was a symmetry between the issues, that is, an implicit deal to be had. We wanted the Americans to support European plans on certain conditions; and the US wanted us to do the same on missile defences, again on certain conditions. And that is what happened. The bargain was struck in the joint statement.

The visit ended on a note of farce. The returning helicopters carrying the British team touched down at Andrews Air Force Base, where the Blairs' Concorde awaited them. The VIPs and the red carpet were all in place for the brief farewell ceremony. Suddenly, the cry went up: Cherie's hairdresser is missing! He had been left behind at Camp David. A helicopter brought him post-haste to Andrews as the rest of us kicked our heels.

In my report to London the next day, I said, 'Mission accomplished.' We had opened our account with the new administration and opened it well. The way was now clear for British–American cooperation based on a close personal relationship between Prime Minister and President.

As I signed off the cable, I reflected on the long and winding road that had ended so satisfactorily in Britain's occupying pole position with Bush and his team. For a start, it had been the closest of close-run things that it was Bush on the other side of the table, and not Al Gore.

20

Ten Days that Shook the World

Washington

'I met Mr Bin Laden this morning,' said John Major. It was 11 September 2001; we were having lunch on the residence terrace in the shade of the great columns of the portico. That morning, four aircraft, seized by terrorists, had crashed into the World Trade Center, the Pentagon, and the Pennsylvania countryside. The loss of life would run into thousands. America had experienced nothing like it since the Japanese attack on Pearl Harbor in 1941.

Catherine and I had just returned from our summer break. The political season in Washington officially starts after Labor Day, which falls on the first Monday in September. We were always tempted to take our holiday in the early autumn, when the crowds had left the mountains and beaches; but I hated to be away when the politicians and government returned in force to the nation's capital.

We were threatened with a visit from John Prescott, the Deputy Prime Minister. I sent a report to London, mainly for Prescott's benefit, which summarized the political situation as I saw it. I despatched it on the evening of 10 September.

I said that Bush's honeymoon was over. His approval ratings were down. The economy was anaemic, with tax revenues falling and unemployment rising. The politics of the economy were starting to look toxic. The White House was about to embark on its annual trial of strength with Congress: the negotiation of the budget, a protracted and byzantine business at the best of times. I had extensively trawled my contacts since returning from leave. I told London that the Republicans were starting to get rattled. The Democrats were rather looking forward to the budget battle. Clinton had been a master of the game. He usually outmanoeuvred Congress. They hoped Bush would suffer by comparison.

The administration had lost momentum. Three of its members came in for particular criticism: Paul O'Neill at the Treasury, Don Rumsfeld at Defense, and Colin Powell at State. Many thought that O'Neill and Rumsfeld would be the Cabinet's first casualties. O'Neill in the event was. He recorded his unhappy experience in a bitter book. Rumsfeld was under fire for his supposed lack of grip in completing a radical review of defence policy. At the beginning of September Powell was on the front cover of *Time* magazine, over a story suggesting that he had not lived up to expectations. There was also, I said, muttering about Bush himself. Typical was a remark from a Republican senator, who said to me that Bush was still not the commanding national figure he needed to be.

The shelf life of my report proved to be only a few hours. The events of 9/11 blew it to smithereens. Osama Bin Laden transformed American politics and radically refashioned Bush's presidency. Al Qaeda did for Bush what the Argentine invasion of the Falklands had done for Margaret Thatcher: turned him into a commanding national figure and rescued his government from loss of purpose and momentum.

Since their first meeting at Camp David the previous February, Blair and Bush had been given several opportunities to get to know each other better. These were at a series of international meetings in the summer of 2001: a summit between the European Union and the US, a summit of NATO leaders, and a conference of the so-called G7/8, comprising the seven advanced industrial countries plus, for political reasons, Russia.

Just before the last, which was to take place in Genoa, I presented the Jacob Epstein bust of Winston Churchill to the President at a short ceremony in the Oval Office. I asked Bush beforehand how he was feeling about going to the Genoa meeting. His reply was trenchant and typical. He was not looking forward to being locked in a meeting room for several hours, listening to 'bullshit' and surrounded by several thousand demonstrators. Having endured many of these windy, hot-air fests myself, I felt the President's pain.

Bush had already acquired from his first EU–US summit in Sweden a pronounced aversion to European politicians *en masse*. He had resented being lectured at Gothenburg on the environment and the merits of the Kyoto agreement. At some point in the summer

Condi Rice remarked to me that Bush was much happier in the company of Latin-Americans than Europeans. A later summit with the EU in Washington, at which, according to a friend in the White House, Bush had been lectured by Chris Patten, then an EU Commissioner, was an unmitigated disaster.

It was after the G8 meeting in Genoa that Bush and Rice had their Pauline conversion about Putin. They met up with him in Slovenia. Afterwards, Bush said that he had looked into Putin's soul and decided that this was a man he could work with. There was an echo here of Margaret Thatcher's reaction almost twenty years previously on first meeting Mikhail Gorbachev. This dissipated much of the earlier Bush/Rice suspicion of Russia, to which Tony Blair had been exposed at Camp David. In a conversation that summer, as we were having lunch after a game of tennis, Condi agreed with Catherine that Putin was an attractive man who walked 'like an athlete'.

In July, on their way to Genoa, the Bushes spent the night with the Blairs at Chequers, the Prime Minister's official residence in the Buckinghamshire countryside. I returned to London for the visit. The Queen gave a small lunch for the Bushes and their party at Buckingham Palace, to which I was invited. It was lively and enjoyable. I felt that I was in the presence of two tribes, so different that it might have been Martians and Earthmen meeting for the first time. The Bushes were accompanied by Condi Rice, Andy Card, Karen Hughes and Karl Rove. There was also the brand-new American ambassador, Will Farish, to whose stud farm in Kentucky the Queen was apparently a regular visitor. As ambassador he proved as agreeable as he was invisible.

Over lunch I observed a lady-in-waiting and Karl Rove amiably hunting for each other's wavelengths. The Duke of Edinburgh was in animated conversation with Condi. She charmed everyone by her unconcealed pleasure at being at the Palace. Liz Symons, the Foreign Office Minister of State, sat on one side of the President like a teenager in the presence of Brad Pitt.

Later that day the Bushes left for Chequers by helicopter. There were to be talks in the afternoon, followed by a private dinner just for the Blairs and Bushes. Rumour has it that Cherie Blair took the opportunity to berate the President over his support for capital punishment. If true, at some later point Bush received the other barrel of Cherie's shotgun. He told me just before I left Washington that Cherie had once had a go at him for America's rejection of the International Criminal Court.

I arrived at Chequers just before the Bushes. I found an anxious Blair with Sawers and Powell. He appeared to express relief at my arrival.

'Where have the Americans got to on missile defences? And what do I say?' Blair asked me urgently about the top issue of the moment. I was baffled. Twenty-four hours previously I had sent No. 10 the latest in a series of reports on just these questions. Why do I bother? I thought to myself.

The answer, incidentally, was that the administration was in a mess. It had still not worked out how to reconcile its twin ambitions of a new 'strategic partnership' with Russia and the creation of defences against ballistic missile attack, to the latter of which the Russians were vehemently opposed. A few days earlier I had put the question to Bush at the Churchill bust ceremony. He was blithely confident. There would be a deal with Putin before the year was out: 'Betcha, Ambassador.'

As I began to speak, we heard the clatter of helicopter rotors. Blair rushed out of the room to find Cherie and meet the Bushes. I never did get to finish my briefing.

That evening I went with the White House and No. 10 teams to a grand local hotel for dinner, leaving the Blairs and Bushes at Chequers. It was another friendly meal, with plenty of political war stories from both sides. It was also an important occasion. David Manning, now ambassador to the United States, had just been appointed successor to John Sawers as the Prime Minister's Foreign Policy Adviser. He sat next to Condi Rice, whom, as his opposite number, he needed to get to know. This was the start of a close relationship that was to be at the core of British–American planning and coordination for the Iraq war.

Once the summer holidays were out of the way, David wanted to follow up his first meeting with Condi and visit her in Washington. She was equally keen. We fixed this for 10 September. At the end of the day Condi and her deputy, Steve Hadley, who looked more like a British diplomat than a British diplomat, came to supper at the residence with David and me. We laid a table for four on the terrace. It was a warm, balmy evening. Catherine joined us for drinks beforehand. She remarked that this had been one of the few Augusts when some international crisis had not blown up. Thank God, we all said.

Catherine left and we sat down to supper. We ranged at length over some of the main issues of foreign policy. I remember that there was an awful lot about the Balkans and Russia and very little, if anything, about international terrorism. But Manning and Rice were clearly going to get on.

By the time I got up next morning, 11 September, David Manning was already on a plane to New York to connect with a flight to London. I have no recollection why he did not go directly from Washington. But the result was that he became one of the very few to have an aerial view of the World Trade Center on fire.

It was the most perfect of days in the most perfect of Indian summers. Washington is usually plagued by humidity. But there are moments in the spring and autumn when high pressure purges the atmosphere of its dampness. A dry, crisp warmth prevails, with cloudless skies and perfect visibility. The light is almost unbearably bright. It was like this all along the eastern seaboard of the United States.

We also had John Major and his personal assistant, Arabella Warburton, staying with us. John had made both a name and money for himself on the American speaking circuit. Away from the tensions of the Westminster political cockpit he was a relaxed and witty speaker. He was also Chairman of the European arm of the Carlyle Group, one of the most powerful private equity firms in the United States. Carlyle had always had close links with the grandees of the Republican Party. I assumed that it was through his personal friendship with George Bush the elder, which continues to this day, that John had been introduced to Carlyle.

After breakfasting as usual with Catherine in our upstairs flat, I joined John and Arabella for coffee. I was feeling relaxed and at ease with the world. The benefits of our summer holiday had not yet worn off. This was my favourite time of year.

John Major was about to head off to a downtown hotel where Carlyle was holding its annual meeting for clients. I had been to one once and they were big affairs. John was one of the featured speakers. I started to get up to go to my office when Amanda Downes, our social secretary, burst onto the terrace.

'An aircraft has crashed into the World Trade Center,' she said in urgent alarm. Amanda was not one to panic. But my first reaction was to assume that this had been some small private plane that had wandered off course or had got into mechanical difficulties. Then Catherine came downstairs and went into her office, which had a door opening onto the terrace. She suddenly called out and urged us to come in to watch her television: 'Something terrible has happened,' she cried. This was the second aircraft, United Airlines 175, hitting the South Tower just after 9 a.m.

John and I went into Catherine's office where she and Amanda were glued to the television, their faces masks of distress. Smoke was pouring from the twin towers of the World Trade Center. I went straight to my office. One crash could have been an accident; two had to be something else. I too sat transfixed by the television images. The word 'terrorism' began to fill the ether. Forty minutes later my private secretary, John Casson, came in to say that an aircraft had crashed into the Pentagon. There were rumours of other aircraft in the hands of terrorists flying towards Washington. I snapped out of my horrified reverie.

This was getting dangerously near home. The Pentagon is only three or four miles from the embassy. The exploding aircraft was clearly audible. Catherine and Amanda went up to the roof of the residence and saw the Pentagon in flames. The smell of blazing kerosene drifted on the light breeze. If the terrorists had other targets in Washington, such as the White House or the Capitol, those were even nearer to us. The Vice-President was our next-door neighbour.

Catherine noticed from her vantage point that an almost complete silence had fallen on Washington. Cars and people had vanished from the streets. Airspace above the city was closed. The familiar and often irritating sound of Washington's Reagan Airport had ceased. It was eerie and threatening. The residence staff began to close all windows and doors.

Catherine and Amanda urged John Major not to go downtown. But he did. He returned at lunch time to say that there had been a brief gathering of the Carlyle Group people, who had then gone their separate ways. He never gave his speech. Among those present was a major investor in Carlyle, a Mr Bin Laden from Saudi Arabia. He was, of course, one of Osama's many siblings. Osama Bin Laden was already being linked in the media with the attacks.

John Major was stuck at the embassy until the end of the week.

The Americans had closed their airspace to all airline traffic. This caught David Manning also, who was stranded at Kennedy Airport in New York. He was forced to spend a night in what sounded like a motel of ill repute, where rooms were rented by the hour. For twenty-four hours we lost track of him. His mobile did not work in the US and all the land lines had gone down. Thanks to our UN ambassador in New York, we eventually got him back to the embassy to join our involuntary house party. At one stage we thought that the Duchess of York would also seek refuge with us; but she managed to get out through Canada.

Major and Manning finally returned to London at the end of the week, thanks to the British intelligence services. A special aircraft had brought all three intelligence chiefs to Washington – Dearlove of the Secret Intelligence Service, Manningham-Buller of MI5 and Richards of the Government Communications Headquarters – for urgent consultations with the Americans. After their meetings we had a drink together on the terrace late on the Thursday night. The worry was a further strike by Al Qaeda. There were rumours of trucks carrying 'dirty' nuclear devices. Major and Manning hitched a ride with them back to London.

Immediately after the strike on the Pentagon I summoned a council of war comprising a core team of embassy staff, who would be needed to run our essential services. I sent everyone else home. I was anxious for our people, who were in turn anxious for their families. Schools had closed. No one knew what would happen next. Wild rumours spread. There was a sense of foreboding and menace in the air. No one knew where the President was. Had he been killed? Was the United States at war? Where would the enemy – who was the enemy? – strike next? I had no idea whether my people would be safer at home or in the embassy compound. My instinct was that families should be together, and at home.

There was no shortage of volunteers who wanted to stay behind; but in an emergency, the scale of which is simultaneously enormous and unclear, you are probably better off not having too many people around. I needed core staff to cover the political, security, intelligence, military, and consular sides of things. We had to find telephonists who would provide cover twenty-four hours a day, seven days a week.

In the end, on 9/11 and in its aftermath, many, many of my

staff put their shoulder to the wheel in Washington. Some simply disobeyed the instruction to go home. Others were back within twenty-four hours. It became a prolonged period of huge stress and tension, of days punctuated by bomb scares. To track and mark what the Americans were up to meant working the same intolerably long hours as they. With the passage of the weeks, I worried as I saw faces getting more and more drawn and eyes pouched by lack of sleep. Adrenalin and sheer professionalism kept people going. I was never prouder of a team. We did not get to ease off a little until the end of the year.

On the morning of 9/11 there were multiple things for our small team immediately to do: establish what exactly had happened and who was responsible; start coordinating responses with the Americans; find out how many British citizens were missing in New York and prepare for the anguished enquiries of relatives and friends; check whether any British military had been at the Pentagon that morning (there had been two Army officers who emerged unscathed); and get some physical protection from the police and Secret Service for the embassy.

A protective cordon had been rapidly thrown around the US embassy in Grosvenor Square by the British police. Days passed before we could get a police presence to control access to our compound. It needed an appeal from me to the Deputy Secretary of State, Rich Armitage, to get the resources diverted to give us a measure of protection. Even then it was modest compared with the Grosvenor Square fortifications. This made our staff very jumpy. Catherine and I did not like it too much either. We knew how easily the low wall between our garden and Massachusetts Avenue had been breached in the past by down-and-outs and deer from the nearby woods.

In the middle of this frantic activity I happened by chance to see live on television the collapse of the two towers. Afterwards I felt that my emotions had failed to rise to the horror of the moment. They had been dulled over the years by a diet of Hollywood disaster movies.

At the end of the week I decided to call a 'town' meeting of embassy staff. People wanted to know: were they in danger? I could not give them the straight answer they craved. We just did not know enough. I sought to be as candid as possible, trying to separate truth from rumour, analysing as best I could the nature of any continuing threat to Washington, explaining what we were doing to ensure the physical safety of the compound, and describing what was unfolding in New York. It was only as I started speaking that I realized it was quite an emotional moment: something to do with the release of tension. But it was nothing to the emotion of a similar event the following week in New York.

The Foreign Office meantime impinged little on my life. Liz Symons, the Foreign Office minister, called to find out how we were getting on. I appreciated that. But that was the only contact I had in the week of 9/11 with anyone in the FO. Indeed, between 9/11 and the day I retired at the end of February 2003 I had not a single substantive policy discussion on the secure phone with the Foreign Office. This was in contrast to the many contacts and discussions with No. 10.

After my council of war on the morning of 9/11 I called Condi Rice. I offered condolences for the thousands of Americans who must have died. We feared that British casualties could run into the hundreds. We were ready to help in any way we could with the search for victims at the World Trade Center (which was rapidly rechristened Ground Zero). Who did she think had been responsible? The names Al Qaeda and Osama Bin Laden were already in circulation. She said that the early evidence suggested that it was them. But there could also be a connection with Iraq. That would need investigating.

Condi sounded very cool and collected. There would, she said, be no knee-jerk reaction from the United States. I said that the Prime Minister would like to speak to the President as soon as possible. She immediately agreed to set this up. Bush would welcome an early contact with Blair.

I passed this immediately to London. My staff were in the meantime in almost constant contact with the National Security Council at the White House, the State and Defense Departments and the intelligence agencies. A stream of information went back to London. The underlying message from the Americans was that there would definitely be retribution for the attacks, but nothing hurried or ill-considered. This was a message that strengthened as the week wore on.

Bush was caught in Florida when the attacks happened. His

security people forced him to take a circuitous route back to Washington until the nature of the threat was clearer. Bush was unfairly criticized for not getting back sooner. That, and a rather stumbling performance on television, started the Washington tongues wagging again. Could he rise to this moment, the supreme crisis of his presidency?

Blair did not get through to Bush until the following day. They spoke again two days later on 14 September. Several things emerged from these conversations. Blair would visit Washington the following week to discuss the attacks and what to do about them. Bush himself confirmed that he would retaliate, but not in any precipitous way. It was now virtually certain that the attacks had been carried out by Osama Bin Laden and Al Qaeda, based in Afghanistan under the protection of the Taleban. As to Iraq's possible complicity, there was no compelling evidence and strong scepticism on the British side. Blair urged Bush to focus to the exclusion of all else on the job in hand: Afghanistan, Al Qaeda and the Taleban.

Blair reiterated this point in a cogent written message. It also set out an international strategy for tackling Al Qaeda and terrorism. It rehearsed themes and arguments which were to become familiar over the next eighteen months: the importance of getting public opinion on side, of creating international coalitions, of avoiding a war of civilizations between Muslims and Christians. It was a first-rate piece of work, apparently from Blair's own pen.

Blair and Bush were agreed on the importance of rapidly getting the UN and NATO four-square behind the United States in condemnation of the attacks: this would provide a legal and political framework for military action. The British remembered how important it had been in 1982 to get a similar resolution out of the UN early in the crisis with Argentina. It provided the indispensable framework for driving the Argentines out of the Falklands by force of arms.

The UN Security Council and NATO responded rapidly and sympathetically in America's hour of need. For the first time in its history Article 5 of the NATO treaty was invoked. This says that an attack on one member state is to be considered an attack on all. The stage was therefore set for military support to the US from the NATO countries. But the Pentagon was scarred by the 1999 Kosovo war, where they felt that military effectiveness had been sacrificed to the constant need to consult NATO allies. The American military were determined not to repeat the experience: thus Rumsfeld's talk of the mission defining the coalition, not the coalition the mission. Fair enough; but it was clumsily handled. What looked like ungrateful American indifference to the many offers of help from allies led to the first signs of international disillusionment. In due course this would come to replace the initial outpouring of sympathy.

New York

As the week wore on, and the situation in Washington began to stabilize, I turned my attention to New York. To be fair to the Foreign Office most of its energies were consumed by the situation there. That was also where media attention was increasingly focused.

We had little idea how many British had perished in the Twin Towers. UK citizens are not required to register with their nearest consulate. What we did know was that the financial services industry, of which New York is the American capital, employed thousands of Brits. It was possible that we had lost several hundred at the World Trade Center. If so, this would be the single greatest loss of civilian life since the Second World War.

The British consulate-general in New York, located in midtown Manhattan, took the brunt of the atrocity. It is also the headquarters of our US-wide commercial network, promoting trade and investment between the UK and US. It fell under my authority as did all the consulates in the US.

Britain was fortunate in having as its consul-general the hard-driving and energetic Tom Harris. Tom's sometimes abrasive style did not make him everyone's favourite, but I liked and admired him. In an age when the Foreign Office is criticized – sometimes rightly so – for not standing up forcefully for British interests, Tom was resolute in pursuing what was right for Britain.

Tom and I spoke regularly that week. My overriding concern was, first, that he had the resources to handle the situation, second, that he and his staff were not coming under too much strain. As the days passed it became plain that things were going to get more difficult. I sent him reinforcements. With no British casualties in Washington, our fears that we would be swamped by enquiries from the UK were not realized.

The challenge was that scores of relatives and friends of the missing were going to arrive in New York within days of the atrocity. It was going to be harrowing in the extreme. 'Missing' meant just that. In most cases it was impossible at that stage to confirm death. To compound the misery, even where there could be no hope of survival, in most cases no physical remains would ever be found.

Catherine and I decided to go to New York on the following Monday, 17 September. We wanted to give moral support to our staff at the consulate-general. We wanted also to review the arrangements being put in place to receive the British relatives. These were going to have to be as sensitive as they were practical. She and I always associate New York City with cacophony. It came as a shock to walk out of Penn Station into a sombre, eerie near-silence. There was little traffic, few pedestrians. We were met by Tom Harris, who took us immediately to the offices of the consulate-general.

All the staff were gathered, some thirty in all, I suppose. They were a mixture of British and Americans. All of them were New Yorkers of one kind or another, some transient, some adopted, some native. They told extraordinary stories: of children from a school nearby watching the bodies fall from the Twin Towers and thinking they were birds; of people pursued by dust storms as they ran for their lives from the falling towers; of a member of the consulate staff who had got on his bike and pedalled towards the smoke and chaos to try to find out what had happened.

To the best of my recollection none had lost family in the Twin Towers. But we heard stories of friends, and friends of friends, who were missing, presumed dead. The atrocity had hit the consulate hard and personally.

I did not talk to the staff for long. I thanked them for their heroic work. I thanked them for their dedication. I paid tribute to Tom's leadership and, above all, to their team spirit. For many, who had slept little for six days and were starting to run on empty, it was a cathartic moment: to pause and hear someone from the outside tell them how well they were doing. As I was speaking, I looked up and saw that some were weeping silently. I found it hard to go on.

Afterwards Catherine and I went round talking to people individually. The usual bureaucratic hierarchy had been dissolved by the urgency of the crisis. Everybody mucked in. Only two things mattered: to try to find out who had died in the Twin Towers and to be ready for the relatives from Britain who were about to arrive. Once or twice, as Catherine and I were discussing practical details with someone, we would suddenly see emotion well up, triggered by some word or thought. Conversation would have to stop; and then, a moment later, it would resume its practical, almost mundane, course.

Later that morning, with Tom, we went to inspect the arrangements for receiving the relatives of the missing.

We were blessed to be working closely with a cooperative and highly effective city administration, led by Mayor Rudolph Giuliani. This proved to be the controversial Giuliani's finest hour. If he throws his hat in the ring for the Republican nomination for President in 2008, it will be largely on the strength of how he rose to the challenge of 9/11.

The New York authorities had moved swiftly to set up a DNA centre at Pier 94 on the Hudson River. This was where relatives of the missing could leave DNA samples to be matched with whatever human remains were retrieved from the burning ruins. This was our first port of call.

It was still perfect autumn weather. I wished that it were otherwise. The bright sunlight and crystalline air mocked the warehouse of suffering that we were about to enter. On the fence outside were scores of pitiful photographs of the missing, with plaintive appeals for help in tracing them. Desperate people wandered in and out of the centre holding placards of their loved ones. The hall was enormous. It was well organized. The New York officials went out of their way to be helpful. We discussed in detail the arrangements. There were stands in several languages. It was clear where the British had to go. Charities and non-governmental organizations were also helping. But nothing could conceal that this would be an intensely difficult experience for those who had to give samples of DNA. It was, I think, at this moment that, for the first time, Catherine and I fully grasped the enormity of what had happened.

We had decided not to add to the burdens of an overstretched city administration by asking to see Ground Zero. Access to it was severely restricted. It was still a rescue zone in which subterranean fires were burning strongly. We got to see it the following month with Prince Andrew and Rudolph Giuliani.

The Prince had come to New York to discharge duties that had been intended for his elder brother, the heir to the throne. The Prince of Wales was patron of an event called 'UK in New York'. This had been planned long before 9/11 as a fortnight in October to promote British business in the Big Apple. Despite being patron Prince Charles had been unable to come to New York for the event, much to the chagrin of the organizers. I was told by a deep throat not a million miles from the Prince's household that shooting at Balmoral had taken precedence. Prince Andrew stepped into the breach. By the time he arrived in New York, after 9/11, the event had changed its name to 'UK *with* New York' to underline Britain's solidarity with the city. Andrew did a fine job representing Britain. He bathed in the warm appreciation of New Yorkers. It would have been a golden opportunity for the Prince of Wales to escape the shadow of Princess Diana and make a fresh start with America – something, so I was told by a courtier, he and his advisers earnestly wanted.

During his visit, Giuliani took Prince Andrew and the rest of us to Ground Zero. We stood on the roof of a high building looking down onto the site. Next door was an empty, but undamaged, block of flats. Giuliani told us that body parts, torsos strapped in aircraft seats, and severed heads had been found on its balconies. Over a month after the atrocity the fires were still burning. It was a vision of Hell, with workers crawling over the site like small figures in a Hieronymus Bosch painting.

Tom Harris had rightly surmised that some of the relatives would want to get as near as possible to Ground Zero. Tom and his wife Mei-Ling had discovered a little church nearby which the priest had agreed to put at the disposal of British relatives. It was a place where they would be able to pray, to grieve or just take the weight off their feet.

Tom, Catherine and I travelled there from the DNA centre by subway. It was the best way of getting close. The southern tip of Manhattan was shut to traffic and security was ultra-tight. The subway cars were unnaturally quiet. We talked in subdued voices to a few passengers who were curious about the TV camera crew following us around and the large wreath in Tom's arms.

The little church was a marvellous choice, quiet and cool. We talked a while to the priest and thanked him warmly. He had agreed that outside there could be a place for relatives to leave flowers *in memoriam*. We left the wreath that Tom had been carrying. Then

Catherine and I were briefly interviewed by British television. We were asked how we felt. Emotions started to rise to the surface again. Catherine found it hard to speak. I suddenly felt angered by the question. I said that what I felt was as nothing compared with those who had to confront the horror of loss.

We walked as near as we could to Ground Zero. The air was heavy with the stench of burning.

Our final stop was at the hotel where the relatives would be housed. It was also the headquarters of a police team from Britain. They were drawn from several forces, family liaison officers trained to give advice and support to people in situations of extreme distress. We were hugely encouraged by their good-humoured, no-nonsense approach.

We stayed that night with Tom and Mei-Ling at their flat near Fifth Avenue. They invited a few of the consulate staff to an informal supper. The unwinding of stress was palpable. The conversation was just a little too loud, the good humour pitched a little too high. It gave me another opportunity to congratulate and thank Tom and his team. I could think of no way in which the arrangements for the British relatives could have been bettered. Tom was later to receive a knighthood and many of his staff honours in the Queen's New Year list. I was delighted for them.

Catherine and I went to bed, drained. Our emotions had been stretched too far. What we had seen, heard and smelled that day marked us for life. Sleep did not come easily. And three days later the Prime Minister would be arriving.

'Grief is the price we pay for love'

Blair's meeting with Bush was rapidly fixed for Thursday, 20 September, at the White House. But by the beginning of that week the Prime Minister's visit was getting increasingly complicated and elaborate.

Over the weekend of 15–16 September we began to hear from the White House that on the day of Blair's visit to Washington the President might make an address to a joint session of Congress. If so, Bush would want him to be his guest of honour.

There was a strong imperative for Bush to address the nation and to assert his role as leader in a time of grief and peril. He had not started too well in the first forty-eight hours. He had done much better by the end of the week. At a packed Washington Cathedral, in a memorial service for the 9/11 dead, we had heard him make an eloquent and moving speech. He had also done very well on a visit to Ground Zero, where he had spoken impromptu through a loudhailer to firefighters, police and rescue workers. But the nation needed something more. The choice, the White House told us, was between an address on television or to Congress. It was the latter that won out.

All this coincided with Blair's and Britain's reputation rocketing to stratospheric heights. Immediately after 9/11 Blair had shown his true genius as a politician in expressing sympathy and support for the United States with an eloquence and emotion which could not have been better crafted to resonate with Americans. The words had an almost magical potency: 'This is not a battle between the United States of America and terrorism, but between the free and democratic world and terrorism . . . We, like them, will not rest until this evil is driven from our world.'

I was all over the American television networks in the slipstream of Blair's oratory.

Later, in early October, Blair was to give a speech at the Labour Party Conference, which in its sweep, ambition and neo-Churchillian oratory would be without rival in his career. There was one line in it that touched Americans at their core: 'We were with you at the first. We will stay with you to the last.' I repeatedly quoted it in my own speeches. The reaction was invariably a thunderous standing ovation, suffused with emotion. It is a great line. But Americans tend to hear these things literally. It became a line with consequences.

The American media reported the carpet of flowers that had been laid by the British people in Grosvenor Square. Then something happened that seized the American imagination like nothing else. On Thursday, 13 September, at the ceremony of the Changing of the Guard at Buckingham Palace, the band of the Coldstream Guards played the 'Star-Spangled Banner'. This was something without precedent. At the embassy we were inundated with phone call, faxes, letters, and emails of gratitude and appreciation. Condi Rice later recounted how she had returned to her apartment that evening after another exhausting day, turned on the television, saw the Coldstreams playing, and, for the first time since 9/11, wept.

This was heady, emotional stuff; but it was not all. Blair was also to attend a memorial service for the British and other victims of 9/11 at the vast church of St Thomas in midtown Manhattan. This was the brainchild of Tom Harris and others of the British community in New York. It was scheduled to take place in the early afternoon, to be preceded by Blair's visiting a nearby fire station which had lost men in the Twin Towers. Then Blair would fly down to DC for his meeting with Bush.

I smelled a logistics nightmare; but the emotional power of the moment swept all before it. I wondered about Blair's endurance. He would arrive in New York having just visited Schröder of Germany and Chirac of France in quick succession. I need not have worried. This was what Tony Blair liked doing. He was on a high. This was a moment when Blair must have thought that a Franco-German-British directorate of Europe, with Britain in the lead, was a real possibility. Robin Cook, as Foreign Secretary, had been the first back in 1997 to articulate the notion of a three-power European directorate. In late 2002 Jack Straw began to talk about Britain as Europe's leader in the fight against terrorism. Hubris was in the air. Nemesis would in due course follow.

While I was in New York with Catherine on Monday, 17 September, I took a call from Alastair Campbell. I always liked talking to him: to the point, no nonsense, exceptionally perceptive, with a good grasp of foreign policy. My eternal memory of him will always be his standing over Blair, on some flight or other, gesticulating forcefully while the Prime Minister sat meekly in his seat like a schoolboy under instruction.

Campbell was candid. He was worried about Blair's attending Bush's speech to the joint session of Congress. Some Labour backbenchers were getting restless about Blair's aligning himself so unreservedly with a Republican President.

'Chris, does he have to do it? Couldn't he slip away before the speech?'

I said: 'Look, Alastair, this is going to be a huge occasion. He's going to be guest of honour and he'll sit next to the First Lady. It won't go down at all well if he says no. It's a moment in history.'

I understood the political sensitivities; but my unreserved recommendation was that Blair should be there. And so he was.

Catherine and I returned to New York by train on the evening of

19 September. I recall spending most of the journey talking to Downing Street about the logistics of the visit and, in particular, the New York leg. There was, I was told, friction between the No. 10 advance team and Tom Harris. That did not surprise me: it was the irresistible force meeting the immovable object. I looked forward to the following day like a hole in the head.

We woke up to torrential, unrelenting rain. I chaired a meeting with Tom and the No. 10 people led by the admirable Kate Garvey. We agreed a plan of action. The main thing that bothered me was that Downing Street insisted on bringing to the church the large party of Lobby journalists and cameramen who were travelling on the Prime Minister's aircraft. The timings were terribly tight. In vain I pointed out that the British press were already in vast numbers in New York and would be at the church. From my time as a press secretary I knew that a travelling press party would complicate everything. I also knew from my previous experience that, unless you warned them well in advance, a travelling press party would cause merry hell if you cut them out of a major event. They were, after all, paying for the privilege of travelling with the Prime Minister.

During our meeting I was handed a draft of the Queen's message that I was to read out at the church. It was not quite right. I suggested some changes to the order of sentences. I would like to be able to record that I insisted on its most poignant phrase – 'Grief is the price we pay for love' – being placed at the end. But I cannot remember if it was there already. In any case, whoever conceived the phrase should be placed on the same pedestal as the genius who told the Coldstream Guards to play 'The Star-Spangled Banner'.

The rain would have caused gridlock at the best of times; but at many intersections, for inexplicable reasons, the lights had been switched off. Traffic was being directed instead by the police. I noticed that many of them were from out-of-town forces like San Francisco and Chicago. Apparently most of the New York Police Department had been detailed to look after a congressional delegation of major importance. The congressmen had come to see Ground Zero for themselves. They were to vote on how much money to give New York to help clean up and rebuild. A British Prime Minister, however popular, could not compete with that.

Kate Garvey and I crawled out to Kennedy Airport, my anxieties increasing with each minute that passed. The traffic in the return direction looked as bad. We got to Kennedy with not a lot of time to spare. I heard Kate discussing the arrangements for the journalists.

The Blairs' aircraft arrived. I greeted them as usual at the foot of the aircraft steps. I saw the travelling press party clambering onto buses. The Blairs and I got into the limo and the cavalcade set off for Manhattan. The Blairs were sombre and, I thought, quite emotional. I went through the New York programme with them. Blair told me that at the church service he was going to read something from Thornton Wilder's *The Bridge at San Luis Rey*. Unfortunately I had never read it. I told him about the Queen's message. Then I briefed them in some detail about the British missing and the first wave of relatives who would be at St Thomas's.

We had a police escort to help us through the traffic, but it was slow, ponderous going. The press coaches slowed us down badly. It was still raining. The nearer we got to Manhattan, the worse it became. In the city itself the long cavalcade had to fight its way through serial gridlock.

We were late, very late. I was getting anxious. I talked several times by mobile phone – thank God it worked – to Tom Harris, who was already in the church. The huge congregation had been in place for a good half-hour already. I told Tom that we were going to have to sacrifice the fire station and come straight to the church. We could not keep so many people waiting indefinitely, including relatives for whom this was ordeal enough already. The Blairs did not demur. They sat holding hands, looking worried and nervous. A jolt of sympathy for them passed through me.

The fire station was not completely ignored. After the service Cherie and Catherine visited it in the unexpected company of Bill Clinton.

St Thomas's is a massive, high-vaulted, neo-Gothic Episcopalian church in the middle of Manhattan. It was full to bursting. We hurried to our seats at the front. They were long benches. I took my place alongside Catherine. I looked along our bench and saw Bill and Chelsea Clinton, Kofi Annan and his wife Nane, and the Blairs. Hillary Clinton, now a New York senator, was in the congressional delegation visiting Ground Zero. The service was very moving. I heard occasional sobbing from the congregation. There was a good choice of hymns. The choir was superb. Alastair Campbell sang loudly and tunefully behind me. During the prayers and addresses I looked at the Queen's message. I had had no chance to read it through since we had suggested some cosmetic changes to the Palace. Now it was a crumpled piece of paper, with ballpoint balloons and squiggles to mark the changed order of sentences.

In due course it was my turn to go to the lectern. I looked down on a vast sea of faces. 'A message from Her Majesty The Queen,' I said. Then I read out the brief but eloquent text. It had some ringing phrases. I paused before the talismanic final sentence: 'Grief is the price we pay for love.' Bill Clinton came up to me afterwards and, like one pol to another, said, 'Hey, great speech. I loved that last sentence.' The ultimate accolade, I thought to myself. The line is now carved in stone at St Thomas's, as also at a memorial in Grosvenor Square.

After the service the moment came to meet the British relatives of the missing who had been in the congregation. A large room had been set aside in the church. Catherine and I went in with the Blairs. Bill and Chelsea Clinton followed us. Somebody told me that Giuliani had raced from escorting the congressional delegation and had been present for part of the service. I went out to find him and brought him back with Governor Pataki of New York State. For Catherine and me it was a case of our already heavily bruised emotions taking another battering. We talked to several relatives. I have never felt so useless and inadequate in my life. Some were inconsolable. Others, perhaps because the service had been so up-lifting, wanted to talk almost cheerily about their lost children, brothers, sisters. Catherine, unlike me, with her empathy and keen, intuitive sense, knew exactly what to say to the bereaved. I was tongue-tied and awkward.

This was not an occasion to rush. The Blairs, all of us, were reluctant to leave. We lingered with the relatives in the hope of being able to offer some crumbs of comfort; but time was pressing desperately. I said goodbye to Catherine and Cherie and escorted the Prime Minister to our limo. Once again we had to struggle through the New York traffic. Once again we were running late. It was as nerve-racking as the inward journey, but I reckoned that we could just about make it on time to our meeting with the President, so long as there were no further hold-ups.

After what seemed like several lifetimes I finally slumped into my seat in the first-class cabin at the front of the aircraft with Blair and his entourage. I was looking forward to a strong cup of tea as soon as we took off. But nothing happened. No 'Fasten your seat belt' sign, no sound of engines revving, no nothing. What on earth had happened?

The word came down. As a result of new security measures introduced while we were at St Thomas's, the airport authorities had decided to subject the travelling press party and all their equipment to meticulous search. They said that, because the press buses had got separated from the rest of the motorcade, they were not 'clean'. The result was to delay us so much that the meeting at the White House planned for the afternoon had to be scrubbed. That just left the supper with Bush.

Meantime, unknown to me, the blame game was in full swing further back in the aircraft. Some of the No. 10 people were panicking. They tried to pin the blame on a member of my staff and told her to go and explain herself to the Prime Minister.

In the first-class cabin all was fret and impatience. Blair was in a huddle with Jonathan Powell and Alastair Campbell. Powell came up to me. 'Tony would rather have Alastair at the supper with Bush than you. I'm sorry.' After the tensions and fraught exertions of the last ten days, and on this day of all days, that was not a terribly well-judged thing to tell me. In fact Powell might as well have punched me in the solar plexus. For a moment I could not find the words to respond. When they came, they were furious and expletive-laden.

'If this happens, you will cut me off at the fucking knees for the rest of my fucking time in Washington. Is that what you want?'

It is a well-established diplomatic convention that prime ministers and presidents frequently confer with each other either with just one adviser each or sometimes just the two of them alone. This reflects the intimacy of the relationship and makes candour easier. It has become the pattern for the Blair–Bush meetings. I could not expect to be present on these restricted occasions. I had to rely on being briefed in detail afterwards. Fortunately the British system is good at doing this. But when the meeting broadens to include a small group of principal advisers, it should include the ambassador. I had to provide the continuity and carry the weight of the relationship between prime ministerial visits. It could not all be done by phone from London. If I had been absent from these wider meetings – and the President's supper was one such – then I would have lost credibility in the eyes of the President and senior members of the US administration. They would have concluded that I did not enjoy the Prime Minister's confidence. If, on 20 September 2001, they had made that judgement, then the effectiveness of the embassy would have been damaged at just the moment when the British Government had rarely needed it more.

Anyway it was unnecessary. A junior White House official appeared to have told a junior No. 10 official that supper would be for the two principals plus three on each side. This was not holy writ, as, of course, we were to find out. All Blair had to say was that he wanted four: his three advisers from No. 10 and his ambassador; but Jonathan Powell just looked embarrassed and shrugged his shoulders.

The aircraft finally took off, we sped to Andrews Air Force Base, and immediately on arrival we jumped into limos and raced to the White House. Blair and I were alone in limo number one. I had a series of phone calls with the embassy. I was told that there could be a problem about Campbell attending the supper, because there would be no one there from the press side of the White House. The Americans had not yet hoisted on board Blair's dependence on Alastair as a senior adviser. I said that we had to be four because Alastair was indispensable to Blair. The Prime Minister was listening to all this. 'I don't mind who goes to the supper between you and Alastair,' he said weakly.

That's no help, I thought to myself. 'Prime Minister,' I said, 'you don't have to choose. A team of four is perfectly reasonable. You have a right to select whom you want. The President will not conceivably object.' As, indeed, he did not.

When we arrived at the White House, Don Ensenat, the good-humoured Head of Protocol, immediately approached me with a worried face. 'Ambassador, we have been told not to include you in the Prime Minister's party for the President's supper. I don't know what to say.'

'Who says?' I asked, the anger rising in my gorge. 'Somebody called from the cavalcade, while you were driving into town,' Don replied. I had a pretty shrewd idea who that had been. Matters came to a head over this type of thing during Blair's visit to the President's ranch in Crawford the following year. The thought passed through my mind to resign if I did not get into that supper; but I was saved from this extreme step by Condoleezza Rice. Her European adviser, Dan Fried, came up to me and said: 'Don't worry. Condi wants you there. We've laid another place.' What have things come to, I thought to myself, when the British ambassador has to depend on the Americans and not his own Prime Minister to do the right thing?

The rest of that extraordinary day is history. As soon as we arrived at the White House, we were ushered into the Blue Room. Colin Powell, Condi Rice and Andy Card were waiting for us. Bush immediately took Blair by the arm and, out of earshot of the rest of us, they had a private word.

We ate supper in the small dining room on the ground floor. In the end, with our principals, we were five a side. Besides myself, Blair was flanked by Jonathan Powell, Alastair Campbell and David Manning, Bush by Condi Rice, Colin Powell, Andy Card and Dan Fried. It was a calm, workmanlike discussion. Bush showed not the slightest sign of impetuosity in seeking retribution for 9/11. He and Blair agreed a strategy for the next few weeks, which would include presenting the Taleban with an ultimatum. Bush unveiled some of the military planning. Blair offered British troops and other military assistance. There was discussion of international support, in which Pakistan would have to play a leading role. Blair was eager to fly wherever and deploy his personal diplomatic skills. He rapidly discovered that in insisting on an exclusive focus on Al Qaeda and the Taleban, he was pushing at a door already opened. The President and his advisers had taken that decision the previous weekend. Iraq was for consideration another day. I heard nothing that evening to suggest that Bush and Blair had agreed to attack Iraq after Afghanistan.

Little was lost by having arrived late. Bush and Blair covered all the required ground over supper. As the meal drew towards a close, I became increasingly aware that within an hour or so Bush was going to have to make the speech of his life to the joint session of Congress. He displayed no trace of nerves. He seemed in no hurry to leave the table for a last run through the text. I began to get nervous for him. As we finally left the table, Bush invited Blair to accompany him upstairs to the private apartments and then to travel with him to Capitol Hill. It was a singular and flattering mark of friendship. The rest of us got into a minibus with a jolly, wise-cracking Karl Rove.

Bush rose to the occasion beyond all expectations. If there had been doubts remaining about his ability to lead the country at a time of crisis, they were dispelled that night. He was given a roaring, stomping reception by senators and congressmen of both parties. Almost every sentence was an applause line. The atmosphere was one of intoxicating, intense patriotism. For me, two things jumped out of the speech: the Manichean division of the world into states that were with America and states that were against – no room for neutral ground; and the challenge not simply to terrorists but to regimes that harboured them.

The speech was delivered in the grand chamber of the House of Representatives. Not only were several hundred senators and congressmen in the audience, but also the diplomatic corps, the justices of the Supreme Court and the entire military leadership of the United States. Guests were packed into galleries high above the chamber. I was seated a little behind Blair in the VIP gallery. The Prime Minister was next to Laura Bush. On the other side of her was Governor Tom Ridge of Pennsylvania. He was about to be announced by Bush as the new Director of Homeland Security. Bush had told us at dinner that he would have something nice to say about Blair. And so he did. At the outset of his speech he paid lavish tribute to Tony Blair as 'our truest friend'. The compliment was received with thunderous applause. What a climax to Blair's extra-ordinary twenty-four hours!

Blair left for the UK immediately after the President's speech. His relationship with Bush had been transported to a new and higher level of trust and friendship. It was a sea change. Blair had become an American hero. More than any other European politician he seemed to have understood the shocking impact on the United States of 9/11: on the President, on the administration, on the intelligence services and on the American people themselves. Over two centuries of invulnerability had been shattered: 20 September 2001, the tenth day of the crisis, had been his day of American triumph.

Catherine and I bathed in the reflected glory of Blair's heroic status. It was a good time to be British in America. People, if they knew who we were or heard our accents, would stop us in shops, restaurants or on the street to thank us for our support.

I saw Blair off at Andrews Air Force Base. He and his entourage were euphoric. I staggered home to Catherine after one of the longest days of my life.

Tartan Day, 2002. I am speaking on the Capitol steps. Note Senators Lott and Allard (middle two, front row) with their kilts more or less correctly positioned.

Sir Sean Connery, Catherine and I under the portico of the Great House. Tartan Day, 2002.

Sharing a joke with John Cleese and his wife at the Embassy garden party for the Queen's Jubilee.

Labour's Foreign Secretary Jack Straw and I give Plácido Domingo (far left) an honorary knighthood at the Great House, 2003.

Catherine and I at the Great House with Lady Thatcher, Senator Jesse Helms and his wife Dot.

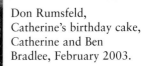

Don Rumsfeld, Catherine's birthday cake, Catherine and Ben Bradlee, February 2003.

I give Steven Spielberg an honorary knighthood for his contribution to the British film industry.

Colin Powell and (on his right) the great Rich Armitage, his deputy at the State Department.

Karl Rove, sometimes known as Bush's brain.

Saying goodbye to Paul Wolfowitz in February 2003.

Farewell call on Vice-President Dick Cheney, February 2003.

Farewell call on Colin Powell in February 2003. I look grey.

Laura Bush's farewell lunch for Catherine and the Italian ambassador's wife at the White House in February 2003.

The Bushes' farewell dinner for us, 17 February 2003: Condi Rice, Colin Powell, Alma Powell, the President, the First Lady, me, Catherine, Kitty and Mel Martinez.

21

The Big Beasts

For a new ambassador Washington can be daunting. Your task is simple to describe: find things out and influence decisions. Where to begin?

In most countries you pop down to the Foreign Ministry to see the minister or one of his senior officials. Occasionally, you will take an appointment with the Prime Minister or President. Much day-to-day business is still conducted through the exchange of formal notes, with their rigid, formulaic preamble: 'Her Britannic Majesty's Embassy presents its compliments to the Ministry of Foreign Affairs and has the honour to state the following ...'

This was how things were done when I first became a diplomat. In Moscow and Madrid, as a lowly third secretary, I spent hours of my life drafting these notes for my superiors' approval. This was traditional diplomacy, done in accordance with strict rules of protocol. It is still an image which clings to the profession, along with the fallacy that diplomats inhabit a rarefied world to which ordinary mortals are admitted only with difficulty.

In Madrid over thirty years ago, whenever my ambassador, Sir John Russell, gave a formal dinner, I would go to see a lady in the Spanish Foreign Ministry who was an expert in protocol. I would show her the guest list. It would inevitably have several members of the Spanish aristocracy. It might include as well one or two ex-crowned heads of Europe, in exile in Madrid. I recall a good many dethroned Romanians, Bulgarians and Yugoslavs. There seemed also to be an inexhaustible supply of French, Italians and Spaniards, all of whom were pretenders to their respective thrones. All these people had to be seated at dinner in the right protocol order. Particular care had to be taken with the Spanish nobility and its strict rules of precedence. A *duque* or *marques* would walk out if he felt that he had been given a seat beneath his rank. The lady in the Foreign Ministry, having consulted a great tome, would set the names in their proper order. The rest of my day was then devoted to reconciling the protocol list with a seating plan for ten round tables with ten guests each. It was a task to challenge Einstein. With the help of a school compass, a pencil stub and a fountain pen, I would spend hours drawing the tables and writing in the names on a large sheet of shiny white card. This would then be mounted on an easel for the guests' perusal as they went in to dinner. Two hours beforehand Lady Russell's phone would start ringing with people wanting to know who their dinner partners would be. These calls would often reveal ancient feuds and hatreds, not to mention liaisons both active and extinct. More often than not the whole thing would be thrown into disarray by someone's successfully lobbying to have their seating changed. I would then start again with a fresh piece of card.

My reward for organizing these occasions was to be allowed to circulate with the guests before dinner and to circulate with them again afterwards. I was not sufficiently grand to be invited to the dinner itself; but I still had to put on black tie. While the guests dined, I would go off to the nearest cafeteria for a bite to eat, where I was indistinguishable from the waiters.

When I joined the Foreign Office in 1966 I was given a book which was supposed to lead new recruits through the maze of diplomatic protocol. It addressed tricky questions like who goes through a door first: the male ambassador or his junior female assistant? If I remember well, the ambassador prevailed. This was at a time when, in the American embassy in Moscow, diplomats' wives would sometimes be asked to wait at table at formal dinners (the Russians did the same in London); and, as the ambassador's private secretary in Moscow, I would ring our own diplomats' wives and tell them whose turn it was to take charge of the embassy laundry.

I once had an ambassador who disconcerted me by farting loudly and repeatedly in my presence. The Foreign Office handbook on protocol offered me no guidance. Should I feign indifference; or, on the principle that imitation is the sincerest form of flatulence, should I join in?

In Moscow I had a small box that buzzed on my desk. This was activated by the security guards in the embassy reception area.

Whenever they spotted the ambassador either coming down the stairs from his private apartment or arriving at the front door in his Rolls-Royce, they pressed the buzzer. Like a greyhound from the slips, I then raced into the entrance hall to enquire solicitously of His Excellency whether there was any task I could discharge for him.

Three decades later in Washington there were only the faintest traces of the old ways. They could be discerned among the more traditional embassies whose reflex was still to channel business through the US Foreign Ministry, otherwise known as the State Department. 'State', which has a vested interest in holding the reins of US foreign policy, did not discourage this.

If only it were that simple. The influences that shape American foreign policy are scattered across Washington. Partly this is a consequence of the US Constitution's formal separation of powers between executive, legislature and judiciary. Partly it is a result of the sheer number of government departments, agencies and congressional committees, who have a stake in overseas policy. Partly it flows from the ever-shifting balance of power between personalities at the apex of government. You should add to the mix the press, where heavyweight foreign policy commentators like Jim Hoagland of the *Washington Post* and Tom Friedman of the *New York Times* can have a material impact on the formulation of foreign policy. They have no equivalent in the United Kingdom.

Having surveyed this daunting scene, the new ambassador notes with dismay something else. Big, contentious issues can take for ever to resolve; they provoke intense debate. This draws in the plethora of interested administration departments and congressional committees, not to mention the White House itself. Turf wars abound, including within departments. It is multidimensional chess on the grand scale; or, as Rich Armitage, Colin Powell's Deputy Secretary of State, used to say to me: 'It's a soup sandwich.'

It should be fairly evident from this that if you want to send a crisply accurate report to your government on where American policy rests on, say, the Middle East or North Korea, a formal note of enquiry to the State Department is not going to do the trick. Nor even, on its own, will a conversation with the Secretary of State, though that will always be illuminating. To establish where a policy debate has got to, where it is likely to go, and, along the way, how to influence it, you have to advance on a broad front. Day in, day out, my staff would spread out across Washington like an army of prospectors. Each evening they would return with what they had discovered. We would then examine the raw material like panhandlers looking for gold dust in the dirt. Then we would put what we thought valuable, together with comment and recommendations, in an encrypted report, which was sent electronically to London overnight. The Foreign Office still calls this instant form of communication by the quaint term 'telegram'. The American equivalent is 'cable'. No one in the FCO talks about 'memos'.

I applied the concept of the club sandwich to that of the soup sandwich. Embassies are hierarchies: in descending order, ambassador, minister, counsellor, desk officer. I wanted everybody at their different levels to develop their own contacts across the US administration and Congress. It was not necessarily the case that the more senior the contact, the better the information. Sometimes the first intimations of a policy decision would come from a relatively junior source.

My own contribution to this process was to deal with the 'Big Beasts', their deputies and their closest advisers. This meant the National Security Adviser to the President; the Vice-President; the Secretary of State; the Secretary for Defense; the chairmen and senior members of key committees in the Senate and the House of Representatives; and the top newspaper columnists. These were the people whom Catherine and I regularly invited for meals, drinks or tennis. They were usually more unbuttoned when we got them inside the Great House.

I found this intensely enjoyable and satisfying. It was also risky. It is one thing to find out and to influence, quite another to get so close that you risk being drawn into Washington's interdepartmental rivalry, like a sleeve caught in a piece of machinery. I had to be very careful not to let this happen and damage the embassy's reputation for trustworthiness and impartiality. Throughout 2002 I heard the whirr of the machine at my elbow. I enjoyed that too. It made the adrenalin pump.

George W. Bush had installed at the core of his administration an exceptionally seasoned and heavyweight team of beasts to handle foreign and defence policy. Vice-President Cheney, Secretary of State Powell and Defense Secretary Rumsfeld went back a long way. In the 1970s Cheney had been deputy to Rumsfeld when he was President Ford's chief of staff. Rumsfeld had once considered a shot at the presidency. In his memoirs Henry Kissinger describes with reluctant admiration Rumsfeld's ruthless effectiveness in Washington's turf wars. Both Cheney and Rumsfeld had been congressmen. Rumsfeld had already been Defense Secretary once. He has the distinction of having been both the youngest and oldest Defense Secretary in American history.

During the First Gulf War of 1991 Cheney was the elder Bush's Defense Secretary. Colin Powell was his Chairman of the Joint Chiefs, approximately equivalent to the British Chief of the Defence Staff. Before that Powell had been President Reagan's National Security Adviser, the post that Condoleezza Rice was to occupy in George W. Bush's first term. The National Security Adviser is the head of the National Security Council, which from inside the White House advises the President on foreign and security policy. It was established in 1947 under President Truman with the deliberate intention of creating a resource independent of the State Department.

Cheney, Powell and Rumsfeld were already Big Beasts when Rice was a relatively junior Soviet specialist in the National Security Council. Her talent and personality rapidly marked her for higher things. She became also a close friend of the Bush family. During the elder Bush's presidency she was an important member of the team that negotiated Soviet withdrawal from East Germany, so opening the door to the reunification of the Federal Republic. This was one of the great achievements of twentieth-century American diplomacy.

When I arrived in Washington as ambassador the Beast I knew best was, through a strange quirk of fate, Don Rumsfeld. In 1990, during my first incarnation in Washington, I was invited to take part in a white-water rafting expedition on the section of the Colorado River that passes through the Grand Canyon. The expedition comprised foreign diplomats and American businessmen, politicians and government officials. On the principle that there was no such thing as a free expedition, it was to end with a seminar on international trade in a hotel on the South Rim of the Grand Canyon. The organizers' idea was that the conference would be better if the participants had bonded for five days and five nights in the Canyon.

It was often bonding in the face of common adversity: ejection from the rafts into icy water as we passed through enormous, thundering rapids; discovery each morning of animal and snake tracks in the sand around our open-air sleeping bags; ingenious though primitive sanitary arrangements, the result of our having to take our waste with us. The expedition leaders sought to encourage the bowel movements of the more fastidious and constipated among us by putting the portable loos and showers in places of great natural beauty. Many an evening you would find me atop a cliff, sitting dreamily on my loo seat and watching the sun set over the ochre walls of the Canyon and the vast expanse of the Colorado desert.

The expedition comprised a number of rubber rafts, each with a boat captain and six of us. Rumsfeld was on my raft. From the outset there was a struggle for supremacy between the boat captain and the once and future Defense Secretary. The boat captain's orders to paddle left or paddle right were under constant challenge from the irrepressible Rummy. In between he would lecture us interminably on the merits of the artificial sweetener aspartame, manufactured by a pharmaceutical company for which he then worked. His rasping voice would echo from one side of the Canyon to the other. It would have been intolerable but for his sense of humour.

The ancient gods of the Canyon soon answered the boat captain's fervent prayers. We stopped one afternoon in a lagoon with the other rafts. A water fight broke out. Rumsfeld was hurling water from a bucket with the best of them. Suddenly he fell, a muscle pulled in his back. To his mortification he remained incapacitated for the rest of the expedition. He was transferred from our raft to the greater security of the large rowboat which carried our provisions. It also transported our waste in a sealed box, from which, towards the end of the expedition, noxious odours began to seep. To watch Don Rumsfeld, strapped near-horizontal as the rowboat navigated a rapid, was like observing the last rites of a great Oriental potentate heading for the funeral pyre.

Rumsfeld can be an intimidating presence. He is a former wrestler and Navy pilot. He is compact, fit, muscular, a regular squash player who looks far younger than his seventy-odd years. He is blunt and to the point. He liked and respected George Robertson, Blair's first Defence Secretary who went on to become NATO Secretary

General. Rumsfeld once told me off for trying to imitate George's Scottish accent. It proved harder to find a common wavelength between Rumsfeld and Robertson's successor, the amiable Geoff Hoon. In fact it was like getting pandas to mate. Hoon got nervous in Rumsfeld's presence.

One Sunday in March 2002 Paul Wolfowitz, Rumsfeld's deputy, came to lunch at the residence. There were just the two of us. We discussed what could be done to get Hoon and Rumsfeld closer. After all, by that time, Britain and the US were fighting together in Afghanistan. Neither of us had an instant solution. I believe that as a result of this conversation Rumsfeld invited Hoon to travel with him on his aircraft to a NATO meeting in Brussels.

In my report to London I omitted any mention of our discussion of the Hoon–Rumsfeld relationship. I did record what Wolfowitz and I had to say to each other about handling Iraq. Part of that letter, which was very highly classified and addressed only to two or three people in London, was later leaked in 2004 to the *Sunday Telegraph*.

Like the Cheneys, Rumsfeld and his pleasant wife, Joyce, were sociable. Colin Powell and Condi Rice were less so. Don and Joyce Rumsfeld came to one of our very last dinners before we left Washington. Though it was big and black-tie, with over a hundred guests, it was a light-hearted affair with a lot of our personal friends – those made after five and a half years in America and some from London. Typical was Catherine's table. Rumsfeld, as a senior member of the Cabinet, had the place of honour at Catherine's right. Then there was a bunch of friends of long standing: Ben Bradlee, former editor of the *Washington Post*, who broke the Watergate story; Eve Pollard (Lady Lloyd), former editor of the *Sunday Express*; David Westin, the head of ABC News; Barbara Taylor Bradford, the author; Leo Melamed from Chicago, the genius behind the Chicago Mercantile Exchange, who, with Milton Friedman, had invented the financial futures market; Lynn Wyatt and Al Montna from Texas and California respectively; and Claudine Ward, a French friend of Catherine's for over thirty years.

This was early 2003. Washington was awash with anti-French sentiment. Rumsfeld soon embarked across the table on a vigorous debate with Claudine about France. She had introduced herself to him as a representative of the Old Europe. As he got into his stride, wagging his finger, she had forcefully to interrupt him to get a word in. These serial acts of temerity aroused the intense admiration of the Americans at the table.

After dinner Rummy took Claudine to meet Joyce. 'I'm afraid that I may have upset you with what I said about France,' said Rumsfeld rather gracefully. 'Not at all,' replied Claudine with a twinkle in her eyes. 'You are so handsome that when French women see you on television they forget what you are saying.' Witnesses relate that this was the first time that they had ever seen the Defense Secretary lost for words.

Quite soon after Catherine and I arrived in Washington I resumed contact with a close friend, the journalist and writer Elizabeth Drew. I had first run into her and her late English husband, David Webster, almost ten years previously in my first Washington incarnation. She was, and remains, an outstanding analyst of Washington politics. At the time of our first meeting she had her own politics show on television and a weekly column in the *New Yorker*. I told her that I found her column so good that I had no hesitation in plagiarizing it. That, as they say, was the start of a beautiful friendship. In those days Elizabeth and David had a political salon. She regularly held court over small dinners to which the powerful of DC flocked. She often invited my first wife and me. It was at her table that, long before I became ambassador, I met the likes of Alan Greenspan, Vernon Jordan, Al Gore, John McCain and leading members of the Senate and House. The rule at her dinners was that there could be only one conversation, which she controlled. Thanks to Elizabeth, I learnt a lot about Washington politics.

One summer evening in 1998 Elizabeth invited Catherine and me to supper. There were only two other guests: the veteran conservative columnist for the *Washington Post*, Bob Novak, and Dr Condoleezza Rice.

This was the first time we had met Condi. I knew her by reputation. She was judged to have done a fine job in the elder George Bush's administration, where, under the wing of her mentor, General Brent Scowcroft, the National Security Adviser, she had been a White House specialist on the old Soviet Union and Eastern Europe. Condi was now Provost of Stanford University in northern California. She is extraordinarily gifted. She can play the piano to professional standard. She has been a fine ice skater. She had a brilliant academic career. As a small girl she had moved with her parents from a racially troubled Birmingham, Alabama, to Denver, Colorado. It was at Denver University that, under the teaching of Madeleine Albright's father, Joseph Korbel, a Czech immigrant, she first took a serious interest in international affairs and political science.

Before the age of thirty she was appointed to the faculty of Stanford University. As a board member of the Chevron Corporation she had an oil tanker named after her. Unlike most African-Americans she found her political home in the Republican Party. So did Colin Powell; but he once told me that he was 'only just a Republican'.

That evening at Elizabeth's we had quite a debate about Russia. Being half-Russian herself, Catherine has a passionate interest in her mother's country. I had had four years of personal experience in Moscow. Condi was already questioning the venerable policy of *détente*, the elaborate framework of rules and protocols drawn up by the US and the Soviet Union to avoid nuclear war in a period of ideological hostility and Great Power rivalry.

I recall in particular her antipathy towards the US–Soviet Anti-Ballistic Missile (ABM) Treaty, considered to be the cornerstone of *détente*. The treaty sprang from the doctrine of 'mutual assured destruction' or, to you and me, the balance of terror. The treaty limited the number of anti-missile systems the Americans and Russians could put in place to defend themselves against nuclear attack by each other. The theory was that neither country would be irrational enough to launch a ballistic missile strike if it knew that cataclysmic retaliation would be the response.

Condi questioned the relevance of all this in the age of Yeltsin and the dismantling of the Soviet Union and the Warsaw Pact. It was a harbinger of the younger Bush's decision three years later to withdraw from the ABM Treaty and build missile defences against all comers, including rogue states.

Later, when she had become National Security Adviser, Condi would come to the embassy from time to time to play tennis. It was usually on a Sunday. Before 9/11 she would often have the time to stay for lunch. On the tennis court she was a powerful hitter without quite the ice skater's elegance. I am no better than a journeyman slugger, whose best shots are the bastard offspring of squash. There was a certain brute strength to our partnership and a fierce sense of competition. After losing a point, I once remarked to her flippantly that there was no place in our game for the plucky British loser. 'No there is not,' she replied with a certain severity. We went on to win.

Our opponents were always Catherine and a male partner, sometimes Mel Martinez, the Cabinet Secretary for Housing and Urban Development (now a Florida senator), sometimes Steve Atkins from the embassy's press section, one of the best amateur players in Washington. Catherine and I had once played against Alan Greenspan, Chairman of the Federal Reserve, and his wife Andrea Mitchell, the NBC television correspondent. Greenspan's game rested on the devilish slicing of the ball. We called him 'Greenspin' from then on.

The biggest Beast of the lot – the President aside – was our next-door neighbour, the Vice-President. In 2000 Cheney had been given the job of finding a suitable running mate for George W. Bush, who would then become Vice-President were Bush to win. I knew a couple of Republicans who fancied their chances of being chosen. It came as a shock to them, as to everybody else, when Cheney in effect chose himself. From there he went on to become the most powerful Vice-President in living memory. He was considered by Republican chieftains the ideal foil to George W. Bush, bringing to a neophyte President a depth and breadth of experience that no other candidate could offer. From the outset of his presidency George W. lunched alone with Cheney every week. The only question mark over Cheney was his health. He had had several heart attacks. There were coronary incidents after he became Vice-President. He is, I think, fitted with a pacemaker.

Catherine and I decided early in 2001 to give the Cheneys a dinner to welcome them, as it were, to the neighbourhood. A couple of days before the dinner, Cheney checked himself into hospital with some kind of heart irregularity. We were plunged in gloom. That would put paid to the dinner, we thought. A large number of Washington's great and good were coming, drawn by the magnet of rubbing shoulders with the Veep. But, to our surprise, he came. Not only that – he ate a large dinner, including a chocolate pudding, drank coffee and stayed late. That helped lay to rest any stories of his being incapacitated.

In my toast to the Cheneys I expressed the hope that the Vice-

President would be an improvement on his predecessor in the helicopter department and not allow their engines to idle interminably on his helipad. In return I promised to moderate my ripe language on the tennis court. Other neighbours, including Hillary Clinton, had already commented on my command of Anglo-Saxon.

In his own way many people found Cheney as intimidating as Rumsfeld. He put the fear of God into John Prescott and Jack Straw, who are not best equipped to deal with tough, right-wing Republicans. The Vice-President is not naturally talkative. He waits for you to speak first. Sometimes he just remains silent. Catherine, who at dinners would sometimes be seated next to him, at first found Cheney a tough nut to crack; but with time, when the ice was broken, we always found him affable and drily humorous.

There were also the slightly smaller Beasts, who were indispensable contacts: for example, Paul Wolfowitz, Rumsfeld's deputy, a soft-spoken intellectual who had been gunning for Saddam Hussein for years and years. Wolfowitz was one of the few genuine 'neocons' in the administration: that is, born into an intellectual tradition at once conservative, fiercely anti-communist and strongly pro-Israel, which in an earlier generation had found its home in the Democratic Party. Paul had idealism and a mission, which was why he was sometimes called a 'democratic imperialist'. As ambassador to Indonesia, he had seen how democracy, albeit imperfectly, had come to Asia. There was no reason, he thought, why the same could not be encouraged to happen in the Middle East. It should start in Iraq.

When I arrived in Washington, Paul was Dean of the Paul Nitze School of Advanced International Studies, my old alma mater from my days as a postgraduate student in Bologna. In that admirably uninhibited American fashion he soon came calling to see what I was ready to do for the School. I was happy to lay on a dinner at the embassy for the trustees. The evening turned into a powerful and illuminating debate on American foreign policy.

After that we saw each other from time to time. I recall a conversation just after Saddam Hussein had forced the UN inspectors to leave Iraq at the end of 1998. Paul thought that the proper response should be to occupy Basra and the southern oil fields of Iraq. From there it would be relatively easy to foment rebellion in the country at large until Saddam was toppled. I thought at the time that this was sheer fantasy; but I wondered how much longer the UN could go on being manipulated and humiliated by Saddam Hussein without losing all credibility.

Then there was the barrel-chested Rich Armitage, deputy Secretary of State and one of Colin Powell's closest friends. Colin and Rich had first met in Vietnam, where both had seen active service. The official White House biography of Rich Armitage tells us only that during the Vietnam war he served on a destroyer and 'completed three combat tours with the riverine/advisory forces'. By all accounts this bald sentence covers a narrative of extraordinary heroism. I was told that after the fall of Saigon, he had stayed behind to help Vietnamese friends of America escape.

To talk to Rich was a joy. As I walked into his office, he would greet me with an offer of coffee and a demand for 'red meat', that is, high-grade information. He was himself frank to a fault, his language enriched with a tumbling flow of jokes and colourful images, many of which could not be repeated in polite circles. Behind all this was one of the shrewdest brains in Washington. Wolfowitz apart, Armitage had bottomless contempt for the senior civilians of the Pentagon. He once described them to me as weirdos akin to the strange creatures in the bar-room scene of the first *Star Wars* movie.

Lewis 'Scooter' Libby, Cheney's chief of staff, was another of the slightly lesser beasts. I found him tough, quirky, very right-wing and amusing. He had written a thriller called *The Apprentice*. Years before he had been taught by Wolfowitz at Cornell. I had never come across a vice-presidential staff more capable and influential than those in Cheney's employ. Like his boss, Scooter was implacably hostile to going to the UN in the winter of 2002 to deal with Iraq.

In principle this was the most impressive foreign policy team at the disposal of a President since the days of George W.'s father twelve years previously; but the whole was always less than the sum of its parts. This was because of the deep fault line that ran through the team. Even at the very outset of George W.'s administration journalists were itching to write a Powell versus Cheney and Rumsfeld story. At first I cautioned London to treat the speculation with care. It was far too soon to tell how the new administration would settle down.

But the press guessed right. Journalists are often accused of trivializing public affairs by concentrating on personalities, not policy. The plain truth is that, in Washington as in London, it is impossible to disentangle the personalities, the politics and the policies. After all, the complex relationship between Tony Blair and Gordon Brown has been the axis on which British government policy has turned since 1997.

Personalities, politics and policy were all in play around the Washington fault line. It pitched Colin Powell and the State Department, sometimes with CIA support, against the Vice-President's Office and Rumsfeld's Defense Department. The President's instincts were usually with the latter. So were Karl Rove's. Condi followed her President. She did not see her role as that of banging heads together in the Principals' Committee, where the Big Beasts met. She once told me that she had no intention of becoming, like some of her predecessors, a rival Secretary of State. Powell, in a separate conversation, said that this was something that he would never allow to happen. In any case, Cheney, Rumsfeld and Powell did not have the kind of heads that would have been amenable to banging. They were just too big.

Colin Powell was a towering personality. In poll after poll he was voted the most popular figure in American public life, something of which he was inordinately proud. His story and career were an inspiration. He was the son of humble Jamaican immigrants who had settled in New York. Through sheer talent and application, he had risen rapidly through the ranks of the military. By the time he retired in 1993 he had become Chairman of the Joint Chiefs, the most senior position in the US armed forces. We gave him an honorary knighthood for his role in the First Gulf War. Powell was eloquent, charismatic, and imposing. There had been talk of his running for President on the Republican ticket in 1996. In private life he had made a fortune as a motivational speaker. He had once come to London at the Government's invitation to make a speech about minorities and the military. Politically, his appointment by Bush as Secretary of State had been a masterstroke. But when, during Blair's visits to the US, we saw Bush and Powell together, it was the impression of all in the British team that this was not a relationship made in heaven. I saw a great deal of Colin Powell. He was instantly likeable, straightforward and always on top of his brief.

With hindsight the fault line was all too predictable. In foreign policy Powell sprang from a mainstream Republican tradition, in which allies and pragmatism ruled and multilateralism had a legitimate, if limited, place. It was the 'realist' school of diplomacy. It had dominated US foreign policy since the Second World War and did not change much when the Democrats were in power. In Washington, as in London, foreign policy had tended for decades to be an essentially bipartisan pursuit. The presence in key positions in the Bush White House, Defense Department and State Department of tough nationalists and right-wing ideologues, with their visceral suspicion of international institutions, broke with this tradition. It was a repudiation not only of Clinton but also of Bush's father. Colin Powell was always going to be out of sympathy with this. Before he took office he was often heard to express scepticism about missile defences and invading Iraq. These became two of the signatures of George W.'s foreign policy in his first term.

Europeans analyse this as the struggle between unilateralism and multilateralism in US foreign policy. I told London that this was too crude and simplistic. So was the fear that the US might relapse into isolationism. You would sometimes find in Congress and the great American hinterland a nostalgic yearning for some golden age when isolation from the world might have been possible. But, today, it was not practical for a global power with global interests; and most Americans knew this.

The debate in the United States, I said, was over the terms of its engagement with the outside world. Since the American Revolution at the end of the eighteenth century, unilateralist reflexes had been hard-wired into the US world-view, Republican or Democrat. International commitments were judged against a national interest cost–benefit analysis, as much drawn by Congress as the administration. There was a preference for informal alliances and coalitions of the willing over the sovereignty-limiting provisions of international treaties, unless, as with NATO, the US was firmly in the driving seat.

There was something else that separated Colin Powell from his Cabinet colleagues. Cheney, Rumsfeld, Wolfowitz and Libby had signed up in the 1990s for something called the Project for the New American Century (PNAC). Its principles for foreign policy were aggressively nationalistic, interventionist, and pre-emptive. They emphasized the modernization of US forces, increases in the defence budget, and a global Pax Americana. Richard Perle, Chairman of the Defense Policy Board, was also a founding member, as were senior members of the National Security Council. The principles were the major intellectual underpinning of US foreign policy in Bush's first term.

The British government and the British ambassador found themselves forced to straddle the fault line. It mattered less before 9/11. There is a long tradition of internecine warfare between the State Department and the Defense Department. Up to a point the embassy expected it and was used to dealing with it. But, after 9/11, it was different. The issue was war and peace. This heightened and exposed the tensions inside the US administration. It sharpened and deepened the fault line. It made the challenge to British diplomacy immeasurably more complicated. It forced me to operate in a way that took me to the limit of what is permissible for an ambassador. My sleeve began to touch the machinery.

22

War

What follows below is about wars in Afghanistan and Iraq in 2001–3. Given the fog of controversy that still hangs over these events, I have done my best to separate hindsight from what I saw, heard and thought during this period. Except where otherwise stated, or where it is chronologically obvious, this chapter's descriptions of key incidents, conversations and judgements are to be found in the regular reports I sent to London at the time.

In July of 2002 I was invited by Leo Daly, a close friend, neighbour, and one of America's foremost architects, to spend a long weekend at something called the Bohemian Grove.

The Bohemian Grove is an institution that has its origins in the nineteenth century. It started out as a club in San Francisco for writers, artists and intellectuals. It purchased a large tract of virgin land in northern California for summer retreats. There, among the giant redwoods, the members of the club could draw inspiration from nature and discuss the meaning of life over campfires in the evenings. It was and remains for men only. Over the decades the summer retreat has grown into an elaborate phenomenon. It now comprises a series of weekends to which the elite of the entire United States flock. But the Grove itself remains largely unspoilt and undeveloped. Its hundreds of denizens are lodged in dozens of individual camps, each with its own name and traditions. The accommodation varies from spartan to very spartan. There is more than a whiff of the English public school.

It is considered a great honour to be invited. Despite the scale of the summer weekends, the Grove is an exclusive club. To join you must be proposed and seconded in the usual way by members; but the wait can then be so long that by the time the Grove is ready to admit you, your proposer and seconder may be dead. The members and their guests are among the most powerful and famous men in America: politicians, including ex-Presidents, captains of industry, Hollywood notables and artists of all kinds. There is a smattering of foreign guests. The rules of the Grove forbid the conduct of business; but it is hog heaven for the professional networker like an ambassador.

There is a multitude of events to keep everyone amused and intellectually nourished. Each year an original musical is commissioned and performed. Distinguished guests are invited to give outdoor lectures alongside a lake. I stretched out on the grass and listened to the film director William Friedkin talk fascinatingly about movie-making. I heard talks on genetic engineering and astronomy. The individual camps organize their own events, to which other camps are invited. Often the event is musical. There is a lot of jazz at the Bohemian Grove. The veteran rock artist Steve Miller is a member and performs most evenings. The most distinguished member of my camp was David Rockefeller, who organized an epicurean dinner at which we drank jeroboams of Petrus 1962.

As is the way of the world, some camps have greater lustre than others. Invitations to them are highly prized. Fortunately, Leo Daly and my official host, the winemaker Walter Sullivan, had access everywhere. One morning we went to one of the great institutions of the Bohemian Grove, the breakfast lecture given by Henry Kissinger. He was flanked by former President Bush and Jim Baker, Bush's Secretary of State. Part of the tradition is that Henry should be interrupted at the start of his talk by a Mariachi band. This is apparently in homage to his weakness for Mexican music. As usual, after playing a tune, the band withdrew and Henry continued his talk.

In 2002 Henry Kissinger's theme was Iraq. He agreed that after 9/11 pre-emptive action against threats to the nation's security could be justified. It was the beginning, he said, of a new era in international relations. It marked the end of a period inaugurated by the Treaty of Westphalia in 1648. The Treaty had concluded the Thirty Years War, which had ravaged continental Europe. One of the Treaty's principles was the sanctity of national sovereignty: on this basis the modern nation-state had come into being (I am not sure that the sixteenth-century monarchs Elizabeth I of England or

Henry IV of France would have agreed with this). Now, in certain circumstances, continued Kissinger, action violating a national frontier could be justified. (The historical reference, so typical of Kissinger, was appropriated by Tony Blair in a 2004 speech, when to the surprise of many to whom Blair the historian was a revelation, the Prime Minister referred to the Treaty of Westphalia.) This was prologue to Kissinger's saying that a war in Iraq could be justified. But he set out three conditions: Military action must be brought to a rapid and successful conclusion – a prolonged war would be very dangerous for America; the US had to get the diplomacy right; and it had to arrive in Baghdad with a clear plan for the succession to Saddam. It would be disastrous to begin debating a successor regime after deposing him.

This was a powerful and convincing presentation. I said as much to one of my neighbours at the table, Jim Woolsey. He had been Director of Central Intelligence under President Clinton. (He was also a champion ballroom dancer, as I had once witnessed at the embassy.) He had become one of the leading hawks on Iraq. He looked at me fiercely and said that the invasion would take place that autumn. I said, Impossible, nothing was ready. He brushed me aside in his fervid eagerness, as did other Washington hawks who were pressing hard for an invasion before the end of 2002.

Kissinger's standing was such that he continued to be consulted by the White House. When I told some of my closest contacts in Washington what he had said at the Grove, they took careful note. In the event, none of Kissinger's conditions was met.

When it is the hour of the generals, the diplomats usually leave the stage. We observe the ebb and flow of combat and air strikes, all the more anxious for knowing that our skills are mostly redundant for the duration of hostilities.

I remembered that from the time when I was in Washington during the First Gulf War of 1991. But for sheer nail-biting anxiety there had been nothing to compare with sitting in the Moscow embassy during the Falklands War of 1982. Every morning and evening I would glue my ear to the BBC World Service. *Sheffield* sunk, oh no! *Belgrano* sunk, great! It was no time for nuance. It was my country right or wrong. Who gave a damn for the *Belgrano*'s change of course? We were at war, for God's sake. We did not have a fit of the vapours every time the *Bismarck* changed course in 1941.

The Russians officially backed Argentina, a member of the long-forgotten Non-Aligned Movement, for which the Soviet Union professed support. In private it was another matter. My ambassador, Curtis Keeble, and I were regularly summoned to the Soviet Foreign Ministry. We would be handed a protest about the Royal Navy's expelling Soviet 'trawlers' from the exclusion zone imposed by Britain around the Falklands. These vessels were, of course, not trawlers at all, but spy ships bristling with electronic surveillance and listening equipment.

Once, after delivering a particularly stern protest, Vladimir Suslov, the head of the ministry's Second European Department, muttered to us as we were leaving: 'When are you going to drive those bastards into the sea? For God's sake hurry up!' After the Argentine surrender we were told that Suslov's department had cracked open a bottle of champagne. Another Soviet diplomat remarked to me: 'We would no longer have considered you a serious country if you hadn't defeated the Argentines.' Margaret Thatcher, the implacable foe of Soviet Communism, saw her popularity soar among Russians. Soon after the war's end I was in the back of a cab in Leningrad (now again called by its pre-revolutionary name of St Petersburg). I mentioned to the driver that I was British. 'Ah! Thatcher! *Molodetz!*' In rough translation: 'What a woman!'

Afghanistan and Iraq were different. In both the issue was 'regime change'. The goal was to remove the governments of both countries and to replace them with something better. In Afghanistan this was done with the full blessing of the United Nations and international law; in Iraq it was not. But in each case the task was the same: it was not simply to replace by force one set of rulers with another; it was also to create new democratic institutions, which would take rapid and durable root in unforgiving soil.

Clausewitz, the great nineteenth-century Prussian general and military strategist, said that war was merely the continuation of politics by other means. From the outset the enterprises in Afghanistan and Iraq were deeply political. If it was the hour of the generals, it was also the hour of the politicians and diplomats. The failure fully to grasp this led to many of the difficulties experienced by the US and its allies in Iraq and Afghanistan.

At the end of 2001 the US administration had forgotten Clause-witz. It had a deep-seated aversion to peacekeeping and nation-building. It considered its armed forces to be trained exclusively for war-fighting, a principal reason for its wish to get out of Balkans peacekeeping. This was particularly Don Rumsfeld's view; and in Afghanistan he was calling the shots. But success in Afghanistan meant winning the peace as well as winning the war.

I was concerned that, having, as they saw it, won the war, the Americans would try to leave the peace to others, notably the British, and move on elsewhere. Early in the Afghan campaign I had heard Condoleezza Rice thinking aloud about a division of international labour along such lines. I always had at the back of my mind that British troops were patrolling Kabul with our regimental ghosts from the slaughter of 1841.

As the year drew to a close, there was growing pressure in Wash-ington to do something about Iraq, but as yet no credible plan. There was instead a furious debate between hawks and doves.

I was a firm supporter of calling Saddam Hussein to account, if necessary by war. I have not changed my mind. I had been in the Washington embassy at the time of the First Gulf War in 1991. I had taken great pleasure in seeing the Iraqis driven out of Kuwait. International law may be a feeble creature, but you cannot allow larger states to swallow smaller states with impunity. The pleasure was short-lived. Almost immediately Saddam sought ways of evading the terms of the ceasefire. These were enshrined in a sequence of Security Council Resolutions. The war had left intact Saddam's best military unit, the Republican Guard. The ceasefire also allowed him to continue to use his military helicopters. Soon after the end of the war he promptly used both to execute a bloody suppression of a Shia revolt in southern Iraq. To this day there are those who believe that the US brought the war to a premature conclusion.

Iraq ran like a toxic stream through my time as ambassador, before and after 9/11. From my first weekend in 1997 there were repeated issues and crises to address with the Americans. As I arrived in Washington, Saddam was already playing cat and mouse with the first generation of UN weapons inspectors, making it ever harder for them to do their job. Finally, UNSCOM, as they were called, were forced to pack their bags at the end of 1998. On departure they were still unable to say what had happened to stocks of materials for making chemical and biological weapons that had gone missing after the 1991 Gulf War. To this day their fate is unknown.

This was not just a great humiliation for the UN after years of cumulative indignities inflicted by Saddam. It put in doubt the value itself of what had been achieved in driving Saddam from Kuwait. The Iraqi boulder was rolling back down the hill. I felt strongly that the UN Security Council should have taken its responsibilities after UNSCOM's departure and presented Iraq with an ultimatum: either to come into line with its UN obligations; or to face war. But the will to act was not there. France and Russia were more concerned to secure commercial advantage from a loosening of sanctions. After UNSCOM's departure, the Americans, with modest support from the British, fired some cruise missiles at Iraq in Operation Desert Fox. It was seen, including in Baghdad, for what it was: a half-hearted response to Saddam's increasing boldness.

Over three years later, after the fall of Saddam, the Americans set up the Iraq Survey Group (ISG). Its remit was to find out what had happened to Iraq's 'weapons of mass destruction' (WMD): chemical, biological and nuclear. In September 2004 the ISG issued its final report. After searching high and low for almost two years the group were unable to find any WMD. This seized the headlines. It was hugely embarrassing to Bush. It was more so to Blair, who had rested his case for war exclusively on Saddam's failure to disarm. But in their meticulous investigation, the group discovered much else besides. Most of this went unreported in the media. For example, it is impossible to avoid drawing the conclusion from the report that Saddam bought off France and Russia through supplies of discounted Iraqi oil and the promise of huge oil exploration contracts. The ISG documented how, by 2000, 'prohibited goods and weapons were being shipped into Iraq with virtually no problem'. All this was financed by illegal oil sales, which by 2002 had generated an income of over two and a half billion dollars. The Baghdad International Trade Fair in 2001 was by all accounts a great success.

The ISG also found 'numerous examples of Iraq's disregard for UN sanctions', including violations of the totemic Resolution 1441. This was the Resolution which, passed unanimously in November 2002, was supposed to have given Saddam Hussein a last chance to meet all his UN obligations, accumulated since the ceasefire in 1991.

On the eve of 9/11 the policy of containment was on its last legs, with sanctions crumbling and the oil-for-food programme abused by corruption and incompetence. We knew most of this at the time. This was why tightening sanctions had become a priority for Secretary of State Colin Powell in Washington and Foreign Secretary Robin Cook in London. The ISG's most important conclusion was that all the evidence pointed to Saddam's intention to restart his weapons programmes once sanctions had been lifted. The United Nations looked to be going the way of its 1930s predecessor, the League of Nations: toothless, discredited, its Security Council Resolutions flapping uselessly in the wind. The UN may be no panacea for the world's problems and in desperate need of reform; but, on balance, we are better off with it.

As I discovered from our travels around the US, it was also getting into the popular bloodstream, especially in universities, that the hardships of the Iraqi people were the fault of the US and Britain, not Saddam Hussein. At the University of North Carolina students demonstrating against sanctions interrupted a speech that I was making and presented me with a petition to have them lifted.

Saddam's decade-long corrosion of the UN's credibility was argument enough for dealing with him once and for all. To his credit Tony Blair spotted this as early as 1998, when he warned the international community of the dangers presented by Saddam. There is little difference between what the Prime Minister said then and what, for instance, he said to the House of Commons on the eve of war at the end of February 2003. In addresses to American audiences in 2002 and 2003 I used to quote in particular a Blair speech from January 1998. In a few succinct sentences it made the case against Saddam. You can agree or disagree with Blair on Iraq. But you cannot fault him on consistency. He was a true believer in the menace of Saddam. To make the case against the Iraqi leader, it was never necessary to have the horror of 9/11, never necessary to prove a link between the Iraqi regime and Al Qaeda, never necessary even to show that he had WMD which presented a clear and present danger. Saddam's threat was his ambition and intent, as the ISG report had demonstrated.

*

In 1998, halfway through President Clinton's second term in office, the United States Senate unanimously passed the Iraq Liberation Act, voting to give $97 million to the Iraqi opposition to Saddam. From that moment the overthrow of Saddam Hussein, otherwise known as 'regime change', became the official policy of the United States. Clinton, first fighting for his political life in *l'affaire* Lewinsky and then licking his wounds after surviving impeachment, was in no mood to take risks. He did nothing to implement the policy.

George W. Bush inherited it. Regime change was not a high priority for him in his first nine months in office. Condi Rice said to me a couple of times that we needed to do some thinking about Iraq. She set in train a review of Iraq policy, but nothing appeared to come of it before 9/11. There was, for example, no sign that I could detect of the President's wanting to exact revenge for Saddam's failed plot to assassinate his father.

I had had discussions in 2001 with Republican conservatives on Capitol Hill, who were all for fomenting rebellion inside Iraq by arming Ahmed Chalabi's Iraqi National Congress (INC). I knew that this was firmly resisted in the State Department and the Foreign Office, who considered the INC completely ineffectual. The FO was anyway against the principle of regime change. Chalabi was an Iraqi exile who lived a lot of the time in London. At the time I did not fully grasp his influence among the Republican Right. Nor could I quite understand why, when his name came up in conversation with Richard Perle or Paul Wolfowitz, each would so stoutly defend Chalabi's reputation. They would claim to me that he was a great patriot whose name was being dragged through the mud by the State Department and the CIA. I recall Wolfowitz taking me to one side in the interval of a Kennedy Center concert in late 2002 and hotly condemning the CIA for failing to see that Saddam had allowed Al Qaeda to set up camp in northern Iraq. 'They only see what they want to see,' he said furiously.

It was only later that I came to appreciate how skilfully and assiduously Chalabi had been lobbying in Washington since the early nineties. I was told that his stock-in-trade was to present plans for the overthrow of Saddam, with requests for money to carry them out. A constant theme in these presentations was that Iraq was ripe for regime change. It needed, he said, only a push from the outside and the Iraqis would rise up and get rid of Saddam. Chalabi's hypothesis was put to the test in 1995 when, under Clinton, the CIA helped him try to foment rebellion. It failed dismally; but, with the Republican Right, this did little to diminish his standing, or the potency of his argument that the INC, properly financed and supported by the US, would be able to provoke a successful revolt against Saddam.

The Washington hawks, who had known him personally for years, were eternally vulnerable to Chalabi: he told them what they wanted to hear. He offered a political plan for Iraq after Saddam. He helped sow the fatal seed that 'doing' Iraq would be relatively easy and that the invading forces would be welcomed as liberators. I came across telling evidence of this not long before the outbreak of war.

In January 2003 I found myself at the annual Alfalfa Club dinner. The origins of the club go back to the early twentieth century. Unlike the Bohemian Grove, women had been recently admitted to membership. It is a black-tie event which brings together in a Washington hotel the power elite of the nation's capital, with their guests. There is a long, raised top table, which is ranged at right angles to goodness knows how many other long tables. The top table accommodates the President, the Vice-President, the Secretary of State, the Defense Secretary, other members of the Cabinet, Supreme Court Justices, top White House advisers, some of the military leadership, and a handful of ambassadors, including invariably the British.

Sometimes I think that America is more organized into exclusive clubs than Britain is reputed to be. After the Alfalfa Club dinner there is, three months later, the Gridiron Club dinner. This is when the Washington press corps lay on an entertainment for more or less the same elite group, including again the President with top politicians and administration officials. The dinner and entertainment are twice as long as the Alfalfa Club's and half as amusing – and ambassadors do not get to sit at the top table.

I was also a member of the Metropolitan Club, which I had joined to play squash. It was old and fusty, heavily populated with ancient retainers. I expected Trollope or Dickens to make their appearance. It was another gathering place for the great and good of Washington. I had to submit to extensive interrogation by officers of the club before being judged suitable for membership. Entry into the Garrick in London is swift and simple by comparison.

The Alfalfa Club dinner is an amusing evening of jokey speeches by the President and senators, combined with elaborate ritual. It used to be said that each of the senators' speeches was written by the same scriptwriter for $10,000 a throw. The dinner is also an occasion of intensive networking. Between courses half the enormous room seems to be in motion as people move purposefully from one table to another. This includes approaching the top table in a constant stream, to greet, like supplicants, the President and the other Big Beasts. The top table is so high that usually it is only the supplicant's head and shoulders that rise to the level of the table. I loved the whole thing.

At the 2003 Alfalfa dinner I fell into conversation with the Vice-President. We were joined by his daughter Liz, who had a senior job in the State Department working on the Near East. She had approached the table from below to say hello to her father. She told me that she had been watching some of Tony Blair's parliamentary performances on the cable TV channel, C-Span. It always broadcasts Prime Minister's Question Time, cult viewing for American politicians, who are transfixed in shock and awe at the cut and thrust of spontaneous debate. The conversation turned to how Blair was going to overcome resistance in the House of Commons to going to war in Iraq. Cheney's chief of staff, Scooter Libby, had come to see me at the end of the previous year to find out about British parliamentary procedure. But I still worried that the US administration was underestimating Blair's difficulties. It had already obtained from Congress the previous October the authority to go to war. Blair needed something similar from the British Parliament. It was not certain that he would succeed. If he lost the vote, it would be regime change in London. I explained this to Cheney. He was dismissive: in a few months' time these difficulties would all be history. Bush and Blair would be fêted as heroes and liberators in Iraq.

Nine days after the attacks on the World Trade Center and the Pentagon, at the President's dinner for Blair in the White House on 20 September 2001, Bush had acknowledged the debate among his principal advisers at Camp David the previous weekend whether to go after Saddam Hussein at the same time as Al Qaeda. They decided against. The debate has since been described in detail by some of the participants. It was not difficult therefore for Bush to agree with Blair that the priority was Afghanistan, with Iraq put aside for discussion at a later date.

What did this portend for Iraq? It was not clear. But I was instinctively certain that it did not mean talking further about 'sharpening' sanctions and clamping down on the smuggling of Iraqi oil. This was a policy that had not so far been a roaring success for Colin Powell and Robin Cook. Iraq would be back.

Blair's second flying visit to Washington on 7 November 2001 did not take matters much further. Over dinner conversation was dominated by Afghanistan and the Middle East. There were anxieties about the progress of the Afghan campaign. We were alternately worried that it was going too slowly or too fast. Our allies against the Taleban were the warlords of the shaky Northern Alliance. We did not want one of them to overrun Kabul to the detriment of the authority of the future President, Hamed Karzai. But that was exactly what happened when five days later the Taleban fled the Afghan capital.

On the Middle East Colin Powell was eager to make a significant speech on American policy, something that had been on the stocks since before 9/11. The Saudis, as their ambassador in Washington, Prince Bandar, had told me at length months earlier, were deeply upset at the lack of American activity in the Middle East (sometimes when the Saudis wanted to reinforce a message for the US administration, Bandar would invite me to tea and tell me something which he knew I would report to London and London might then take up with Washington).

Blair too wanted to hear something that signalled greater American involvement in the perennial issue of Israel and the Palestinians. It was a leitmotiv of his foreign policy. But the President's antipathy towards Yasser Arafat was undisguised. The body language between Bush and Powell that evening was not great. Powell made a joke about resigning, Bush about Powell's being unsackable. The failed badinage fell to the floor with a thud.

After the capture of Kabul, as the sounds of battle in Afghanistan began to subside, the hum of speculation about Iraq became audible. There were, of course, other urgent foreign-policy issues to be addressed: 2002 was the year in which Pakistan and India came close to nuclear war; the intifada between Israel and the Palestinians had exploded into shocking and seemingly unstoppable violence; but at the beginning of 2002 the 800-pound gorilla lurking in the dark corners of chancelleries in Washington and London was Iraq.

On 29 January 2002 George W. Bush delivered the annual State of the Union speech to the usual joint session of Congress. As ever, it was an evening of great political theatre, with members of the Cabinet, the Supreme Court, the military leadership and the diplomatic corps in attendance. There was a large audience in the upper galleries. One gallery was reserved for the First Lady and special guests. The ambassadors are placed in the chamber in order of precedence. New arrivals sometimes have to stand at the back, as I did at my first State of the Union in 1998. By 2003 I had graduated to a seat among congressmen. The speech is invariably drafted to arouse optimism, confidence and patriotic fervour not only among the party faithful, but in the nation at large. Senators and congressmen of the President's party rise to applaud and cheer after almost every other line of the speech. Such is the respect for the office of the presidency that every now and again members of the opposition party will do the same, though for the most part they sit on their hands.

On this occasion it was the Axis of Evil speech. As soon as I heard the phrase I was taken back almost twenty years to the kitchen in my Moscow flat. It was there, with my short-wave radio wired up to a central-heating pipe to improve reception, that I heard on the BBC World Service President Reagan describe the Soviet Union as the Evil Empire.

Bush's speech made the world sit up. The reaction in Europe was almost universally hostile. Reagan's Evil Empire had evoked similar snorts of disdain. Yet those of us who had dealt with the Soviet Union in the 1980s would not easily forget the sophistication and expertise of American negotiators at that time; or that, far better than Britain and France, the United States had spotted the opportunity to induce the Russians to withdraw their forces of occupation from East Germany. Powell, Cheney and, especially, Rice had all been part of a team that had secured the reunification of Germany, a landmark in late twentieth-century history.

Even before the Axis of Evil speech mutual disenchantment between America and Europe had begun to grow. The transatlantic solidarity immediately following 9/11 was fast fracturing under the strain of a crude polemic about unilateralism versus multilateralism and how America should comport itself in world affairs. Rhetorical mortar shells flew across the Atlantic in each direction. With all this going on, I thought that the Axis of Evil speech, and the thinking behind it, demanded more than a knee-jerk reaction.

The speech had caught almost all in the State Department by surprise. Thanks to a source in the White House the embassy had a few hours' notice of what was coming. Rice and Powell told us afterwards that the Axis of Evil passage had been carefully and deliberately drafted, and that it enjoyed the President's personal stamp. I told London that agreeing or disagreeing with what Bush had said was one thing; but to describe it condescendingly as simplistic was itself simplistic. It was the birth of a Bush doctrine. Four months earlier, in his speech of 20 September to the joint session of Congress, where Blair had been present, Bush had depicted terrorist networks and the states that harboured them as the enemy. He had not even mentioned Iraq. The circle of enemies had now been enlarged to include so-called rogue states with WMD which could be given to, or fall into the hands of, terrorists.

The speech, to great controversy, gave Iraq, Iran and North Korea the rogue state label. The choice of these three – as opposed to, say, Libya or Syria – should have come as little surprise. Rice had already identified them in her seminal January 2000 article in *Foreign Affairs*. It put the three on notice that they were marked regimes. As the White House put it to me euphemistically, it was meant 'to change the terms of the debate'.

The United States had been unused to and unprepared for the violence of foreign terrorism. The attacks of 11 September 2001 were a cataclysmic shock to Americans. They had never before known what it meant to be vulnerable and threatened. Even today Europeans find this difficult to grasp. Unless you were living in America at the time it is not easy to imagine the impact on Bush himself. He was responsible for the security of nearly three hundred million American lives. The fear of further atrocity was overwhelming. There was intelligence that Al Qaeda was trying to get hold of technology for producing a 'dirty' nuclear bomb. However fanciful it may seem today, each member of the Axis of Evil was considered to have the capability and will to help Al Qaeda. It was a danger that, in the shadow of 9/11, Bush felt that he could not ignore. He had made it his life's mission to destroy, as he saw it, the nexus of terrorism and rogue WMD, if necessary by pre-emptive action.

With the Taleban defeated, the shadowy network of Al Qaeda was an unsatisfactory enemy. How did you declare victory over it in the war against terror? Rogue states were satisfyingly specific. They played, to Bush's political advantage, to the President's role as Commander-in-Chief. The Republicans had always missed communism and the Soviet Union as the tangible, Manichean enemy. I did not for a moment believe that this meant war with Iran and North Korea. But it had raised expectations of military action against Iraq. This was a new phase. The relative simplicities of overthrowing the Taleban had been left behind, to be replaced by the complexities of nation-building in Afghanistan, where we and the Americans did not always see eye to eye. Now the US had added to the pot the Axis of Evil. These new challenges were not something which could just be sub-contracted to Don Rumsfeld and General Tommy Franks, the head of the US military's Central Command, responsible for Afghanistan and Iraq.

Rumsfeld's dictum that the mission defined the coalition, not the coalition the mission, had always been slick but inadequate. The task was now to demonstrate to the Americans that it was both possible and desirable to reconcile the mission with the concerns of America's friends. It could call for some very plain speaking in private, including with the Vice-President, who was coming through London in March, and with Bush himself at Crawford, Texas, where Blair was due in April. The leverage was there. For all their brave talk, the Americans would always prefer to act in the world with allies than without. The Sheriff and his posse were part of American mythology.

With the Axis of Evil speech several streams of American thinking came together. Their combined effect was to nourish the President's belief that Iraq was too dangerous to be left to containment, that the officially mandated policy of regime change should be actively pursued, and that his supreme calling was to be the nation's Commander-in-Chief at a time of peril. The 'neocon' hawks, like Paul Wolfowitz and Richard Perle, saw Iraq as the anvil on which a realignment of forces in the Middle East favourable to the United States and Israel would be struck. The new Iraq, they argued, would inject stable democracy into a region of autocrats and tyrants. It would offer a haven for US military bases. It would reduce dependence on the Saudis and their oil. Saudi Arabia had for long been a close ally; but across the administration the fear that dared not speak its name was the kingdom's long-term stability. It was unclear who would succeed the ageing rulers of the royal family. As with Pakistan, so with Saudi Arabia, there were deep and possibly insuperable fissures in society and politics. It was a breeding ground of Islamic fundamentalism, the home of Wahabism. Osama Bin Laden was a Saudi. So were most of the 9/11 hijackers.

It was the Hour of the Hawks. Their Middle East vision had been gestating for years in the strategic closet. After 9/11 it burst into the open with all the force of something which had been long suppressed. Colin Powell may have thought that its standard bearers in the Defense Department and elsewhere were 'fucking crazies', and history's verdict looks likely to be that the strategy was terminally flawed both in conception and execution; but at the time, immediately after 9/11, the old pragmatism of 'realist' Republican foreign policy was unable to withstand the intellectual *élan* and polemical skill of the strategy's neocon protagonists. I always found that a debate with Wolfowitz or Perle or Kristol* was the intellectual equivalent of standing in a wind tunnel.

The events of 9/11 allowed the notion of pre-emption to insert itself into the hawks' strategic vision. I remember a conversation with Perle towards the end of 2001. He argued forcefully that the United States could not afford to wait and see whether Saddam would give WMD to terrorists. The risk was too great. National security demanded pre-emptive action. The argument was very similar to Tony Blair's in a speech made in Texas in the spring of the following year.

Soon after 9/11 it became clear that the fault line in US foreign policy between hawks and doves would henceforth run through Iraq and the Middle East. The hawks were in furious pursuit of evidence linking Saddam to the atrocities. Even Rice did not rule out the possibility that Al Qaeda had had a little help from Iraqi

* Editor of the neoconservative journal, *The Weekly Standard*.

friends. The State Department under Colin Powell and his deputy, Rich Armitage, were far more cautious and sceptical. Open warfare broke out in the media between surrogates of Wolfowitz and Powell. Wolfowitz told me that he was fed up with being demonized as an extremist by the State Department. The vision of Wolfowitz and his colleagues appealed to the President because of its democratic ambition. I heard Bush say at Camp David in September 2002 that putting American troops in harm's way would be justified if it brought democracy and freedom to the people of Iraq. He said it again, when Catherine and I dined with him at the White House just before we took leave of the United States. His words took us back to the little two-minute speech that he had rehearsed with us in the Governor's office in Austin, Texas, in 1999. Bush's concept of democracy and freedom has been at the heart of every speech that he has made on Iraq.

Something else also appealed. Early in 2003 I went with Jack Straw to see the Vice-President at the White House. Jack said something that triggered an unusually animated response. Cheney listed in detail a sequence of provocations and attacks by terrorists over the years against America. It had begun in 1996 with the blowing up of the US Army barracks at Al Khobar in Saudi Arabia. Then there had been the bombing of the USS *Cole* in Aden harbour and the attacks on US embassies in East Africa. America, said Cheney, had failed forcefully to respond, to the detriment of its reputation and interests in the Middle East. The time had come to change all that, to show that no one attacked America with impunity.

Meantime, Ahmed Chalabi and other INC spokesmen, exploiting their close links with the hawks, were frequent visitors to Washington – apparently stoking the fires of war, playing up the threat from Saddam, telling the US that it would be welcomed with rose petals in Baghdad.

Later, at the end of 2002, when, as used to be required of all ambassadors, I submitted my annual review, I said that the pressure for war came from groups inside the administration and political elite playing on a receptive President; but it did not come from the American people at large. All year I had been addressing groups big and small across America. Apart from an oil man in Houston I had failed to find anyone keen to go to war; but most Americans trusted their Commander-in-Chief and would follow where he led.

This drew me to a broader point. None of Bush's signature policies – on missile defence, tax cuts or the partial privatization of the federal government's pensions system – had much resonance with the mass of voters: they were policies driven from the top. But each was enormously attractive to the Republican Right. If there was one lesson which George W. Bush had learned from his father's failure to win a second term, it was not to alienate the Right as the elder Bush had done.

Looking back at the eighteen months between 9/11 and the invasion of Iraq, one question dominates all others. It is about the inevitability of war. The integrity and reputation of Bush and Blair depend upon it. The timing of the Iraq campaign, the wisdom or otherwise of the way in which the war was executed and its aftermath managed, the controversy in Britain over the September and 'dodgy' dossiers, and the final outcome in Iraq and Afghanistan – all these are huge issues that will help shape history's judgement on Bush and Blair. But they are qualitatively different from that of inevitability.

If, as many allege, Bush and Blair decided come hell or high water to go to war at their White House meeting on 20 September 2001, or at the Crawford summit in April 2002, or at the Camp David summit in September 2002, each can be justifiably charged with duplicity on a grand scale: with deceiving his public and using the UN both as smokescreen and facilitator for a conflict that was the first option, not the last. Those who believe Bush and Blair guilty as charged see a straight linear progression from, say, the start of military planning in early 2002 to the outbreak of war on 20 March 2003. A number of highly classified British documents, including one that I had authored, were leaked in 2004 and 2005, presumably to help make the case against Bush and Blair. But, sitting in Washington, working at the coal face, talking to contacts, the road to war looked to me at the time anything but straight or the destination preordained. Tracking the twists and turns in the debate around Iraq was for my staff and me the supreme challenge throughout 2002.

I had a handful of especially important contacts in the higher echelons of the US administration. They were also personal friends. The history is too recent for me to name them. They were at the heart of planning for the Iraq campaign. They were loyal and patriotic servants, committed to carrying out the President's policies.

Their overriding goal was that these policies should succeed. They saw that there were ways in which I could be of assistance to them. Because a trade was involved, absolute trust was the indispensable ingredient in our relationship. I wanted a clear understanding of where each of the main players in the US administration stood. I needed to know about the arguments, the tensions, and who would prevail. Members of my staff, both civilian and military, had similar relationships at their levels.

I was told things that were highly sensitive. I was always anxious about what would happen to the reports I sent to London. So were my American contacts. I would give the reports a very high security classification and address them only to two or three named individuals in No. 10 and the Foreign Office. I enjoined the recipients to handle them with the greatest care and, above all, not to quote them to other American officials or foreign diplomats. I knew Whitehall, its photocopying machines and the propensity of officials to flaunt sensitive information to show that they were in the know. If any of my contacts had been 'outed', they could have got into serious trouble. After each conversation one of them would always say: 'Don't get me burned!' Fortunately no one was burned.

Sensitive information was not given to me because my friends liked the colour of my eyes. I had to give something in return. My contacts followed closely what was going on in London. From a very early stage they assumed – rightly – that whatever Bush chose to do, Blair wanted to be with him. But these contacts knew the political difficulties that this would cause in Westminster and inside the Cabinet. They saw the tension between No. 10 and the Foreign Office. They always wanted to know where the centre of gravity lay in London.

The answer to that question was, invariably, in No. 10, Downing Street. As with Margaret Thatcher and the Falklands War, Blair and his staff dominated political and military strategy for Iraq. They did so to a greater degree than the White House and National Security Council chose to do in Washington. There, wide powers were delegated to Rumsfeld, as Secretary for Defense, and to General Franks. It was impossible to conceive of Geoff Hoon or General Sir Peter Wall being granted similar powers by Tony Blair. I found myself repeatedly answering the question: did something said by Jack Straw or Geoff Hoon represent the Prime Minister's views? Sometimes it did not.

There were wheels within these wheels. Blair and Bush spoke quite often on the phone. I would receive the records of these conversations. They too were highly sensitive, though in my time they had a tendency to be broad-brush rather than specific. One of my contacts, at the heart of contingency planning and sympathetic to British concerns, had a necessary operational interest in knowing what had passed between the President and the Prime Minister. American records of these conversations could emerge slowly, if at all. But the records that I received from London were of conversations only a few hours old. This meant that I was often better informed of how policy was moving inside the White House than my contact. An important part of the trade was to give him the gist of what had passed between Prime Minister and President. I thus found myself in the curious position of telling him what was going on in his own government as well as in mine. In return I received invaluable information for London. I did not say exactly how I had acquired it.

People forget that in the first few months of 2002 the violence between Israel and the Palestinians was as much a concern in Washington and London as any contingency planning for war in Iraq. This was in large part because the two were seen to be linked. It was a period of flux and uncertainty in American diplomacy. But, by the summer break, US policy had settled on a number of positions: the path to peace in Palestine lay through the liberation of Baghdad; the United States would not actively promote negotiations between Israel and the Palestine Authority (the Palestinian government) until its institutions were reformed and democratized, including by the replacement of Chairman Yasser Arafat; and Bush would for all practical purposes give Ariel Sharon, Israel's Prime Minister, a free hand in how he dealt with the intifada in the West Bank and Gaza. This included confining Arafat to an increasingly insanitary and battered headquarters in Ramallah. In the meantime, any outside diplomacy to unwind the violence would be left on a care-and-maintenance basis to Colin Powell.

This was not what Britain had wanted. We had sought the energetic re-engagement of the United States in the moribund Middle East peace process (diplomats' jargon for a negotiation which would lead to a final political and territorial settlement between Israel and the Palestinians, culminating in the establishment of an independent state of Palestine). We failed to get it. This underlined the limits of British influence – and the extent to which, by contrast, Israel had Washington's body politic in its grasp.

As Palestine blazed, the sound in Washington of debate about Iraq had become deafening. Blair was due to visit Bush at his ranch in Crawford, Texas, at the beginning of April. The British press had started to call the meeting a council of war. As is the way before such summits, officials on both sides prepare the ground. Some of the preparation on the British side was leaked to the press. It was a strange experience to see a photo in the *Sunday Telegraph* of the report that I had sent to London about a conversation over lunch at the embassy with Paul Wolfowitz.

It was by now clear that Bush was determined to implement the official American policy of regime change in Iraq; but the how and the when of it were uncertain. It made war probable but not inevitable. I had picked up from our military staff in the embassy the beginning of contingency planning in the Pentagon. Debate inside the administration was fuelled by a growing awareness of the political risks and practical difficulties of going to war. There were one or two people in Washington, whose judgement I greatly respected, who thought that when Bush fully realized the scale of his Iraqi ambition, he would see that the risk was too great.

It was time to put our fix into American thinking before it coagulated and Blair arrived at Crawford. David Manning, the Prime Minister's Foreign Policy Adviser, came to Washington in mid-March to see Condi Rice. A few days later I gave lunch to Wolfowitz. It was reports of these two sets of encounters that were leaked in 2004.

The central issue was to influence the Americans. Blair had already taken the decision to support regime change, though he was discreet about saying so in public. It would be fruitless to challenge a fixed, five-year-old policy that had bipartisan support in the US. It was hard to see how Saddam could be de-fanged without being removed from power. Blair was also firmly wedded to the propositions that, to have influence in Washington, it was necessary to hug the Americans close; and that the world would self-evidently be a better place without Saddam Hussein.

Support for regime change caused deep concern inside the Foreign

Office. The King Charles Street legal experts' advice was that regime change, however desirable, could not alone justify going to war. Then there were the questions, valid enough, of *realpolitik*. These boiled down to uncertainty and risk: how reliable was the Iraqi opposition? how did we know that a successor to Saddam would be an improvement? if it came to military action, how much international support would there be? what would be the wider effects in the region? what about the Israel–Palestine conflict? where did the UN fit into all this? did regime change necessarily mean war? and so on. These were the tough questions on which we wanted the Americans to focus; they provided David Manning's and my scripts. But we did not want just to put questions. We also wanted to suggest answers that the Prime Minister could press when he came to the President's Texas ranch two weeks later.

Having taken my cue from the Manning–Rice exchanges on 12–13 March, I distilled the messages for my lunch with Wolfowitz on 17 March. I liked Paul Wolfowitz a lot. I admired his formidable intellect. I always enjoyed a conversation with him. Sunday lunch did not disappoint.

To reinforce my credentials as someone who had something to say worth listening to, I emphasized the Prime Minister's commitment to regime change. I wanted Wolfowitz to know that we were starting from the same premise and that in Britain it was not without political cost. It was the diplomacy of 'Yes, but . . .' I had learned it in Brussels in the late seventies when working as a foot soldier in our Permanent Representation (i.e. embassy) to what was then called the European Communities. I was always struck by how much more successful than the British the French were in winning arguments with the other member states or the European Commission. The French had, of course, the advantage of being a founder-member of the European project, while Britain was seen already as a grudging late-comer. If some policy was proposed to which the UK had objections, we had a habit of saying straight out that we rejected it for the following half-dozen reasons. Backs went up all round the meeting room, where Anglo-Saxon plain speaking was not widely appreciated. The French, by contrast, if they wanted something blocked or amended, would welcome the proposal for its brilliance and ingenuity and suggest that it might be improved still further by a few technical amendments. The French would then reel off a list of problem areas no less than our own. But bathing in the warm sunshine of extravagant French praise, the meeting would be far more inclined to make the changes acceptable to France.

With Paul Wolfowitz, I went through the 'buts' in our 'yes, but ...' approach. Of course, if it came to war, the US had the military power to go it alone and prevail; but if it wanted to go into Iraq in company, it would need to take on board the concerns of potential coalition partners and the international community. Attacking Iraq would be a tough sell in Britain and continental Europe. There had to be a strategy for building international support. So what was needed was a clever plan which convinced people that there was a legal basis for toppling Saddam and that the US was taking into account international opinion. The UN had to be at the heart of such a strategy. We would need to wrongfoot Saddam in the eyes of the Security Council. This, anyway, was long overdue. One way was to demand the readmission of the UN weapons inspectors into Iraq. If he refused, this would not only put him in the wrong but also turn the searchlight onto the multiple Security Council Resolutions of which he remained in breach.

As part of this strategy, I stressed the critical importance of making progress in defusing the violence between Israel and the Palestinians. Wolfowitz listened carefully; but he was noncommittal. On Iraq itself he was more interested in reminding the world of Saddam's savage barbarism. He was, he said, less attracted to fomenting a military coup against Saddam than to replacing the regime with a democratic alternative.

Two weeks later, on the eve of Blair's visit to Bush's Texas ranch, the escalating violence between Israel and the Palestinians had reached such a pitch that for a while it pushed Iraq into the background. There had been hideous Palestinian suicide bombings. Israeli tanks had moved into the crowded Palestinian towns on the West Bank. There were almost daily civilian casualties on both sides. International opinion, including in Britain, was clamouring for the withdrawal of Israeli armour from the towns.

As an old press secretary I was focused on the joint press conference that Bush and Blair would have to hold after their Crawford talks. Unless the Americans called also for Israeli withdrawal, the press would drive a coach and horses between the two leaders. There had to be common ground on which the two of them could stand. I said this to anyone who would listen in the administration.

In the usual assessment sent to Blair just before his visit, I said that the Americans were only now starting to look at the hard questions on Iraq: the need for international support; the how and the when of removing Saddam; above all, what would happen afterwards. These were the issues on which the Prime Minister should focus; but they included also the feasibility of bringing Saddam to book while Palestine burned. Blair needed to find out from Bush how far the Americans were prepared to let Sharon go on the West Bank in the name of fighting terrorism.

On 4 April 2002, a couple of days after my report, the President made a statement on the Israel–Palestine crisis. It was extremely tough on the Palestinians and Yasser Arafat. It rightly condemned terrorism and suicide bombings, but it also called for the withdrawal of Israeli tanks from the West Bank towns. Immediately afterwards the Israelis said that this was fine by them: they would leave when the job was finished. I nagged the administration to impose a time limit. Twenty-four hours later the administration was briefing that withdrawal meant 'without delay'. I was pleased. The statement provided the necessary common ground. It envisaged a final settlement in which two states, Israel and Palestine, would cohabit. It introduced some much-needed balance into America's public treatment of Israel and the Palestinians. The President and Prime Minister could now get through the press conference in good shape.

Obviously the White House had not wanted what would have been seen as a major row between Bush and Blair. They needed Blair's support for whatever the future held for Iraq. Bush had also been coming under criticism at home for inconsistency in his approach to Israel/Palestine. This was the result once again of public differences between Colin Powell and administration hawks. The 4 April statement was supposed to draw a line under all that; in fact it started to fall apart as soon as Blair left Texas the following weekend. In my time it marked the high tide of American willingness to get tough with Sharon.

I had had my first inkling of what was to come in a conversation during the Crawford summit with one of the President's senior advisers. I had remarked on how useful the 4 April statement had been. This had been greeted with a gloomy face and a curt, 'We shall see.' The gloom had soon been explained. The 4 April statement had come under fierce criticism from the Republican Right. Bush was being charged with losing 'moral clarity' in the war on terrorism, for not seeing that Arafat was the moral equivalent of Bin Laden. The decision, taken almost jointly by Blair and Bush at Crawford, to send Colin Powell immediately to the region to try to tackle the violence had been greeted on the Right with intense suspicion.

The problems went beyond the Right. The instinctive pro-Israel reflex of the US Congress was a constant of American politics. The Israelis did not like being told to get out of the West Bank towns without delay; they were also intensely suspicious of Powell's mission. Their lobbyists had got to work on Capitol Hill. The former Israeli Prime Minister, Binyamin Netanyahu, who walked and talked like an American, had come to Washington to help them. To a background of bloody suicide bombings in Israel he had fanned the flames of anti-Palestinian sentiment and belittled the significance of Powell's mission. Several senators had said to me that the 4 April statement had been a mistake. Richard Haass, Powell's Head of Policy Planning in the State Department, had described to me the mood in Congress as 'more Likud than Likud'.

All this was having its effect on the administration. Netanyahu, despite his criticism of Powell's mission, had been received by Cheney and Rice. There had been little sign of compensating high-level public backing for Powell from inside the administration. His hand had been weakened with Sharon and the Palestinians. The White House spokesman had started to retreat from 'without delay' for the Israeli army's withdrawal from West Bank towns; he had even described Sharon as a 'man of peace'. The administration was reverting to its instinctive, heavily pro-Israel position, where it felt most comfortable.

Powell's mission to reinvigorate the peace process and quell the violence between Israel and the Palestinians failed. It was a failure also for what Britain wanted in the Middle East. One of Powell's closest aides said to me that Powell would not make further visits to the region if he was to be 'fucked again' by his enemies in Washington while he was away. I told London that hell was more likely to freeze than Bush threaten Sharon with a big stick.

Among another set of highly classified documents leaked to a British newspaper in 2005 was a Cabinet Office note of July 2002. It recorded that Blair had told Bush at the Crawford ranch in April that 'the UK would support military action to bring about regime change, provided that certain conditions were met: efforts had been made to construct a coalition/shape public opinion, the Israeli–Palestine crisis is quiescent, and the options for action to eliminate Iraq's WMD through UN weapons inspectors had been exhausted'.

At the end of July, when the note was drafted, none of these conditions was anywhere near to being met. Leave aside the precise meaning of 'quiescent', it had been clear since April that we could not expect decisive intervention by the US administration to unwind violence in the Middle East. With the passage of the months, the US position had moved even further in the other direction.

In late June Bush made another *ex cathedra* statement on the Middle East. This replaced the ill-fated predecessor of 4 April. It followed further suicide bombs against Israel and fresh evidence of Arafat's links with terrorist organizations. It was so contentious in the writing that, with the usual battle between the State Department and almost everyone else, it had run to almost thirty drafts.

The British government welcomed the statement, though from London's point of view it was hardly ideal. It was, to be sure, a plan, signalling some measure of US engagement in the peace process; but, more than ever, it put the onus on the Palestinians to create the conditions for peace and political negotiations with Israel. It was infused by a recent idea (acquired, so I was told, from Sharon's people) that there had to be democratic reform of the Palestinian institutions before anything could move. This was code for getting rid of Arafat. The Republican Right and the Israelis were cock-a-hoop at the statement; so was Karl Rove. He wanted to raise the Jewish-American vote for Bush from around one-fifth to a third.

For Britain the statement proved, in fact, to be a step backwards. By putting the onus so heavily on the Palestinians to move first, it meant that there would be no early progress. In the end it took death to remove Arafat two years later. The statement said nothing about how the plan would be implemented; this was to be left to Colin Powell. But Powell was now being regularly outgunned by his opponents in the administration. The plan dribbled into the sand.

So much for the Middle East. Nor, at the time the leaked Cabinet

Office note was drafted, had we left the starting gate in pursuit of the UN or building an international coalition.

Since the Crawford meeting a question had been growing in my mind. When is a condition not a condition? Had Blair said in terms to Bush at Crawford that he would be unable to support a war unless British wishes were met? I doubted it. I was not present for the two leaders' exchanges at the ranch. For long periods of time they were alone together. David Manning was there for some of the time, particularly when Israel–Palestine was under discussion.

On the Sunday morning of the Crawford weekend, the Blair cavalcade went by road to College Station, home of Texas A. and M., the great public university. Here the Prime Minister was to meet President Bush senior and make a speech at the Presidential Library where the elder Bush's presidential archive was housed. I had had no time to debrief either the Prime Minister or David Manning on the Crawford talks; but it was never really necessary. Blair revealed much of his thinking in a well-written, well-delivered speech that never got the press attention it deserved. I was seated between Condi Rice and ex-Secretary of State Jim Baker (not a man easy to please). Both were in raptures afterwards.

The speech was Blair's doctrine of pre-emption. The lesson of 9/11 was, he said, that you did not wait to be hit if you saw a threat coming. You dealt with it before it materialized. Saddam Hussein was such a threat. Doing nothing about him was not an option. The speech cut Osama Bin Laden and Saddam Hussein from the same piece of cloth. The conflation of the war against terrorism with a war to be rid of Saddam was one of the areas where Blair later became most vulnerable to criticism. For the first time in my hearing, Blair embraced regime change.

The speech contained a passage that made me sit up. In a reference to democratic values, Blair said that when 'America is fighting for those values, then, however tough, we fight with her – no grandstanding, no offering implausible and impractical advice from the touchline'. To an American audience it was another uncon-ditional statement of solidarity among several that Blair had uttered since 9/11. Had he not said on 4 October 2001 at the Labour Party Conference: 'We were with you at the first. We will stay with you till the last'? Blair's words at the Presidential Library were heard, as they were meant to be, as a commitment to stand by America and

George W. Bush, however the cards fell; but the commitment was not the same thing as an operational decision to go to war in the spring of 2003, even if war was the probable outcome.

Preconditions do not mix easily, if at all, with a commitment like that. They become instead what you would like to have, if possible, rather than what you insist on. There comes a point where, if you hug too close, it becomes an end in itself. As the outcome of the Crawford summit began to percolate through the American administration, this became rapidly apparent. In the middle of May I had a conversation with a senior contact at the heart of contingency-planning for Iraq, who warned me that the 'buts' in our 'yes, but' position were being forgotten. People were hearing what they wanted to hear. Little work was being done on the UN dimension and getting the weapons inspectors back in. With great prescience my contact said that the nightmare would be if Hans Blix, the leader of the then dormant UN weapons inspection team, to be reactivated in November, judged the Iraqis to be cooperating and the US did not.

My anxieties mounted through the summer months. I banged away to the Americans with our post-Crawford message. If it came to war, the UK would be with the US; but it would be indispensable to build a public case for attacking Saddam. Exhausting UN processes on inspections and unwinding the violence between Israel and the Palestinians had to be part of this. The usual reply was that, with active UK–US contingency planning moving ahead, British 'conditions' were getting less and less traction.

By early July I told London that the UK risked being taken for granted. We were getting too little in return for our public support. The Prime Minister's prescription for handling Israel–Palestine looked to be going nowhere. The Americans were being churlish and difficult about giving British steel companies exemptions from tariffs that should not have been imposed in the first place. I gave other examples of unfriendly American behaviour. This was a lousy backdrop to taking part in any military action against Iraq. There needed to be a plain-speaking conversation between Prime Minister and President to get these issues out into the open.

Later that month Blair sent a message – one of a pithy series in his characteristic short-sentence, short-paragraph style – that, among other things, set out a strategy for tackling Iraq which included the

UN. David Manning followed in person a little later, at the end of the month, when he was able to lay out for both President and National Security Adviser what was at stake for the UK and how we saw the way ahead.

Despite these efforts, we entered the summer holiday period with no agreed approach on either the UN, or on putting together an international coalition, or on what would happen if and when Saddam were removed. The Iraqi pulse was beating faster in Washington; but on key issues there remained an absence of policy and detail.

The UN became the focus of all our, and Colin Powell's, concerns. Taking the UN route – that is, giving Saddam one last chance to come into compliance with his UN obligations – looked to be a panacea. It offered: a way to refocus international public opinion on Saddam's iniquities; the means to create an anti-Saddam coalition of states; legality for any attack on Iraq; political cover in the UK from those, mainly in the Labour Party, who were both anti-war and anti-American; the reintroduction of the weapons inspectors into Iraq; a bridge to post-war Iraq, where the UN would have an indispensable role; and for some in the Foreign Office and the State Department, a means of avoiding war altogether.

At the beginning of September 2002, Bush announced what London so desperately wanted to hear. He would go to the UN to seek support for tackling Saddam. He would consult Congress and seek authority for war, if that was what it came to. He would consult also with foreign leaders. Phone calls to Paris, Moscow and Beijing were mentioned. Tony Blair would be coming to Camp David on 7 September for an afternoon's talks.

Bush's initiative got him off the defensive. It followed another period of drift and confusion. A fierce public polemic over Iraq had been waged during August; great figures from the elder Bush's administration, like Brent Scowcroft and Jim Baker, had emerged in the press to enjoin caution and the importance of dealing with Iraq through the UN. The Vice-President had responded towards the end of the month with a speech to war veterans so dismissive of UN weapons inspections that, so I was told, it embarrassed the White House.

Bush had let the polemic run through August, even though he

had apparently accepted already that, at least in principle, American interests would be better served by taking the UN route. It is hard to gauge Britain's influence on his decision. A private meeting between Colin Powell and George Bush on 5 August looks to have been decisive. A note of this meeting later fell off the back of a lorry into my hands; it recorded Powell's compelling description of the likely damage to American interests around the world, if the US chose to go it alone against Saddam. It also showed once again that Bush's conservative and hawkish instincts were tempered by a strong sense of *realpolitik*.

One of Powell's arguments was that Britain needed UN cover. Jack Straw, who had built a solid relationship with Powell, had made this point in spades. Something then occurred to me: Britain was acquiring the status of indispensable ally. I had depressed myself by the thought that Tony Blair's unconditional support for Bush had destroyed British leverage; but it dawned on me that the Americans really needed us by their side if it came to war. Scooter Libby, Cheney's chief of staff, said to me later that we were the only ally that mattered. That was a powerful lever.

I took stock on the eve of Blair's arrival: Bush's decision to go the UN route was welcome, as far as it went; but it left a host of questions unanswered. He was going to disclose his thinking on Iraq the following week in a speech at the annual opening of the UN General Assembly. But there was an unresolved debate at the highest levels of the administration about what should go into the speech. Should the President propose a new Security Council Resolution? Should he canvas the possibility of more than one? Should any Resolution be 'light and short' or 'heavy and coercive'? Either way should it demand of Saddam the re-admission of the weapons inspectors? Or should his speech, as the hawks wanted, simply exhort the UN to take its responsibilities towards Iraq, or else?

Weapons inspections were especially controversial. Even Colin Powell had once said to me that the worst outcome in Iraq would be a sequence of 'Potemkin' or phony inspections, which led to Saddam being given a clean bill of health and sanctions lifted. Washington's view of 'exhausting UN processes', before military action could be undertaken, might prove very different from our own. The UK could find itself in an awkward two-way stretch between the Americans and others in the Security Council.

There were other policy gaps to be filled. Biggest of all, post-war Iraq was a blind spot in Washington. The White House appeared to have bought fully into the neocon idea that with the overthrow of Saddam, all would be sweetness and light in Iraq, with automatic benefits elsewhere in the Middle East. In my view post-war Iraq would make pacifying Afghanistan look like child's play. The US was in greater need of coalition and UN support for what was likely to be a protracted post-war phase than for the attack itself.

Bush had, on return from his summer break, repeated publicly that his policy was the removal of Saddam Hussein. If he could have followed his instincts, he would, like Cheney, have moved to attack Iraq tomorrow; but his head had told his heart to go to the UN and launch a process of consultation at home and abroad. To a degree Bush would be bound by its dynamic. The US would not have full control over the timetable. My final, not very original, thought was that it was more important to get Iraq right than to do it fast.

On the Friday night before Blair's Saturday arrival a familiar voice came through on the phone in my study. It was one of the most experienced and prominent foreign policy practitioners of Clinton's administration. The voice warned me that Dick Cheney would be present throughout Tony Blair's discussions with the President the following day.

'How the hell do you know?' I asked.

'Don't ask, don't tell,' was the enigmatic reply. 'But Blair had better watch out.'

The voice was right. When we got to Camp David the following day the Vice-President was there to greet us with the President. He attended all the meetings, both in restricted session (Bush, Blair, Manning, Rice) and plenary. It brought home to me as never before Cheney's influence in the Bush administration.

While Bush, Cheney and Blair met in restricted session, the rest of us began discussing how to make the public case against Saddam: on the British side, Jonathan Powell, Alastair Campbell and I; on the American Karen Hughes, Dan Bartlett* and Steve Hadley. Two weeks later the first of the British dossiers would be published. The original plan was for the Americans to publish their own more or

---

* Counsellor to the President.

less simultaneously; but it became entangled in a bureaucratic jungle.

Our deliberations were interrupted by the emergence of Bush and Blair from their conclave and the start of the plenary meeting. The President announced that the Prime Minister had *cojones*. I may have been the only member of the British team who understood that this meant 'balls'. It was a tribute to Blair's unequivocal reaffirmation to Bush of his earlier commitment to stand by the Americans, including in a war. That was what the Americans wanted from the Camp David summit. Bush, in return, would go to the UN to give Saddam one last chance to come into compliance with his international obligations. It was understood that, if he failed to take his chance, military action would ensue.

Once again this was not an irrevocable operational decision to go to war in early 2003; but, since the two leaders had last met five months previously, contingency planning had moved up several gears.

At his meeting with Bush, Blair pressed the case for a fresh Security Council Resolution to secure the weapons inspectors' return to Iraq. As they had got off the aircraft from London, the No. 10 team were divided whether one or two Resolutions would be necessary to bring Saddam to book, but Blair, like Colin Powell, was clear that re-engaging with the UN was meaningless without the return of the inspectors. That would require a further Resolution.

Bush did not share Cheney's adamantine hostility to the UN. He had already talked in public earlier in the year about getting the weapons inspectors back into Iraq. But he was not quite ready to sign up to Blair's prospectus. There would have to be further debate with his advisers, notably Cheney, whom he gently teased from time to time in the meeting. Cheney seemed to enjoy it, his lop-sided grin spreading across his face. As the meeting broke up, Bush asked Blair to soft-pedal on the inspectors until he had got things sorted out in Washington.

Tony Blair had come to Camp David to pin down the President's commitment to the UN path. In this he succeeded, so meeting a main 'condition' for going to war; but the devil, once again, was in the detail. As Blair's aircraft took off that evening from Andrews Air Force Base for the UK, much of the detail remained unsettled. The crucial debate had yet to be concluded inside the administration.

*

As soon as Blair left, battle was fiercely re-engaged among the Big Beasts. Cheney continued to argue against mention in the President's UN speech of another Security Council Resolution and the return of the inspectors. He feared that this would play into Saddam's hands. Powell argued the opposite. It was a close-run thing. I was in daily contact with someone involved in the drafting. As usual the speech went through innumerable drafts. In some versions the reference to a Resolution was in, in others it was out.

By the eve of the speech, I was pretty clear that Powell and Blair were going to get what they wanted. There was a last-minute hiccough when, apparently innocently, the wrong version of the speech was put on the President's teleprompter in New York. It omitted the reference to a Resolution. But Bush adlibbed its reinstatement, talking about Resolutions in the plural. This was to cause some confusion in the coming months.

There was considerable rejoicing in London and elsewhere about Bush's General Assembly speech on 12 September. It was remarkably emollient in tone towards the UN. People were astonished at Bush's announcement that the US would rejoin UNESCO (it had left in 1984, in protest at the body's waste and incompetence). Had he had multilateral brain surgery? Diplomacy is sometimes like mountaineering. As you scale one ridge, falling exhausted at its summit, you look up to see another in front of you. Back in Washington the struggle between hawks and doves simply moved to other battlefields. For two months Colin Powell led US diplomacy in the negotiation of what emerged on 8 November as UN Security Council Resolution 1441. In the process, not only was he engaged in stubborn and intricate bargaining with other members of the Security Council; but he had constantly to watch his back in Washington, where there were strongly competing views about the content of the emerging Resolution.

The struggle had so far been about the principle of a Resolution and the desirability of seeking the return of the weapons inspectors. On these Powell, with a little help from Blair (and two other strongly pro-American Prime Ministers, Aznar of Spain and Howard of Australia), had prevailed. The debate now moved to the trigger for war and how it was to be defined in the Resolution. This was to make the earlier arguments look mild by comparison.

In October I had a long conversation with Scooter Libby, the

Vice-President's chief of staff. It was typical of the resistance in Washington to the British view of a new Security Council Resolution. Like his boss, Scooter started from the proposition that there was no need at all for a further Resolution. Saddam was already in violation of so many that to add another to the pile was superfluous; but if there had to be another, it should require only that Saddam make a full and accurate declaration of his WMD holdings. Since he was bound to cheat, this would be reason enough to go to war. All this was delivered in Scooter's quirky, caustic style in an office once occupied by Teddy Roosevelt. I replied that the British would never accept that a defective declaration on its own could be a *casus belli*. There had to be a pattern of Iraqi non-cooperation as well.

For two months the front-line action was all in New York, where my UN colleague Jeremy Greenstock bore the brunt of negotiating for Britain. My job was to monitor the instructions being sent from Washington to America's negotiators and, where possible, to try to influence them in the direction that London wanted.

In early October, a month into the negotiations, agreement on a new Resolution looked a distant prospect. Meantime Bush had duly secured from both Houses of Congress authority for the use of military force in Iraq. The war pulse began to beat faster. I took stock again. I went back to basics and asked the question: will the President go to war? The answer was not straightforward. There were some interesting cross-currents.

Some things had not changed. Bush wanted to be rid of Saddam. He was the prime mover of US policy; he believed it impossible to disarm Saddam without eliminating him. Attempting the UN route offered the best conditions for this. Nobody could rest secure until he was gone. Even highly intrusive inspections were unlikely to be enough. They would more likely be the tripwire for war.

But, from talking around the administration and Capitol Hill, I thought that those arguing for more haste, less speed had acquired some traction. Bush himself had toned down his bellicose rhetoric. There was less overt talk of regime change, more of the threat presented by Iraqi WMD. It had helped him secure the large congressional majorities authorizing war. Senators and congressmen were in turn being told by the polls that their constituents would be far happier going to war in international company and under UN cover. Those focusing on Iraq after Saddam were becoming acutely conscious that going to war without UN cover was one thing; ruling Iraq without benefit of UN backing quite another.

This had sharpened the dilemmas for the White House. The conventional wisdom in Washington envisaged two scenarios, each leading to war: the Security Council negotiations collapsed, in which case, in Bush's eyes, the UN would have failed the test; or Saddam defied a new UN Resolution, so bringing upon him the full force of the international community.

There was a third way, however, of particular concern to the hawks, but not only to them. This was that Saddam might fold his cards, accept inspections, and force the US to take 'yes' for an answer. If Saddam was as cunning as his reputation, he would give UNMOVIC (the acronym for the latest group of United Nations weapons inspectors under Dr Hans Blix) and the Security Council no cause for complaint before the US presidential election campaign of 2004. Once that began Bush would not be able to go to war.

Bush's patience was meanwhile being tested by the slowness of negotiation in New York and what was seen as French obstinacy. The diplomatic arm-wrestling in New York continued with tortured slowness, as the protagonists argued over paragraphs, sentences, words and even punctuation. I continued to fear that British and American views of what constituted exhausting the UN process could suddenly diverge. In discussion with the White House of a possible trigger for war, they had conceded that there would have to be a pattern of non-cooperation by Saddam to justify military action. But I did not think that this was bankable. Towards the end of September, on a visit to London, I warned No. 10 to prepare for everything going wrong at the UN in New York.

In early October I had visited the great US naval base at Norfolk, Virginia, and spent the day on the massive nuclear-powered aircraft carrier USS *Harry S. Truman*. The captain told me that they were ready to sail to the Gulf as soon as the order came. As I left the vessel, I was struck by the thought that, if you were inside the war machine, it must be very difficult to think anything other than that war was inevitable. This raised the most crucial question of all: had US mobilization reached such a point that there was already an insoluble contradiction between the planned timing of military action and the timetable for weapons inspections, if and when the inspectors got back into Iraq?

When I put this last point to a White House contact, I was told that the President had not yet signed off on going to war. Nothing was yet irrevocable. Powell gave Straw a similar answer when the Foreign Secretary visited Washington in October.

So, as of early October, we had not yet arrived at the moment of truth. I knew that I was in a tiny minority in thinking at the time that if it all went wrong in the UN negotiations in New York, and the US was faced with going to war alone, Bush might blink. Or, to put it another way: what Britain decided to do in such circumstances could be the decisive factor in the White House.

At first blush United Nations Security Council Resolution 1441 of 8 November 2002 was a triumph against the odds. It had taken two months of arduous negotiation. It passed unanimously. It was a battle with the hawks that Britain and Colin Powell had won, at least on paper. The Resolution made clear that, to use the UN jargon, a 'material breach' of its provisions would require from Iraq both a defective declaration of its WMD holdings and a failure to cooperate with the inspectors.

The Resolution put Saddam Hussein well and truly in the dock. It offered him a final opportunity to comply with his disarmament obligations, as set out in almost a dozen earlier Resolutions going back to 1991. It required Iraq to provide 'an accurate, full, final, and complete disclosure' of all aspects of its WMD programmes. The Resolution threatened 'serious consequences' if Saddam failed to meet these demands. It further demanded that, so as to gauge Iraq's compliance, the weapons inspectors should have 'immediate, unconditional, and unrestricted' access to sites of their choosing. A few days after its passage, Saddam accepted the terms of the Resolution. He had already agreed in October to the return of the UN weapons inspectors. Later in November the inspectors went back to Iraq after a four-year absence.

Jeremy Greenstock, with some back-seat driving from Jack Straw, had done a first-rate job in near-impossible conditions. In Washington there was a bull market in Colin Powells. There was a feeling that Saddam might be brought to heel without going to war.

The triumph was short-lived. It carried the seeds of its own destruction. As so often in diplomacy, the price of unanimity was ambiguity. The Resolution fudged the trigger for war. It failed to explain what the 'serious consequences' for Iraq would be if it were found in 'material breach' of the Resolution. In UN-speak the phrase 'all necessary means' was the customary code for war. 'Serious consequences' was a diluted substitute that did not enjoy the same pedigree. It had emerged as a hard-fought compromise between, mainly, the French and the Americans. As a result, the French, Russians and a majority of other members of the Security Council were able to claim that a breach of 1441 could not alone constitute the trigger. There would be, as they put it, no automaticity. They would need, they said, a further meeting of the Security Council and a second Resolution to authorize war. The US, by contrast, maintained with equal authority that if Saddam failed to meet the demands of 1441, no further Resolution would be necessary. In Washington I sought to paper over the crack by saying that since Dr Blix would have to give progress reports on the inspectors, there would be further Security Council discussions in any case; that would be the time to decide on a further Resolution. But the ambiguity proved to be the rock on which UN Security Council unity foundered on the eve of war the following year.

The Washington hawks hated Resolution 1441, the more so for its having been agreed unanimously. They feared that it would turn out to be just another UN process which Saddam would be allowed to manipulate with impunity. From the beginning they sought to interpret it as belligerently as possible. Condi Rice's deputy, Steve Hadley, told me that there would be 'zero tolerance' of any deficiencies in Iraq's cooperation with the inspectors. The hawks, and not just the hawks, started to look for ways of short-circuiting the inspections process.

The brief period of hope that Saddam could be disarmed peacefully ended a month after the passage of Resolution 1441 with his declaration on 7 December of his WMD holdings. During this interlude I had asked Condi Rice what were the best and worst outcomes of the crisis. The best, she said, was the implosion of the Iraqi regime under the pressures to which it was now subject. The worst was for Saddam to prevaricate with sufficient skill to split the Big Five in the Security Council: the US, Britain, France, Russia and China. The self-evident conclusion was that war lay somewhere between the two in the hierarchy of preferred outcomes.

The atmosphere in Washington changed sharply after the Iraqis' 7 December declaration. Despite its voluminous size, it was judged to be a defective and mendacious re-hash of earlier declarations. Bush continued to say that he hoped for a peaceful outcome. Those who also nurtured this hope saw that the declaration had played into the hands of the hawks. As for the latter, there was relief that Saddam had scored such an own goal. The Iraqi declaration swung the pendulum back towards a war in the spring. Against the background of intensifying military preparations, anxiety gripped the administration. It feared a prolonged inspection process that failed to reveal Saddam's WMD; troops going stale as they kicked their heels in the Gulf; allies going off the boil; and a once-and-for-all opportunity to be rid of Saddam slipping through American fingers.

The issue of the moment became how to find the 'smoking gun' and ensure quickly that Blix caught Saddam red-handed with concealed WMD. It was the only way to short-circuit the inspections process without alienating the UN Security Council. There was a debate in Washington whether to give Blix sensitive intelligence to help him find the WMD. There were doubts about his ability to use it well. There were doubts also about whether Blix would be tough enough himself. The administration wanted to 'extract' Iraqi scientists to somewhere like Cyprus. There they could spill the beans about Iraqi weapons without, it was hoped, the threat of retribution from Saddam. Hans Blix did not appear at all keen on doing this, much to the Americans' irritation.

American anxieties were not groundless; but the risk was that, through impatience and excessive pressure on Blix, the US would alienate the UN, bust the 1441 consensus, and fragment any international coalition for war before it had even got started. The crisis was getting nearer the moment of truth. It could mean rough waters between the UK and the US. The worst case would be one where, so as to meet the unforgiving timetable of an early spring campaign, the US were to devise a *casus belli* which most did not recognize as justified. In which case, I asked London, did we go with the Americans or didn't we?

I no longer thought that, in the event of opposition to war from Kofi Annan and most of the Security Council, Bush would blink. Yet, absent Saddam's demise, Bush would still have an agonizing decision to take early in 2003. If it was agonizing for him, it would be doubly so for Blair. The advice the British Prime Minister then gave the US President would never have been more important in my time in Washington. It could even be the swing vote for war or peace.

The pendulum never swung back again. If the President had left himself any space to step back from war, he closed it down early in 2003 with his State of the Union speech on 29 January. As long as Saddam remained in power, the die was now cast for war. Even by Bush's standards the speech was unusually messianic in tone. The destruction of Saddam was a crusade against evil to be undertaken by God's chosen nation: 'This call of history has come to the right people.' It was an appeal to the anxious and unconvinced in the country at large. It was a call to rally to the flag, to the Commander-in-Chief, and to the military. It was a recipe which never fails to stir the deep-seated patriotism of the American people. It was the speech in which Bush claimed that, according to British intelligence, Saddam had tried to acquire 'yellow cake' uranium from the sub-Saharan country of Niger. The TV cameras apparently focused on me at this point. Fortunately I looked reasonably alert. A few minutes later and they would have caught me in a slack-mouthed doze. The yellow cake claim later turned out to be false.

The speech was also notable for announcing that the following week Colin Powell would go to New York to present to the Security Council evidence of Saddam's weapons programmes and collaboration with Al Qaeda. He would show that Iraq's declaration of last December was false and that Saddam was already in violation of Resolution 1441.

That shook me out of my semi-comatose state. Only a couple of days previously Dr Hans Blix had made the first of his inspection progress reports to the UN in New York. Though preliminary, it was fairly negative about Iraqi cooperation. The Americans jumped on it like seagulls after sardines. The pressure was mounting inexorably inside the administration as they saw the coming train wreck between their timetable for war and UNMOVIC's for completing its inspections, which potentially stretched way beyond the spring. Powell's presentation was intended to exploit Blix's report and deliver the *coup de grâce* to Saddam, so making further inspections otiose.

I told Rich Armitage after the speech that all this looked in too much of a hurry. He was unrepentant. He and his boss could now see that, unless Saddam left the scene somehow, war was inevitable. Their task was to ensure that America embarked on hostilities in the most advantageous circumstances possible. There was a distinct hardening in the State Department; and it came from the top.

The French had not helped. A week or so previously, their Foreign Minister, Dominique de Villepin, had 'ambushed' Colin Powell in New York. To the intense inconvenience of both Powell and Straw, de Villepin had implored them both to attend a Security Council discussion of global terrorism on 20 January. For Powell this coincided with Martin Luther King Day, an important occasion for African-Americans; for Straw it meant two visits to the United States in one week. They agreed nevertheless to attend. Predictably the meeting was an occasion for the worst kind of UN flatulence. As Powell was returning to Washington from New York, de Villepin used a press conference to launch an intemperate attack on the US over Iraq. When I saw Powell and Armitage soon afterwards, the air was blue. I doubted that de Villepin had intended this disastrous consequence for US–French relations.

Much later, a very senior French diplomat and close friend told me that de Villepin's style, in its audacity, was like a French cavalry general of the Napoleonic Wars, who had told his men that if they lived beyond the age of thirty they should consider themselves a disgrace to the nation. My French friend added that in this respect de Villepin was much like President Chirac: they egged each other on in one misjudgement after another.

I just hoped that Powell would have something really compelling to offer the Security Council on 5 February. My fear was that he would go off at half-cock. I had not been encouraged by Armitage's telling me that a first draft of the presentation had been unusable in its unsubstantiated accusations against Saddam. As we were later to find out and Colin Powell himself to acknowledge, much of the information that he presented to the Security Council, even after editing by State and the CIA, was wrong. It was hardly surprising that Powell's presentation, though quite well received at the time, was not the knock-out blow that the Americans intended.

*

Blair paid one more visit to Washington before the outbreak of war. The meeting with Bush, on 31 January 2003, took place against a deeply unpromising background. Transatlantic relations were in a trough. Blair's famous bridge between Europe and America was sinking beneath the waves. Chirac and Schröder remained vocal critics of the impending war. British diplomacy in Paris, Moscow and Berlin was wholly ineffectual, though through no fault of the ambassadors. Rumsfeld enraged the French and the Germans by dividing Europe into the Old (bad) and New (good). Paris and Berlin were all the more angry because the American policy of divide and rule in Europe worked.

Meanwhile, Blix's second report to the UN, this time more favourable to the Iraqis, left the judgement on Saddam's compliance with Resolution 1441 in a bog of uncertainty.

Blair, I judged, was going to find a pretty implacable Bush, impatient and deeply disillusioned with France and Germany. Unless we had some good ideas for sending Saddam into exile, the Prime Minister's task looked to be to try to ensure that we and the US went to war in the best possible company. That would be made much easier if Blix found the 'smoking gun' or made a sequence of fortnightly reports saying that the Iraqis were still not cooperating fully as required by Resolution 1441. But Bush did not have the time to see if Blix would make the case. As I had always believed, exhausting the UN route was going to mean different things in Washington and in London. The timetables for war and for the inspections programme could not be made to synchronize. Bush was undecided about the merits of going for a second Security Council Resolution to authorize war, something which had become a political imperative in London. Blair was coming to Washington looking also for delay in starting the military campaign, which had been scheduled for mid-February. On both points the President would have to be convinced.

The meeting looked more uncomfortable than it was. Blair won his delay in starting the war for the simple reason that the Americans were not ready to go until the second half of March. I had been hearing this for some time from our military staff at the embassy and from a White House source. The latter had told me as early as October that the notion of going to war in January 2003, the original contingency timetable, was not feasible. The main obstacle had always been the Turks and their refusal to allow troops to pass through their country en route for northern Iraq. Ultimately fruitless negotiations with Turkey continued until almost the last moment. This slowed much American planning.

When, just before their press conference, President and Prime Minister came down from a tête-à-tête meeting upstairs in the White House, it looked at first as if Blair had secured Bush's solid support for a second Resolution. We were all milling around in the State Dining Room, advisers from both sides, as Bush and Blair put the final touches to what they were going to say to the media at the usual press conference in the main lobby of the White House. Bush had a notepad on which he had written a form of words on the second Resolution which sounded to me pretty forward-leaning. He read it out. Ari Fleischer, Bush's press secretary, said that Bush had never said this before and it would be a big story. Condi commented that she and others in the administration had already said something very similar in public. That, said Fleischer, is not the same thing as the President saying it. There was a silence. I waited for Blair to say that he needed something as supportive as possible. He said nothing. I waited for somebody on the No. 10 team to say something. Nothing was said; I had not been in the meeting – but I cursed myself afterwards for not piping up.

At the press conference Bush gave only perfunctory and lukewarm support for a second Resolution. It was neither his nor Blair's finest performance. They looked stressed and out of sorts. Bush immediately got irritable with his first questioner, who tried on him the kind of three-part question he does not like. Then Blair kept giving answers that were too long as he sought to make the case against Iraq from first principles. The British press later reported that they looked to have had a row. This was exactly as Alastair Campbell predicted when we went upstairs to the private dining room to have supper with the President and First Lady.

I left Washington and retired from the Diplomatic Service a month later. The battle for a second Resolution was still being fought. The Americans had finally swung in behind us, but their diplomacy was as ineffectual as ours. We went to war without benefit of a further Resolution and in the company of a motley, *ad hoc* coalition of allies.

I would have liked to be in Washington a little longer for the denouement and war; but heart valve disease got in the way.

23

'Proud to be an A**hole from El Paso'

In 2002 I knew three things about Waco, Texas: it was known as the Buckle on the Bible Belt; it was home to Baylor, the largest Baptist University in the world; and it was nearby that David Koresh and the followers, some British, of his Branch Davidian Sect had perished in flames one day in 1993 under siege by the FBI.

It was also the nearest large town to President Bush's ranch at Crawford. When I told people in Washington that I was on my way there to join up with Tony Blair, there were murmurs of condolence as if I were a Soviet dissident heading for exile in Siberia.

It was April 2002 and Blair was coming to Crawford for a meeting with Bush, the so-called Council of War. He was to spend Friday and Saturday nights at the ranch. On Sunday he would make his landmark speech at the Presidential Library of George Bush Senior at Texas A. and M. University in nearby College Station.

Blair flew to Waco direct from London. He was to be joined by Cherie, her mother, their daughter Katherine and the French hairdresser. They had come, if I remember well, from a charity event in Atlanta, Georgia, where Cherie had appeared with Laura Bush.

Preparing the visit had been a nightmare. The No. 10 advance team had continued to pursue their vendetta against the embassy. At every turn they tried to cut my staff out of the preparations and planning. Things reached such a pass that I had to make a formal complaint to Downing Street.

I took wing to Waco on Friday morning, 6 April 2002. As I waited for the connecting flight at Houston airport, I ran into Karl Rove, who was heading in the same direction. There would be time to kill in Waco before Blair arrived. Karl suggested that I join him in lunch with a friend who was running for the Texas Senate. He also asked me whether I wanted a pair of custom-made cowboy boots. He was going to ask his bootmaker to come up from Austin to fit him for a pair. Would any of Blair's advisers like boots? I said yes for myself but couldn't speak for the others.

'They will be a gift from the White House,' said Karl.

'If they are going to be more than about $200' (I couldn't remember the exact figure) 'I'll have to turn them down.'

'They are going to be way more than $200,' said Karl, laughing.

'It doesn't matter,' I said, 'I'll buy them anyway.'

With that, Dain Higdon from the Texas Clothier in Austin was summoned by phone from the departure lounge to measure us up for J. B. Hill boots.

Texas was a place where I collected clothing and footwear like a magnet does iron filings. I already had a pair of black cowboy boots, courtesy of the Mayor of Dallas. I was to receive in due course a ten-gallon hat from Ross Perot Junior when Catherine and I once had lunch at his ranch. He flew us there by helicopter and, on arrival, we were greeted by a cowboy and cowgirl each sitting astride a steer. It was Perot's father, of course, who had run for President as an independent in 1992, so splitting the Republican vote and allowing Bill Clinton to take the Presidency from George Bush Senior.

The White House and No. 10 advisers were to be lodged at the Waco Hilton hotel. As we checked in, we discovered that rooms were at a premium. Our visit coincided with the annual Miss Teen Texas Pageant. To the locals the visit of the British Prime Minister was of little consequence compared to the pageant. This probably explained why the British press party had been shunted, by their account, to a motel from hell some way from Crawford and Waco. This was the subject of formal complaint to No 10. by the journalists.

The Hilton was full of contestants, parents and chaperones. When I got into the lift to go to my room, I had the sensation of being enveloped in hair. Not any old hair, but Big Hair – no, not Big, but Huge. It was blow-dried, curled, teased, pomaded, set in elaborate neo-mullet constructions: and that was just the girls' fathers.

For lunch Karl drove us out of town to what I remember as a large, anonymous building with no windows, set in a parking lot. This was unprepossessing home to Dan's Bar-B-Q Ribs, reputedly the best in the area. It delivered frequently to the Bush ranch, so I was told. Inside, belying its exterior, it was all liveliness and bustle.

Dan's was doing roaring business. Karl seemed to know everyone personally. I was overwhelmed with Texan bonhomie and hospitality. I ate gluttonously from a massive meal of ribs, coleslaw, apple pie and iced tea. I learned more about Texas politics in an hour than most would in a lifetime.

Once, when Catherine and I made one of our visits to Dallas, Karl suggested I pay a call on a friend of his who was very well plugged in politically. We talked about this and that. Then we got onto Britain's support for the US after 9/11. Like all Americans, Karl's friend was generous in his gratitude. He talked about Blair's heroic status in the US. Then, almost as one professional appraising another, he said, 'That Tony Blair – why, he's as smooth as a teacher's leg.'

I never did get to the bottom of this vivid phrase, which I added to my thesaurus of Texan sayings. Nor was I convinced that the simile was entirely complimentary. I had for the most part been accustomed to teachers' legs that were male and hirsute in so far as they were visible between the grey fabrics of suit and sock. What was the phrase intended to tell you about the quality of the Texan teacher's leg? How did you establish that the limb was rough or smooth? In Texas folklore were teachers the first ladies to resort to depilation? It was obviously not an ironic phrase. Nor, I reckoned, did it refer to legs other than female. If the Texans did not do much irony, they did not do a lot of political correctness either.

As soon as Blair arrived at Waco on the Friday afternoon he was whisked off to the President's ranch. He dined alone with Bush. The rest of us were left to our devices. The White House team invited us to dinner in a Waco restaurant across the road from the hotel. It was good Southern food, with more than a touch of Tex-Mex, the kind of place where you drink your Corona or Dos Equis beer straight from the bottle through a piece of lime on the rim.

It was a high-powered American team: Andy Card, the President's chief of staff; Karl Rove; Karen Hughes, Bush's Communications Director and a Texan; Condi Rice; and her press secretary, Anna Perez. On our side, it was the usual Gang of Three – Jonathan Powell, Alastair Campbell, David Manning – and myself.

As we were ordering, the arrival of the bootmaker was announced. I had warned the No. 10 team of his coming. I had said with my most serious face that it was a signal honour, not to be lightly dismissed, to be offered the possibility of acquiring custom-made, hand-tooled, genuine cowboy boots. Karl asked if there were any takers for the boots. There was an uneasy shifting in the British chairs. There was none. Our national honour was at stake! I retired with Karl to one of the restaurant's storerooms, where Dain Higdon and two Hispanic ladies had set themselves up.

I was shown a catalogue with a bewildering variety of styles, colours, leathers and designs. I had not a clue what to choose.

'OK,' said Dain, 'we'll take it in stages. First thing, we trace your feet.'

I put my feet down gingerly on two pieces of board. One of the ladies traced my feet, which, according to Catherine, are my ugliest feature.

'OK,' said Dain, 'High boot or low boot?' Low? God, no. In for a penny, in for a pound.

'High, please,' I replied. That seemed to please Dain and Karl.

'Pointed toe or rounded?' I looked to Karl for instruction.

'Pointed,' he said.

'Pointed,' I said.

'That means you'll be wanting a high heel,' said Dain.

'How high?' I asked.

'High,' said Dain and Karl.

'High,' I said.

'How much tooling?' asked Dain. By now there was no holding me.

'Give me the full monty, please,' I said, using a piece of British vernacular which had made a temporary entry into American speech thanks to the unexpected success of the eponymous British film.

'If you like,' said Dain, 'we can decorate the pulls at the top of the boots (i.e. leather loops to help you pull them on) with the flags of Britain, America and Texas.'

'Yessir!' I replied.

After a final consultation with Karl and Dain on leather and colour, the deed was done. Within a month or so I would be the proud owner of a pair of custom-made, hand-tooled, cordovan-coloured, genuine J. B. Hill boots. They are magnificent to behold. I wear them from time to time in Europe, where ironically they go down better in France than England.

It took a while to get used to wearing the boots. I shredded a couple of pairs of socks until I discovered that I had to wear a special kind. The boots had a life of their own. So they should. For once I owned some footwear more expensive than Catherine's. They made me walk like John Wayne. They enjoyed phenomenal success all over Texas, where I displayed them shamelessly, especially the pulls. They were less appreciated in Washington.

'You wimps,' I said cheerily to my British colleagues as I returned to the table.

Crawford is not much more than a crossroads with a gas station and coffee shop. You pass through it to get to the Bushes' ranch. Along the road is the local high school, where the White House organizes press conferences in the sports hall for the President and his distinguished foreign house guests. The school was justifiably proud of its unexpected status. I noticed that, after President Putin's visit to the ranch, the Russians had donated various memorabilia, which were on prominent display.

Further along you come to the Bush ranch. It looks pretty isolated. It is heavily guarded by the Secret Service. It is a large, low, unpretentious building. Inside it is roomy, comfortable, and feels like what it is: a real home, not a government guest house.

The high point of the British visit was the dinner at the ranch on Saturday night given by the Bushes in honour of the Blairs. The senior members of the White House and Downing Street teams were invited, along with some of the Bushes' friends, Jenna, one of the Bush twin daughters, and her boyfriend – maybe twenty to thirty guests in all. Dress was 'smart casual', that is chinos, no jeans, for the men.

As I arrived, Laura Bush asked me: 'Where's Catherine?'

'I don't think she was invited,' I replied in some embarrassment.

'Well, no one consulted us and we would have liked to have her here,' said the First Lady.

I had an identical exchange later in the evening with the President. Another manoeuvre, I thought to myself, by the No. 10 advance team, who had told me that Catherine had not been invited. It was of a piece with their (failed) attempt to remove my name from all the events the next day at College Station. God knows what the Americans thought of this odd, obsessive behaviour.

It was a jolly, light-hearted evening. The Bushes were geniality and hospitality personified. A country-and-western band was playing.

The Blairs and family arrived. Cherie's mother was a sweet lady. Katherine Blair was taken in hand by Jenna Bush. Alastair Campbell fell into deep conversation with the President about, I think, running – a joint obsession. I talked to the former US ambassador to Britain, Anne Armstrong, and her husband and daughter Katherine Isdal. They all seemed to own ranches into which Belgium would fit nicely. Out of the corner of my eye I noticed that Tony Blair was wearing jeans.

We were called to dinner. I saw Tony and Cherie talking to each other in consternation.

'I am the only one wearing jeans. I have to change,' I heard him say. He raced back to the guest house.

The dinner was organized in round tables of about six guests each. I was seated on Laura Bush's left with Katherine Isdal on my left. Tony Blair was on the First Lady's right. Karl Rove was also at our table.

The President, at another table, rose to his feet to give a toast of welcome to the British Prime Minister and his wife. To my horror I saw that Blair had not yet returned from changing his trousers. As her husband began to speak, Laura Bush whispered to me,

'Where's the Prime Minister?'

'He's gone to adjust his dress,' I replied.

'Bushie,' Laura exclaimed, 'you'll have to sit down. The ambassador says that the Prime Minister has gone to adjust his dress.'

A few moments later a slightly breathless and embarrassed Prime Minister made his entrance and the President rose once more to give the toast of welcome.

While Tony Blair and Laura Bush talked to each other, I embarked on a lively and amusing conversation with Katherine Isdal. There was a lot of laughter. Then I became aware that Blair had fallen into serious conversation with Karl Rove. Through the hubbub of Texan and British voices words like 'Arafat' and 'Sharon' drifted across our table.

I was now in a three-way conversation with both my neighbours. We got on to the history of Texas and its brief period of existence in the nineteenth century as an independent country. As a historian and fan of Larry McMurtry's books about old Texas, I found this fascinating. Laura Bush and Katherine talked about the different waves of migration into Texas. Meantime, from the other side of the table, 'Jerusalem' and 'Gaza' floated past my ears.

Having gone through the Mexican, African-American, English, German, Irish and Scotch-Irish, our conversation turned to the Jewish migrations of a century previously and their strong influence on the life and culture of the Lone Star State, as Texas is sometimes known. Katherine mentioned that one of the most popular country-and-western bands in Texas was Jewish-American, an irreverent bunch called Kinky Friedman and the Texas Jew-Boys. Kinky Friedman is, incidentally, also a novelist (I have seen his books in British stores), organizer of children's summer camps, and has at least one website dedicated to his *oeuvre*. One of his greatest hits had been 'They Ain't Makin' Jews Like Jesus Anymore', she said. I found myself convulsed with laughter. Simultaneously, I was dimly aware of the intensifying seriousness of the Blair–Rove exchange as 'peace process' and 'West Bank' penetrated the peals of laughter on our side of the table. Laura Bush added that Kinky had also recorded a number called 'Proud to be an A**hole from El Paso', which had sold well.

The laughter decibels on our side of the table increased still further. At which point the clipped syllables of Britain's Prime Minister cut like a knife through the mirth to pose the question: 'What do you think, Chris?'

That put a stop to the laughter. I had no idea where he and Karl had got to in their discussion of the Middle East. I retreated under the carapace of Sir Humphrey, saying, 'I did not quite catch your last point, Prime Minister.'

Soon after, the dinner broke up, we drank our coffee, and departed into the inky-black Texas night. It had been a great evening. I was touched by the evident pleasure of the President and Mrs Bush at entertaining in their newly renovated home. I gave Laura Bush a little enamel box to add to her collection. It had on it a picture of the great Lutyens house in Washington, based on a photograph that Catherine had taken on a bright, snowy day.

24

That's Diplomacy!

In the spring of 2001 I caught a terrible cold. As usual it went to my chest. I developed what I hated most: a wheezing, bronchial cough. Weeks went by, including a break in the Florida sunshine, and I still could not shake off the cough. I do not like to take antibiotics unless absolutely unavoidable. But I had had enough. I went to see our doctor, Michael Newman.

Michael did the usual doctor's thing, listening to my chest through his stethoscope. 'I'll give you the antibiotics and that will soon clear up the bronchitis,' he said. 'But I heard something else: a clicking sound. It could be a heart murmur.'

'A what?' I exclaimed in alarm. This was a bolt from the blue. I was almost never ill and rarely went to the doctor.

'A heart murmur is not necessarily terribly serious,' said Michael. 'Some people have it from birth and go on to lead perfectly normal lives with no impact on longevity. It is quite a common condition. It often runs in the family. It means that one of the heart's valves – the mitral – is not functioning at full efficiency. With each beat of the heart the blood is pumped through the valve, after which the valve closes. If the valve is not working properly, it fails to close fully after each pump and some of the blood flows back through the gap in the valve. It's called mitral-valve regurgitation. It's audible, which is why it's called a heart murmur. I'll make an appointment for you at Georgetown. The first thing to find out is whether this is the problem and how serious it is.'

I was stunned. I had no inkling of heart trouble. I considered myself pretty fit. I had played squash all my life until recently damaging an Achilles tendon. I ran and now played tennis regularly. As far as I knew, there was no history of heart trouble in my family, still less of mitral-valve regurgitation. As I sat in Michael's office and heard him talk of heart 'disease', a shiver ran through me. It was, I thought melodramatically, one of those moments when your whole life changed.

I was put through an astonishing battery of tests at Georgetown University Hospital. The cardiologists confirmed Michael's provisional diagnosis. I had mild to moderate mitral-valve regurgitation. In all other respects I was very fit.

It was decided that my condition was not yet serious enough to warrant what would be open-heart surgery either to repair or replace the valve. The operation was quite common, with a low mortality rate; but, for the time being, the balance of risk favoured my doing nothing.

Michael told me to come back in a year. I sent the test results to the Foreign Office medical adviser, since it was the FO that paid the medical bills. Then I tried to forget the whole thing. It was not terribly difficult because there were no symptoms that I could detect. I went back to jogging and playing tennis.

But my heart came to play into the question of how long we should stay in Washington.

The normal term for an ambassador in the United States is four years. That would have taken us until late 2001. In 2000 the Foreign Office had asked us to extend our posting for a further eighteen months. This was fine by Catherine and me. We were enjoying ourselves in Washington, we loved America, and it was important that, when we left, the embassy should be well broken in with whichever administration emerged from the 2000 presidential election. So our departure date had been fixed for 28 February 2003. It would make me the longest-serving ambassador to the United States since the Second World War.

On one of my regular visits to London in late 2001 – the one during which I warned No. 10 to prepare for a train wreck at the UN over Iraq – Jonathan Powell said at the end of our conversation, 'Tony feels bad about pulling David out of NATO after only a few months as ambassador.* He will want to make up for it by giving him Washington after you. But he will expect David to stay at No. 10 for a full two years. We may have to ask you to stay on even longer.'

* David Manning had been British ambassador to NATO in Brussels for only a few months before he was chosen by Blair to be his foreign policy adviser.

'Jonathan,' I said, 'I'm not sure about that. Five and a half years are already a long time. I'll think about it. But I have very strong family and personal reasons for returning as scheduled in early 2003.'

What Jonathan was suggesting would have meant remaining in Washington until August of that year; but I was getting increasingly concerned about my elderly parents, who were now too infirm to travel to America. In the event, my mother died not long after we returned to London.

An even greater concern for Catherine was that her elder son, Alexander, would be eighteen in the spring of 2003. In Germany that would give him the full independence of an adult. It was vital to her to have established by then a home in London to which he could come easily and cheaply, if he wished. Neither of us had a home in London at the time. As it happened, less than two months after his birthday Alexander came of his own volition to London with his younger brother Constantin. For the first time in nine years mother and sons slept under the same roof. It was the beginning of the end of Catherine's long nightmare.

Several months after my conversation with Jonathan, David Manning himself raised the matter with me during Blair's visit to Crawford in April 2002. He confirmed that the Prime Minister wanted him to follow me in Washington, but that he would not release David until August 2003. Would I be willing to stay on a few more months?

Again I said that I would think about it. I could see that David really wanted the job and I did not want to mess things up for him; but, I said to him, in all frankness I did not think that it was going to be possible.

Things on the home front were deteriorating. My stepfather had just had another fall and was in hospital for the second time in only a few months. My mother, in her mid-eighties and with her own crop of ailments, was increasingly worried about her ability to look after him. Catherine, meantime, was going through one of her worst periods with the German courts. They had now banned her from seeing her children for reasons which plumbed new depths of malevolent injustice. She also had very elderly parents.

Catherine and I talked things over after I returned from the Crawford summit. The pressures were building on us to return home. We even questioned the wisdom of our earlier decision to stay on in Washington for an extra eighteen months. I phoned David Manning to say that I was very sorry, but I intended to stick to my decision to leave Washington and go into retirement on my due date at the end of February 2003. For good measure I confirmed this to the Foreign Office.

Later in the year I was approached by headhunters in search of a replacement for Lord Wakeham as Chairman of the Press Complaints Commission. As twice before, I was drawn like a moth to a flame to a job dealing with the British press. I threw my hat in the ring and in due course was offered the job after I retired.

Formally, matters rested with the letter that I had received from the Foreign Office in 2000, confirming the extension of our posting until February 2003. After that I was never to receive another formal communication about our departure date. But, out of the blue, in the early autumn of 2002, my staff told me that the Foreign Office had officially sought what is known as *agrément* from the US State Department for David Manning to replace me as ambassador in August 2003. This is the process by which governments are asked to approve the appointment of a new ambassador. There had been no warning or prior consultation from London, as there should have been. I had never known of a case where *agrément* had been requested without the sitting ambassador being informed.

I called David Manning. 'What the hell is going on? You and the Foreign Office know that I am leaving at the end of February. Do people understand that there will be a six-month gap if you don't arrive until August?'

David was apologetic. 'I have told the Foreign Office not to rush this. I've tried to speak to the PM, but he doesn't want to listen.'

I began to sniff a stitch-up.

This conversation took place just as I had received bad news about my heart condition. During the summer of 2002 I began to be woken up at night by bouts of palpitation. I went again to see Michael Newman and off I was sent to Georgetown for the same battery of tests.

The diagnosis was that in just over a year the mitral valve had got significantly worse. The regurgitation was now classified as moderate to severe. This was the cause of the atrial fibrillation, or palpitations, when the heart beats wildly out of rhythm. While I was hitched to some piece of medical technology, which showed my heart in 3D, I was surrounded by a small group of American consultants.

One exclaimed, 'Jeez! Take a look at that!'

Thanks a lot, I thought.

Michael Newman said that we should get a second opinion. But he was clear that I needed an urgent operation before damage to the heart became irreversible. He recommended that I go to the Mayo Clinic in Minnesota both for second opinion and, if necessary, operation. It was a centre of specialization in mitral-valve surgery. Appointments were set up.

I now had to get the authorization of the Foreign Office for further treatment, because it was going to be expensive. I reckoned that if I had the operation immediately, I could convalesce over Christmas 2002 and be back at work early in the New Year.

The Foreign Office refused to authorize the treatment. Various arguments were advanced, financial and clinical. Couldn't I find somewhere nearer than the Mayo for a second opinion? Then I was told that the Cardiothoracic Department at St Thomas's Hospital had been shown the test results. They did not agree with the American diagnosis and recommendation for urgent surgery. The condition was not, they said, as serious as the US consultants suggested; an operation could wait. Americans were always too eager to operate etc. etc. I should come in for tests at St Thomas's after I retired. March 2003 would be quite early enough.

By that time, of course, I would be off the books of the Foreign Office. I did not know whether to be relieved or more anxious. Michael Newman and the specialists at Georgetown and the Mayo Clinic were incredulous. 'The reason has got to be financial,' one of them said. 'Otherwise this decision is inexplicable.'

What to do? Who do you believe? With hindsight I should have sought a second opinion at my own expense, in the US or UK. I chose instead to defer to the judgement of St Thomas's.

When, in March 2003, just after I had retired, I went through a battery of equivalent British tests, I was told that the valve was almost certainly too far gone to be repaired. When I finally went under the knife in July of that year, the surgeon was unable to repair the valve and replaced it with one made of carbon fibre. A week after the operation I had open-heart surgery for a second time to deal with a blood clot that almost killed me. The surgeon said to me afterwards that my condition was worse than he had realized. I deduced that the Americans had been right all along.

Soon after I left Washington the Foreign Office introduced a new system of medical treatment for Diplomatic Service staff in the US, intended to cut costs.

If I had had any second thoughts about leaving Washington at the end of February 2003 – and, as war loomed, I did – they were dispelled by the heart business. Catherine and I wanted it fixed as soon as possible, and that was now going to have to be in London. Late in 2002 I was asked by Jack Straw during one of his visits to reconsider my decision. The Prime Minister continued to refuse to release David Manning until August the following year. I declined, again citing private and family reasons, as I had repeatedly done for almost a year.

Immediately after returning to London, in March 2003, I went, as is customary, to say my farewells to No. 10 and the Foreign Office on retiring from the Diplomatic Service. It was just before the beginning of the Iraq war. In Downing Street I saw Alastair Campbell, Jonathan Powell and David Manning. I sought an appointment with Tony Blair, but one never materialized. Catherine and I were, a few weeks later, invited to one of the Blairs' eclectic Saturday night dinner parties at the Prime Minister's country residence at Chequers; but, by then, the Prime Minister and his wife saw me only as Chairman of the Press Complaints Commission and conversation was monopolized by press matters.

In the Foreign Office, among others, I called on Jack Straw, Liz Symons, the minister of state, and Michael Jay, the Permanent Under Secretary. All were fulsome in their praise for what Catherine and I had achieved in Washington. On the evening of the day when I had made one of these calls – I forget which – I went to the Blue Bar at the Berkeley Hotel to meet Catherine. She was having a drink with the Duchess of York. After a while we were joined by Prince Andrew.

He said to me breezily, 'I have just been at the Foreign Office. Someone very senior said that you had deserted your post just when you were needed. I'm not going to tell you who it was.'

Similar stuff started to appear in gossip columns. Journalists spoke to me of 'resentment' in the Foreign Office, where the timing of my retirement was seen as 'tactical', whatever that meant.

A little later I was awarded a bonus of £4000 for my service in the US – taxable, of course.

We were desperately sorry and sad to leave Washington. We said farewell to many good friends, with whom we have stayed in close contact. America had become very special to us. It was a second home where we felt entirely at ease. We still do, even without all the comforts of ambassadorial life. We visit it regularly. Catherine and I had begun our married lives on American soil among American people. There could have been no better environment for a new marriage than the friendship of Americans. As nowhere else, they had shown Catherine unstinting support and encouragement in her efforts to regain contact with her children. The American people are the most generous-hearted on earth.

They have also been better at preserving the old civilities than we in Britain. Once, late at night, I got lost in deep countryside somewhere near the Maryland–Pennsylvania state line not far from Gettysburg, scene of the mighty Civil War battle. I finally saw a light in the pitch-black darkness. I stopped my car outside a small, isolated house. The light was coming through an open door to the rear. In some trepidation I went to ask for directions. I fully expected to have a shotgun stuck in my face at that time of night.

Instead I found an elderly woman humming to herself as she baked cookies. I knocked on the open door. She barely looked up and said, 'Come in. Have a cookie. What can I do for you? Can I fix you a cup of coffee?'

I declined the coffee but ate a cookie, still warm from the oven. I received elaborate instructions on how to get to my destination, a country inn. I thanked her warmly, we said our farewells and I went off into the night. I was minded to close her back door.

'Leave it open,' she said; 'the night air smells sweet.'

By the end, after two months of farewell meetings, dinners, lunches and receptions in January and February 2003, Catherine and I were emotionally and physically drained. She fainted at one of these occasions. In the photos taken at the time my face sometimes looks grey. The bouts of atrial fibrillation were getting longer and more frequent.

The President and Mrs Bush gave us a small, private dinner at the White House just before we left. It was a great honour. We were asked to suggest one other couple. We chose Mel and Kitty Martinez.

He is now one of Florida's senators. At the time he was in the Cabinet as Secretary for Housing and Urban Development. The Bushes had also invited Colin and Alma Powell and Condi Rice.

It was a nice evening. I presented the President with a traditional red despatch box of the kind in which, since time immemorial, the diplomatic papers of the Prime Minister and the Foreign Secretary have been carried. We ate in the small dining room upstairs in the Bushes' private apartment. Conversation ranged back and forth, sometimes light, sometimes more serious. There was no concealing the solemn and heavy burden on the President's shoulders at the prospect of imminent war; but, he said, he was convinced that it was the right thing to do. As I looked across the table at the leader of the world's only superpower, I was once again struck by the thought that, agree with him or disagree with him, he was about as far removed from his European caricature as it was possible to be.

After I had joined the Foreign Office in 1966, and been placed in the West and Central African Department, my first assignment, on my second day, was to go to Heathrow, meet the Foreign Minister of Upper Volta (now Burkina Faso), and accompany him to central London. I was carefully briefed on a number of African issues and told that I would have to discuss them with Monsieur Ouedragou in the back of the car in French. To my astonishment, as he settled into the government limousine, he addressed me in excellent English and asked the result of the previous night's football match between, if I remember well, Liverpool and Lazio.

On my very last assignment for Her Majesty's Diplomatic Service, I paid my final call on Dr Condoleezza Rice, the President's National Security Adviser and the most powerful woman in the world. Our conversation was more personal than official. I asked her what she would like to do next. Condi said that she could think of nothing better than being Commissioner of the National Football League.

That's diplomacy!

Hindsight

Hindsight usually follows failure. In September 2005, when I wrote this chapter, things looked bad in Iraq and worrying in Afghanistan.

At regular intervals over the last two years I have asked the same question of former colleagues in the British and American governments: in Iraq, is the glass half-empty or is it half-full? With one exception the answer has invariably and, given the source, been 'half-full'. The exception was a trusted American friend and government official, who, after paying a recent visit to Iraq, returned to tell the White House: 'We're fucked.'

His pithy prognosis may in the long run prove wrong; but, unlike the late Chinese Prime Minister, Chou En Lai, we cannot wait indefinitely to render judgement. When asked about the consequences of the French Revolution, Chou said that it was too soon to tell. More to the point was the great British economist John Maynard Keynes, who famously said that in the long run we are all dead. Success in Iraq and Afghanistan means reasonably democratic and reasonably stable states, whose democracy and stability become self-sustaining within a reasonable period of time. 'Reasonable' is rough and ready and begs a thousand questions; but in another, say, five years we should know for sure which way the water is flowing in the glass.

I often find myself caught up in a debate between those who would have the troops out of Iraq without delay; and those who do not want 'to cut and run'. My instincts are always with the second. I am haunted by something which Colin Powell once told me. He was talking about the withdrawal of US troops from Somalia in 1993. This was after the deaths of eighteen American soldiers in the Somali capital, Mogadishu (the subject of the book and film, *Black Hawk Down*). The trouble with our withdrawal, said Colin, was that it signalled that the soldiers had died for nothing. As of writing, US deaths in Iraq are approaching 2000, British 100.

Even if the most optimistic predictions are finally realized for Iraq, the question will still be asked: why did the Americans and British make it so hard for themselves and even harder for Iraqis? Why did Washington and London fail so comprehensively to meet the three conditions for removing Saddam that I had heard Henry Kissinger enunciate at the Bohemian Grove in the summer of 2002?

The US and the UK would have stood a better chance of going to war in good order, and of doing the aftermath right, had they planned on an autumn, not a spring, campaign – the next period of cool weather. It would still have been a risky and controversial venture. There would have been no guarantee that it would have avoided the splintering of the Security Council, the transatlantic alliance and public opinion in Britain, but certain things would have become possible that were impossible on the timetable of a spring campaign.

Early in 2002, when I sensed that the option of an autumn campaign was blowing, however briefly, in the Washington wind, I asked Karl Rove how late he thought that war could be left in 2003 without getting unacceptably entangled with campaigning for the 2004 presidential election. His answer was the end of 2003 or very early in 2004. There was, I concluded, no political objection of principle to an autumn campaign.

From the moment that President Bush had agreed with Tony Blair in September 2002 to go to the UN, I had been anxious that the American view of exhausting UN processes would not coincide with our own, still less with that of the rest of the Security Council. Once the famous Resolution 1441 had been unanimously passed in November of that year, this anxiety took specific shape. How could Dr Hans Blix's schedule of UN weapons inspections be synchronized with a military plan for an attack on Iraq sometime in the first quarter of 2003? Unless Blix found something that established beyond reasonable doubt that Saddam was in 'material breach' of Resolution 1441, three months or so were never going to be time enough for Blix or the Security Council to conclude that Saddam's cooperation with the inspections was so deficient as to warrant military retribution.

The Americans spotted this instantly. This was why celebration in Washington of the passage of 1441 was muted and short-lived.

To the hawks the resolution was a potential trap. Their fear that they would be sucked into an endless process of inspections, manipulated by Saddam, was constant. To avoid the trap they had to short-circuit the inspections schedule. To short-circuit the schedule they had to find definitive evidence of Saddam's weapons programmes. This was to turn the logic of Resolution 1441 on its head.

In its essence the Resolution demanded that Saddam prove his innocence. By trying frantically to find the 'smoking gun' of Iraq's WMD between December 2002 and March 2003, the Americans and British shifted the burden of proof from Saddam to themselves. We had to show that he was guilty. This turned out to be a strategic error, which to this day, in the absence of WMD, continues cruelly to torment Blair and Bush.

None of this would have been necessary had the war been planned for September or October 2003. It would have allowed a proper articulation between coercive diplomacy, the inspections schedule and, if it came to it, war itself.

The role of coercive diplomacy is a neglected element in the polemic about the Iraq war. It was a central part of Blair's strategy in 1999 to stop the mass killing of the Kosovo population by the Serb leader Slobodan Milosevic. Blair's argument was that if you wanted to avoid a land war in Kosovo with the risk of heavy casualties, you should intimidate your opponent by letting him see that you are making serious preparations for just such a war. With a little help from the Russians, this was a strategy that worked.

Not without reason, both the White House and Downing Street harboured similar hopes for dealing with Saddam. The opponents of the war in Iraq fail to acknowledge that, without the US military threat, the weapons inspectors would never have been readmitted by Iraq in October 2002. Such cooperation as Dr Blix thereafter received from Iraq was due to the threat of the American and British military presence in the Gulf. But that force, in those numbers and at that state of readiness, could not have been left twiddling its thumbs for months, which is what would have happened if the spring campaigning season had been missed – all of which brings us back to the case for a more deliberate, but equally menacing, military build-up geared to an autumn campaign.

A more deliberate timetable might also have avoided the political pressure which led to the mistakes and misjudgements of the two

British public dossiers and Colin Powell's UN presentation on Saddam's WMD. Because of these pressures the British dossier of September 2002 replaced with a phoney threat of imminent attack Blair's powerful argument for pre-emptive action against Saddam, articulated with such eloquence in his Texas speech of April 2002.

Other things as well could have flowed from a later timetable.

It could have made possible an understanding with France and Russia, Iraq's 'allies', about the trigger for war. Once that had happened Saddam would have known that the game was up. This might have sufficiently ratcheted up the pressure to lead to his overthrow or flight into exile. I never interpreted President Chirac's refusal in March 2003 to accept the draft of a second Security Council Resolution authorizing war as a refusal for ever and a day. In diplomacy you never say 'never'. That, at least, is what French diplomats told me in private. They accused the Americans and British of deliberately exaggerating France's position to justify going to war without further UN cover. We will know the full truth only when the archives are opened in Paris, London and Washington.

A more united Security Council would have been of inestimable value for the rebuilding of Iraq. The case for going through the UN was always as strong for the post-war period as for the war itself. UN backing would have done much to defuse the notion of a Christian crusade against the Arabs and Islam – and the argument about whether Iraq belonged to the 'war on terror' or was something quite separate.

Above all, an autumn timetable could have given Washington and London the time to think through coolly and calmly the running of Iraq after the removal of Saddam, the black hole in Anglo-American planning.

Throughout 2002 the British embassy in Washington had warned that: the linkage between the political and the military components in planning for Iraq was, as for Afghanistan, defective; that the political could not be left to the Pentagon; that planning in Washington for the administration of Iraq after Saddam's demise was rudimentary; and that the timetables of the military and the UN inspectors could not be reconciled. The embassy also said that Britain had the leverage to do something about all this.

What leverage? When I have made this point to former colleagues in the British government, they have disagreed vehemently. They cite Bush's offer to Blair that Britain stay out of the war if it was going to be too difficult politically, or Rumsfeld's apparent dismissal of the British military contribution. But these things were said at two minutes to midnight when war was inevitable.

London was not fertile ground for the notion of leverage or the tough negotiating position that must sometimes be taken even with the closest allies, as Churchill did with Roosevelt and Thatcher with Reagan. Somewhere in the archives of the Foreign Office is a paper written by a former ambassador and adviser to No. 10, Sir Roderic Braithwaite, on how to negotiate with the United States. Just before retiring I commended it to No. 10 and the Foreign Office.

By the early autumn of 2002, despite Blair's earlier expressions of unconditional support, Britain should have made its participation in any war depend on a fully worked-out plan, agreed by both sides, for the rehabilitation of Iraq after Saddam's demise. This would have been the appropriate *quid pro quo* for Blair's display of *cojones* at his Camp David meeting with Bush in September 2002. We may have been the junior partner in the enterprise; but the ace up our sleeve was that America did not want to go it alone. Had Britain so insisted, Iraq after Saddam might have avoided the violence that may yet prove fatal to the entire enterprise.

Unfortunately, and unavoidably, at precisely this moment, political energy in London had become consumed by a titanic struggle, which was to last for six months, to keep public opinion, Parliament and the Labour Party onside for war. The very survival of the government depended on it. There was little energy left in No. 10 to think about the aftermath. Since Downing Street drove Iraq policy, efforts made by the Foreign Office to engage with the Americans on the aftermath came to nothing.

Even in the autumn and early winter of 2002, despite the quickening pace of military preparation, I did not believe that the President had yet taken an irrevocable decision to go to war. This was regularly confirmed to me by White House and other contacts. The military and intelligence staff of the embassy did not agree with me. War was, of course, by far and away the most likely outcome. But that was not the same thing.

I did not see the notorious Downing Street memorandum, recording a meeting between Blair and close advisers on 23 July 2002, until it was leaked to the British press in 2005. The meeting seems to have focused on a report from the then head of the Secret Intelligence Service, Sir Richard Dearlove, who had just returned from Washington. As recorded in the memorandum, Dearlove appears to have concluded that war was now inevitable. He referred to the facts and intelligence being 'fixed' around the policy. I do not know what he meant by this. If it was an allusion to a belief that Saddam had WMD, then I know of no one at the time who did not share that belief. If it was a reference to the assertion that there was a link between Saddam and Al Qaeda, it was, however mistaken, one made with complete sincerity by all the Washington hawks of my acquaintance. If it was a reference to the Pentagon's seeking to sideline the CIA, there is no denying the intense, and long-standing, bureaucratic hostility between the two organizations.

The memorandum has been widely construed, especially in America, as proof positive that Britain and the United States were irrevocably committed to war; and that the subsequent pursuit of UN resolutions was a grand charade to disguise their real intentions. The memorandum certainly exudes a fatalism among those present at the meeting about the unavoidability of war. To a degree this is hardly unreasonable. Those sitting inside the military and intelligence machines, tasked to prepare for the contingency of war, and absorbed in their preparations, were always likely to conclude that war was the irrevocable intention. The more interesting question is whether No. 10, relying heavily – maybe too heavily – on the views of its military and intelligence advisers, as a consequence underestimated its political leverage and ability to affect the course of events.

History will doubtless charge Blair and Bush with a number of sins of omission and commission in Iraq; and its judgement may be harsh. But on the central accusation – that together they conspired from early 2002 deliberately to mislead their publics as to their true, bellicose intentions – they are, in my view, innocent. I believe them to have been sincere when they said that a peaceful outcome was possible and war the last option; but, equally, I had little doubt that Bush and Blair thought that it would come to war. Neither had any confidence in Saddam's doing the right thing. Who did?

Enormous controversy surrounds the intelligence on which Blair and Bush relied. I saw a great deal of intelligence material in 2002. I was myself persuaded that Iraq had WMD. There is nothing of which I am aware that Blair said in public about the intelligence for which he did not have cover either from the Joint Intelligence Committee (JIC) or from its Chairman, John Scarlett. If either succumbed to political pressure, that is another story. Had I been in Alastair Campbell's place, I too would have wanted as categorical a public depiction of Saddam's threat as possible. Equally I would have expected the JIC to be rigorous in telling me how far I could go.

Tony Blair chose to take his stand against Saddam and alongside President Bush from the highest of high moral ground. It is the definitive riposte to Blair the Poodle, seduced though he and his team always appeared to be by the proximity and glamour of American power. He needed little convincing of the desirability of bringing down Saddam. Blair was a true believer before Bush himself.

Tony Blair had behind him the success of wars in Sierra Leone and Kosovo, where, in difficult circumstances, his judgement was proved right and thousands of lives saved. These military expeditions were the embodiment of ideas set out in his speech to the Chicago Economic Club in April 1999, when he had argued the primacy of the humanitarian imperative over traditional national sovereignty. Not many politicians get to put into practice their doctrine of international relations. He must have thought that it would once again prove a true and sufficient guide in tackling Saddam Hussein. That was certainly the thrust of his speech in Texas three years later.

But the high moral ground, and the pure white flame of unconditional support to an ally in service of an idea, have their disadvantages. They place your destiny in the hands of the ally. They fly above the tangled history of Sunni, Shia, Kurd, Turkoman and Assyrian. They discourage descent into the dull detail of tough and necessary bargaining: meat and drink to Margaret Thatcher, but, so it seemed, uncongenial to Tony Blair.

As the French commander Marshal Bosquet said in 1854 during the Crimean War, on observing the charge of the Light Brigade towards the Russian cannon at Balaclava, 'C'est magnifique, mais ce n'est pas la guerre.'

Index